Political Analysis

The *Political Analysis* series provides a showcase for political science in all its variety and a channel for political scientists in different specialisms and different parts of the world to talk to each other and to new generations of students. Written in an accessible style, books in the series provide introductions to, and exemplars of, the best work in the discipline and its various subareas.

PUBLISHED

Colin Hay, Michael Lister, David Marsh (eds)
The State: Theories and Issues (2nd edition)

Jon Pierre and B. Guy Peters
Governance, Politics and the State (2nd edition)

Johanna Kantola and Emanuela Lombardo
Gender and Political Analysis

Vivien Lowndes, David Marsh and Gerry Stoker (eds)
Theory and Methods in Political Science (4th edition)

Dimiter Toshkov
Research Design in Political Science

Keith Dowding
The Philosophy and Methods of Political Science

Andrew Hindmoor and Brad Taylor
Rational Choice (2nd edition)

Gerry Stoker, B. Guy Peters and Jon Pierre (eds)
The Relevance of Political Science

Jean Grugel and Matthew Louis Bishop
Democratization: A Critical Introduction (2nd edition)

David Beetham
The Legitimation of Power (2nd edition)

B. Guy Peters
Strategies for Comparative Research in Political Science

Ioannis Papadopoulos
Democracy in Crisis? Politics, Governance and Policy

Vivien Lowndes and Mark Roberts
Why Institutions Matter: The New Institutionalism in Political Science

Lina Eriksson
Rational Choice Theory: Potential and Limits

Heather Savigny and Lee Marsden
Doing Political Science and International Relations: Theories in Action

Rudra Sil and Peter J. Katzenstein
Beyond Paradigms: Analytic Eclecticism in the Study of World Politics

Cees van der Eijk and Mark Franklin
Elections and Voters

Martin J. Smith
Power and the State

Peter Burnham, Karin Gilland Lutz, Wyn Grant and Zig Layton-Henry
Research Methods in Politics (2nd edition)

Colin Hay
Political Analysis: A Critical Introduction

Democratization

A Thematic Approach

**Stephen Noakes
and
Chris Wilson**

BLOOMSBURY ACADEMIC
LONDON · NEW YORK · OXFORD · NEW DELHI · SYDNEY

BLOOMSBURY ACADEMIC
Bloomsbury Publishing Plc
50 Bedford Square, London, WC1B 3DP, UK
1385 Broadway, New York, NY 10018, USA
29 Earlsfort Terrace, Dublin 2, Ireland

BLOOMSBURY, BLOOMSBURY ACADEMIC and the Diana logo are
trademarks of Bloomsbury Publishing Plc

First published in Great Britain 2023

A catalogue record for this book is available from the British Library.

A catalog record for this book is available from the Library of Congress.

ISBN:	HB:	978-1-3503-2834-1
	PB:	978-1-3503-2835-8
	ePDF:	978-1-3503-2836-5
	eBook:	978-1-3503-2837-2

Political Analysis Series

Typeset by Integra Software Services Pvt. Ltd.

To find out more about our authors and books visit www.bloomsbury.com
and sign up for our newsletters.

Contents

List of boxes

Introduction: Democratization in an era of pessimism and doubt

Planet earth, then and now

Compare any two political maps, one from the early twentieth century and one from the present, and you will notice that the world now contains more democracies than it used to.

Woodrow Wilson, 28th President of the United States, famously waged the First World War to 'make the world safe for democracy', but it would be many more decades before democracies ceased to be in the minority internationally. In 1950, European democracy was primarily concentrated in the western- and northern-most portions of the map. The UK, Ireland, France, the Low Countries and Scandinavia were the continent's democratic standard bearers. Latvia, Lithuania, Estonia, Poland, Czechoslovakia, Hungary, Romania, Bulgaria and East Germany were all satellites of the Soviet Union, with whom they formed the bulk of the 'eastern bloc' – a group of communist countries comprising the main source of opposition to the world's democracies. Yugoslavia and Albania created their own communist governments, limiting democratic prospects in Southern Europe. Italy's experiment with fascism had only recently ended, while Spain's would continue until the 1970s.

In Asia, democratic India was the exception, not the rule, in the mid-twentieth century. The People's Republic of China and Democratic People's Republic of Korea (North Korea) allied themselves with communist states abroad, and were followed by Vietnam, Laos and Cambodia soon after. Meanwhile, strong anti-communist dictatorships were established in

Indonesia, South Korea, the Philippines and Taiwan. Many Latin American countries were likewise embroiled in civil strife between communist insurgencies on the one hand and military strongmen on the other. Democracy was nearly absent in the Middle East and Africa, save for a few non-typical cases.

By the early 1990s, the picture had changed considerably. The Soviet Union had collapsed, transforming the political face of Europe and indeed the globe almost overnight, dramatically increasing the number of democratic states. This surge in the number of democracies worldwide was referred to as the 'Third Wave', the latest in a set of macro-historical processes that witnessed the global ascendance of democracy as a system of government (Huntington 1991). The first wave began in the late eighteenth century with the revolutionary collapse of monarchism and the onset of democratic republics in places like the United States and France. The second wave involved the birth of new democracies in places like Japan, West Germany and Italy after the Second World War, and also included newly decolonized countries in Africa and Asia throughout the 1950s and 1960s. For many scholars, however, the demise of the Soviet Union and concomitant wave of transitions to democracy during the Third Wave signalled 'the end of history' (Fukuyama 1992). With its main rival now eliminated, no practicable alternatives to capitalist democracy remained, and thus it was regarded as the ultimate phase of human political development.

Democratization is the study of what happened during the intervening years – of how and why democracy spread globally to become the widely practised system of government it is today. Democratization studies are concerned with explaining change or stasis in political institutions or *regimes*, where the latter comprise the rules of the game through which politics gets played in a given setting. This understanding of regimes casts them as distinct from *governments*, which are game players. For example, as of this writing, the government of the UK is led by Liz Truss of the Conservative Party. The UK regime, however, is a constitutional monarchy, which evolved over many centuries of rule by kings and queens, now tempered by popular sovereignty.

Thirty years on from the 'end of history', the outlook for democracy and democratization around the world is uncertain. On the one hand, there exists a sort of consensus recognition of democracy's viability. This consensus appears to be so strong that nearly all of the world's countries adopt the terminology and trappings of democracy, even as they remain thoroughly undemocratic in practice (think the 'People's Democratic Republic of Korea', or the 'Democratic Republic of the Congo'). On the other hand, many of the countries that began democratic transitions after the fall of communism never reached their goal. Many have slid back into old practices, and now resemble their former authoritarian selves more than any democracy. As the literature on hybrid regimes indicates, many others did change, but their systems resemble neither democracy nor authoritarianism and instead show characteristics of both, and in a state of fixity, with no signs of tipping or transitioning to one over the other (Diamond 2002). Long-established democracies have encountered significant problems in their functionality and legitimacy, while non-democracies like China appear to be on the rise, developing rapidly with a high degree of orderliness and stability, sowing seeds of doubt that democracy is the best or last way of politics. One 2021 report argues that authoritarianism is on the rise, that 'electoral autocracy' is the most common regime type worldwide and that levels of democracy in the world are at their lowest since 1990. The Covid-19 pandemic has only made matters worse, with two-thirds of all countries imposing media restrictions, one-third using emergency powers with no time limit and many more guilty of a range of more and less serious misuses of power (V-Dem Institute 2021: 6).

This book is about the processes of, and prognoses for, democratization in the twenty-first century. It is intended as a guide for students of democratization, introducing them to the key ideas that have animated scholarship within the *transition paradigm*, the framework that dominated in democratization studies for decades but has now fallen into disrepute due to the large volume of countries that failed to democratize as expected (Carothers 2002). The book also examines emergent trends and challenges that push us to adapt or refine our tools for understanding how or why political systems around the world differ, and why democracy does not emerge in particular cases or with the regularity it was once predicted to. Such trends include authoritarian retrenchment and the prevalence of so-called 'illiberal democracies', democratic decay as a result of populist demagoguery, the rise of extremist groups (some of which have a global reach) and increasing sectarian violence, among other factors. A generation removed from the triumphalism of the post-Third Wave era, the book is as much a study of contemporary barriers and threats to democratization as it is a survey of the ways democratization has traditionally been studied.

What exactly is democracy?

As we note repeatedly throughout this book, measuring democratization is an essential but difficult task, complicated by both the huge range of countries referring to themselves as democratic and the propensity for any country to behave in democratic or undemocratic ways at different points in time.

How do we recognize democracies when we see them? What is it that enables us to distinguish them from other forms of government? The enterprise of defining democracy precisely is of foundational importance but is hardly new. As Alexis de Tocqueville wrote in 1836,

> It is our way of using the words 'democracy' and 'democratic governance' that brings about the greatest confusion. Unless these words are clearly defined and their definition agreed upon, people will live in an inextricable confusion of ideas, much to the advantage of demagogues and despots.
>
> (as cited in Sartori 1987: 3)

This definitional challenge is only compounded by the current consensus for democracy globally – that is, by the common tendency for regimes of all types to refer to themselves as democracies, often in qualified terms. Modifiers such as 'guided', 'limited', 'proto', 'neopatrimonial' and even 'authoritarian' sometimes precede 'democracy' when referencing countries with hybridized political institutions. Prefixes like 'multiparty', 'federal', 'confederal', 'consociational' or 'parliamentary' are often applied to countries traditionally thought of as democratic, but which nonetheless vary widely in their institutional configurations (Collier and Levitsky 1997: 430–2; Schmitter and Karl 1991). Even among countries like the UK, the United States, Canada, Australia, France, Ireland and New Zealand, there is no single model of democratic politics, nor any uniform blueprint for the design and operation of democratic procedures.

So, what do democracies have in common?

Most users of this book will probably associate democracy with voting, a sentiment shared by twentieth-century theorists of democratization. In 1959, the Austrian economist Joseph Schumpeter defined democracy in terms of its 'procedural minimums'. That is, the minimum standard for classifying democratic political systems as such, and for distinguishing them from non-democracies, lies in their procedural characteristics, i.e. elections. Decades later, open, free and fair elections held at predictable intervals are still widely regarded as a necessary criterion for identifying democracies.

However, virtually all theorists now agree that democracies are much more than elections. Individual and collective liberties, including freedoms of the press, belief, speech and internal geographic movement and the right to seek public office, as well as protections against cruel, inhumane or degrading punishment, a relative measure of equality of opportunity, access to social services and representation for minorities are all just as important, and are also broadly typical of democratic systems. Moreover, electoral competition is misleading as an indicator of democracy because many non-democratic countries hold regular elections, often to legitimize incumbent leaders or placate their international critics. However, elections in these cases are not necessarily always free or fair.

To address this problem (sometimes termed the 'electoral fallacy'), later generations of scholars developed new tools for identifying democracies that moved beyond procedural minimums to more fully capture the values and behaviours that separate authentic democracies from imposters. In addition to the formal institutions that define democracy, these theorists argued that it is the informal institutionalization of certain values that causes democracy to emerge and endure. Informal institutionalization refers to the degree to which these values have been internalized and adopted by political actors, including office seekers, voters and citizens at large. The point at which they are so deeply engrained that democracy becomes 'the only game in town' (i.e. at which alternatives to democracy are unthinkable) is known as *consolidation* (O'Donnell 1996: 36).

US political theorist Robert Dahl offered the term 'polyarchy' (lit. 'government by the many') to differentiate democracies from non-democracies and shed light on how values and procedures interact to aid and abet democratization. For Dahl, the essence of democratic systems lay in their patterns of participation in politics, particularly the ability of opposition candidates or parties to seek and gain office, to articulate their preferences and to expect to have these preferences considered reasonably and fairly in the conduct of government (though without assurances that these preferences may be converted into laws). In turn, the appearance and survival of this type of participation depends upon broad-based stewardship for the principles of representation and contestation. Note that in this sense, stewardship does not merely mean 'tolerance', but the guaranteed granting of voice to those participants in politics who might otherwise not be heard.

Dahl's conception of polyarchy envisaged a political system that was not solely determined by majority rule but balanced the weight of majority perspectives with meaningful contrarian viewpoints (Dahl 1971).

In other words, genuine democracies temper competitiveness with concern for the values of fairness, transparency and accountability. Democratic accountability operates both vertically and horizontally. Democratic rulers are held vertically accountable, directly or indirectly, by subjecting office holders to recall or replacement at predictable intervals at the ballot box. Those that fail to meet voters' expectations can lose their post, while those that satisfy voters may keep their office for a further term. However, democracy is also strengthened through horizontal accountability – i.e. guarding against the unrestrained exercise of power by making different branches of the government subject to one another. In the US context, this is usually referred to as the 'separation of powers'. The authors of the US constitution, having waged a war of independence against the British monarchy, sought safeguards against over-concentrations of power in any single branch of government. Thus, they created a bicameral legislative branch consisting of the Senate and House of Representatives, and further distinguished this branch from the executive and judicial branches. This ensured that presidents and judges could not simply pass laws at will but required the assent of the people's duly elected representatives. Of course, not all democracies opt for a US-style 'separation of powers' (in Westminster-style parliamentary democracies, executive and legislative powers are fused). However, most democratic constitutions contain provisions upholding 'checks and balances' of one sort or another. For example, the Canadian Senate exists to provide 'sober second-thought' to legislation introduced by other government branches. In turn, the exercise of horizontal or vertical accountability depends upon freely accessible information – how else would voters make informed decisions about whom to elect, or self-restraining governments identify and call out abuses? The extent to which such information is knowable or shared is called *transparency*. Democracies cannot function properly without it.

One further set of democracy-strengthening values concerns civic participation. While Dahl's discussion of participation centres mainly on the behaviour of competitively chosen legislators, healthy democratic systems require citizens to be active and engaged on a consistent basis. Citizens may exercise their voice on election day, but national elections may only be held at intervals of three or four years, or in some cases even less often. Civil society becomes an important agent of democratization by facilitating sustained, regular representation of varied social interests, whether these are cultural, linguistic, religious, educational or based on gender or sexuality, as well as public-interest watchdogs (pursuit of private interests, as in the case of profit-seeking firms, falls outside the scope of civil society, as we discuss in chapter four). This pattern of sustained representation in turn serves to strengthen transparency and accountability, both vertically and horizontally. Accordingly, civic engagement can be critical for the emergence of new democracies (by, for instance, shedding light on the abuses of incumbent dictatorships), and for their long-term survival.

In laying out the constellations of formal institutions and the informally institutionalized values that sustain them, theorists of democratization also established what democracy is not. First, nothing in the foregoing discussion indicates that democracies are necessarily more economically well-off than non-democracies, or indeed that there is any *prima facie* relationship between democratization and economic development. True, some democracies are wealthier than others. Many of the world's oldest democracies are among the world's richest countries, including the United States, France, the UK and Australia. Yet democracies run the economic gamut. Democracy is well consolidated in places like Mongolia, Jamaica, Ghana, the Cook Islands and many other countries, despite their relative poverty levels. The existence of poor democracies highlights a troubling truism – that democratization may not be a path to prosperity, and certainly isn't the only path.

Relatedly, democracies are not necessarily more economically open than non-democracies. Though in practice there is often an overlap between political and economic liberty, there is no principled or theoretical requirement that this be so. New Zealand has been democratic since its inception, but, prior to the Labour Government-led neoliberalization programme of the 1980s, was one of the world's more isolated economies. Many other democracies are likewise inward-looking or at times even unwelcoming to foreign investment. Meanwhile authoritarian countries such as Singapore or China are increasingly open and developing rapidly. Indeed, in the 1990s many argued that economic neoliberalization and globalization may undercut democratic principles in a variety of ways, not least by having a homogenizing effect on local cultures and imposing restrictions on national sovereignty.

Third, democracies are not inherently more stable or governable than non-democracies. Many are weak states whose governments struggle to turn their preferences into authoritative actions. In Mexico, for example, large segments of the state security apparatus and judiciary came under the influence of criminal gangs once it came to light that transnational drug cartels could offer better pay than most police forces. Particularly in areas where the cartels were strong, multiple levels of the Mexican state were relatively weak, and in some instances unable to provide citizens with the most basic of government services: public safety. The problem of state weakness and ascendant cartel strength became especially pronounced after the Partido Revolucionario Institucional (PRI) was removed from power in 2000 and President Vicente Fox of the opposition was elected.

Some other democracies are failing or recently failed states where law and order completely collapsed and democratic institutions rose from the ashes. Cambodia and Afghanistan are two ready examples. Persistent poverty is a key part of the story, but in both cases building functional states has proven a difficult and complex task. Cambodia's experience was shaped heavily by the Khmer Rouge regime that held power from 1975–9, during which an estimated 1.2 million Cambodians (or about 20 per cent of the pre-1975 population) died as a result of radical social engineering policies. Consequently, Cambodia has struggled to come to terms with human rights abuses, and with the reintegration of former regime officials into Cambodian society, even after a widely publicized truth commission sought to shake the country free from the spectre of its authoritarian past. Afghanistan's democratic institutions, created after the toppling of the Taliban regime by a US-led international coalition in the early 2000s, proved even more fragile. The Islamic Republic collapsed in August 2021 amid the seizure of power by a resurgent Taliban (Murtazashvili 2022).

Even the strongest and wealthiest of the world's democracies are not always so easily governed. The modern versions of France, Canada, Germany, the United States and many others are multicultural societies where plural viewpoints or identities not only exist but periodically bubble over into unrest. The 2022 truckers' convoy and subsequent blockade against Covid-19 vaccine mandates in the Canadian capital, Ottawa, is just one recent example. The demonstration caused major disruptions and highlighted deep divisions over politics within Canadian society. Democracies have chosen from a diverse repertoire of options for accommodating difference. Many of these are discussed in depth later in this book. These discussions demonstrate that there is no 'one size fits all' model of democracy. Rather, democracies may come in many institutional forms but are united and defined by the principles at their core.

Contemporary challenges to democratization

The rise of illiberal democracies

The definition of democracies elaborated above rests on the embeddedness and the protection of liberal values within political institutions. The more deeply embedded and well protected these are, the more resilient a democracy is likely to be. This leaves us with two key problems, however: 1) How can liberal values become embedded and reflected in places having no previous democratic experience (in other words, where do democracy-strengthening values come from)?; and 2) What are we to make of the contemporary trend where democratic institutions exist in the apparent absence of liberal values?

The first question is one which has animated scholarship on democratization for many decades. In the aftermath of the Cold War, much scepticism was expressed about the longer-term prospects for democracy in Eastern Europe. Much of this democratic pessimism centred on supposed cultural differences and experiences separating the countries of Eastern Europe from those of existing democracies. Thirty years later, Poland, the Czech Republic and Slovakia have very strong, consolidated democratic regimes. Back then, however, it was supposed that Czech, Slovak and Polish people had little first-hand knowledge of democratic processes and no cultural background with values that supported democracy, and thus that democratic institutions would never take root. In the 1930s and 1940s, similar arguments were made about German, Italian and Japanese society; all three are now strong, stable democracies. Very similar arguments are still tabled to explain why China has not democratized. Chinese culture, the argument goes, is incompatible with liberal democracy and much more disposed to the kind of authoritarianism China has evolved since 1978.

The problem with these arguments is that the understanding of cultural values employed is excessively static. Cultures and values do not stand still in any country. Rather, they are constantly evolving (the United States of 2022 is culturally very different from the United States of the 1950s, for example). Nor are values necessarily stable, consistent or evenly subscribed within individual societies. Northern Italy, for example, has been shown to have much stronger civic traditions than the south, which explains in large part the observed differences in the way democracy works there (Putnam 1993).

The propensity for changes in values, sometimes even radical change over a relatively short period of time, leads us to question the source of such changes. Since the end of the Second World War, there has been a growing trend towards the globalization of values. Indeed, the global spread of democratic values was in evidence well before that, but the latter half of the twentieth century and the first decades of the twenty-first saw a drastic increase in the rate at which values transited across borders, primarily as a result of rapid technological changes. As a result, many democratic transitions during this period came about because of values learned or observed in other countries. The most obvious examples are the televised toppling of the Berlin Wall, and the opening of the border between Austria and Hungary, both of which became catalysts for the collapse of communism and the rise of nascent democracy across nearly all of Eastern Europe. To be sure, many democratic transitions have resulted from locally based political activity, but nearly all such grassroots movements have in some way obtained resources from beyond their borders and applied these to their struggle at home. This tactic of seeking help from abroad for domestic activism is known as the 'boomerang effect' (Keck and Sikkink 1998).

The second question calls attention to a problem with our conceptual toolkit for understanding and classifying different types of political systems. Democracy has often been viewed in exclusive and binary terms – a given country is either democratic or it isn't, and cannot be both a democracy and a non-democracy at the same time. This framing allows for the possibility that democracies can vary in their institutional features, or that some non-democracies are more repressive than others, with a scale ranging from soft authoritarian countries such as Singapore to totalitarian ones like North Korea. Critically, this framing also allows for countries to slide along the authoritarian–democratic continuum, transitioning from one type of regime to the other if specified criteria are met. On the other hand, it does not allow for the straddling of the point that separates democracies from non-democracies. For many scholars of democratic transition, this 'line in the sand' has traditionally been important for telling real democracies apart from the pretenders.

This approach to measuring democratic change runs into difficulty when states appear to belong to democratic and non-democratic camps or move back and forth between the two, effectively blurring the distinction between them. As already noted, the electoral fallacy is one common manifestation of the problem. If regular elections are the distinguishing mark of a democracy, most of the world's countries could be declared democratic. However, electoral competition might not always be free, fair or open. Democratic processes sometimes exist side by side with undemocratic practices and often seem to facilitate or lend credibility to them. Zimbabwe under Robert Mugabe's ZANU-PF and Malaysia under its ruling UMNO coalition are two ready examples. These and many others are commonly referred to as 'illiberal democracies', 'competitive authoritarianism' or, sometimes, 'hybrid' regimes, to reflect their dual authoritarian/democratic character (Levitsky and Way 2010; Diamond 2002; Zakaria 1997). Throughout the book, we contend that these have become more pervasive over the last twenty-five years, fuelling debate over the future of democracy globally.

The challenge of classifying political systems is further compounded by the fact that all democracies, even those most firmly consolidated, sometimes behave in non-democratic ways. New Zealand and Australia are widely agreed to be democracies, yet the label fails to do justice to practices in both that trample the rights of Indigenous peoples, albeit in different ways and to different degrees. Indigenous Canadians might likewise cast a critical eye on Canadian democracy, which historically has reinforced rather than righted colonial injustices. Given the persistence of racial discrimination and lagging voting rights for more than a century after the abolition of slavery, one could argue that the United States did not democratize until 1965 with the passage of the Civil Rights Act. The point is that talk of 'transition' and especially of 'consolidation' has tended to divert focus from instances of backsliding by the world's pre-eminent democratic exemplars, as though democracy, once consolidated, cannot be lost or weakened. An alternative or post-transition framework might look to remedy this classification problem by pointing out that *democracies are constantly becoming*, and require diligent engagement for their health and survival.

Democratic decay

As a parallel to the rise of illiberal democracies, we also examine the phenomenon of decay or decline in the quality of democracy in consolidated states. This decay, we argue, is related to but distinct from the 'democratic deficits' described by theorists in the 1970s, 1980s and 1990s (Durant 1995). Whereas democratic deficits refer to a structural or functional problem within democratic institutions, we conceptualize decay as a potential but not inevitable consequence of these deficits (for example, residents of Washington DC are obliged to pay federal income tax but lack direct congressional representation; this is evidence of a democratic deficit, but not necessarily decay). The problem was initially described in 1975 by US political scientists, who, writing in the aftermath of the Watergate scandal, warned of a slide into 'anomic' democracy severe enough to be called a 'crisis' (Crozier, Huntington and Watanuki 1975). One could easily argue that after the events of 6 January 2021, when an angry mob stormed the Capitol building to stop the ratification of Joe Biden's Electoral College win, the United States is once again an embattled democracy.

Much of the decay discussed throughout the book results from tension between free expression and protection from harm, values which many democracies inherited from the political thought of Montesquieu, a seventeenth-century French philosopher. To what degree should democracies protect freedoms of speech, thought or action? For Montesquieu, democratic rights were not absolute, but limited by the propensity for such speech or action to cause harm to another. In modern terms, this debate is sometimes conceptualized as a fight between 'freedom to' (act or speak) and 'freedom from' (harm), and has tangible implications for governing and law-making in democratic societies.

The major concern involves use or manipulation of legal loopholes to restrict, undermine or extinguish the rights and freedoms of others. Sometimes the actors involved are politically powerful non-governmental actors or societal interest groups. The gun lobby in the United States is one example. In this case, the right to bear arms, constitutionally protected by the Second Amendment, supersedes the risks to public safety resulting from widespread gun ownership. Ergo, federally mandated controls on firearms remain very weak, even as mass shootings continue. Put another way, in the US context, freedom to own and carry a gun trumps freedom from harm inflicted by guns. This near-absolute commitment to gun ownership is extreme relative to the situation in most other developed democracies, which either ban guns outright, or place tight restrictions on the number and types of guns that can be owned by civilians. In the UK, for example, such restrictions are justified by public safety concerns. There, freedom from gun violence trumps freedom to own a gun – almost the inverse of the US situation. The US approach to free speech is similar, making it an outlier among its democratic peers. Canada, New Zealand, Germany – indeed, almost all European democracies – have much tougher hate speech legislation, owing to differences in demography and historical experience. The key point here is that for many in the United States, failure to adopt stringent gun control laws, even in the face of recurrent mass shootings, represents a failure of democracy to meet citizens' needs or protect them from harm, and thus is a potential source of dissatisfaction in the US system of politics. Naturally, the situation is made all the more politically complex by the fact that gun advocates would no doubt view the adoption of stricter controls as an attack on sacrosanct freedoms, deepening malaise about democratic politics from the inverse side of public debate.

In many other instances, concerns for the health of democracy have been expressed when considering the rise of politicians seeking greater restrictions on the rights of marginalized populations, usually recent or non-naturalized immigrants. Donald Trump's campaign rhetoric around the construction of a border wall to keep out illegal Mexican migrants, the subsequent policy of separating the children of detained migrants from their parents and the seeming legitimation of these policies at the polls in November 2016 have all contributed to a growing sense of decay in US democracy. Similar arguments have been made about Hungary's Viktor Orbán, who acceded to the office of Prime Minister in 2010 and has since introduced a wave of anti-immigrant, anti-intellectual and anti-European Union (EU) legislation, and about Australia's Pauline Hanson. Of course, not all such politicians have enjoyed electoral success. France's Marine Le Pen and the Netherlands' Geert Wilders both experienced notable defeats in 2017. But candidates of similar 'nativist' profiles, once dark horses, are increasingly seen as electable in many democracies.

Sectarian violence and global terror

Our third major thematic focus concerns an issue many previous generations of democratization theorists did not have to consider as closely – the rise of global terror threats and transnational sectarian violence. Civil strife has long been a significant factor in shaping democratic outcomes. In this book, we devote discussion to the challenges to democratization posed by ethnic, religious and linguistic differences, particularly in the immediate aftermath of armed conflict. The range of strategies employed in the service of 'difference management' in new democracies is a particular concern of chapter three.

However, the potential for conflicts to spill over international borders is now greater than ever before. Technology has collapsed space and time, making it easier for diffuse terror cells to link up and form networks with membership numbers undreamt of in decades past. Antidemocratic principles can be disseminated more broadly and more quickly, increasing the likelihood of physical attacks by both large coordinated entities and 'lone wolf' individuals.

Large-scale coordinated terror attacks such as 9/11 are routinely framed as violent assaults on liberal democratic values. Radical Islamist groups like Al Qaeda view violent insurrection against these values and those that practise them as both necessary and just. In academic discourse, this struggle has been conceptualized as the 'clash of civilizations' in which incommensurable belief systems are pitted against one another in a fight-to-the-death struggle for survival (Huntington 1996). In the case of lone-wolf attacks, individuals with extreme views are sometimes able to take advantage of free speech laws and loosely policed online fora to advocate for and plan violent acts against ethnic, linguistic or religious minorities, tolerance for which they regard as abhorrent. One such attack took place in Christchurch, New Zealand, in March 2019, claiming the lives of fifty-one worshippers at the city's Al Noor Mosque and Linwood Islamic Centre. Another occurred in July 2011 when Anders Breivik first detonated a bomb outside the residence of the Norwegian Prime Minister in central Oslo, killing eight, before driving to a nearby summer camp for politically engaged youth and murdering sixty-nine more. Both incidents were described in the media as attacks on the very ideals that sustain liberal democracy.

Structure of the book

Part I: Democratization from within

Part I, comprising the five chapters which follow this introduction, explores approaches to democratization based on within-country conditions, including but not limited to such factors as economic development, education and industrialization; the role of authoritarian incumbents (including the military); civil society groups; and ethnic, linguistic or cultural cleavages. The chief aim is to orientate readers towards the main approaches employed (What is 'modernization theory' or 'transition studies'?) and questions asked (Who are the main actors? What are the main events? How often is there violence? What is the role of elections?) in empirical and theoretical research on democratization. Because these questions have been well studied in recent decades, these chapters can also serve as a kind of intellectual history, giving a sense of how the study of democratization has developed.

Chapter one opens by considering some of the structural preconditions thought to be important for the emergence and survival of democratic regimes – particularly the role of economic development. The association between capitalist development and democracy is perhaps the most consequential and persistent proposition in the study of democratization. We open the chapter by interrogating anew the presumption of democracy's compatibility with capitalism, before unpacking some of the classic hypotheses undergirding the supposed relationship between development and democracy, including the separate-but-related question of economic advancement in the survival or breakdown of non-democracies. The chapter then concludes with a consideration of the 'resource curse', a condition in which over-reliance on natural resource wealth, often but not always relating to oil, can actually create structural barriers to the onset of democracy and limit the chances of its consolidation in some cases.

Whereas chapter one was concerned with exploring how democratization is thought to have arisen from economic structures, chapter two is concerned with historical sociology, a more process-based approach that allows us to see in greater detail how structural conditions are animated, and by whom. For example, consider the role of capitalism introduced in chapter one. Capitalist development produced a stratified class system based on ownership of private property, causing the newly well-to-do to seek political protection for their gains – a phenomenon captured in Barrington Moore's famous dictum, 'no bourgeoisie, no democracy'. However, this chapter also considers the flipside of the coin – that democratization is a by-product of class conflict, and that the critical mass of economically marginalized classes arising from capitalism is the key driving force behind democracy. In this sense, democratization is understood as a drive for greater social equality, a process legitimized by mass participation in democratic revolutions in places as far apart as the United States, France and India, and by the gradual expansion of the franchise in many other democracies. The latter portion of the chapter then examines 'transitions studies', a framework similarly geared towards understanding the interaction of structures, actors and their interests, but which departs from the early structural-functionalist and Marxist-inspired scholarship to highlight the critical role of leaders and coalitions in negotiating democracy's onset, whether these be pro-democracy reformers or authoritarian incumbents. We note the variety of forms transition processes may take, but stress that stable democracy is not always the end result. Accordingly, the final portion of the chapter considers some options available to stalwart dictators seeking to preserve and prolong their own non-democratic rule.

Drawing from detailed case studies in Indonesia, Kenya and India, chapter three deals with democracy and the propensity for violence in divided societies. As we note, a great deal of literature exists to suggest not only that democracies are less prone to engage in interstate wars, but that they tend to be more domestically peaceful as well. However, this theoretical premise is difficult to square with the political realities of many states where violence (or the potential for it) is a salient fact of political life. We identify challenges at both the pre- and post-transition stages. Violence becomes a particular risk in what we term 'dangerous transitions' and quasi-democracies, where participatory representative institutions solidify and deepen existing identities, giving groups that are at odds with one another a vehicle to engage in escalating conflict. In other more advanced democratic cases, vote-seeking elites are incentivized to manipulate identity rifts to their advantage, and may even encourage violence if it helps them politically. This is a tactic known as 'ethnic outbidding'. We also call attention to the more common approaches to ameliorating the potential for future violence through careful constitutional design, a key task in many new and historically divided democracies. The first, which recognizes existing divisions rather than ameliorating them, emphasizes mechanisms for sharing power and is derived principally from the life's work of Arend Lijphart. The second, coined 'centripetalism' by Donald Horowitz, places greater importance on the moderating effects of particular institutional formulas. Both approaches may be important for the establishment of a democracy-supporting political culture in the longer term, a subject to which we turn in chapter four.

Part of the way that structural conditions helped to shape democratic movements was through the aggregation of social interests at the grassroots. Once galvanized into blocs, groups of like-minded citizens mobilized in support of democratic change, often by calling to light the abuses or excesses of authoritarian incumbents, or by lending support to reformist parties and candidates. Yet the ability of these 'civil society' actors to successfully advocate for the emergence and health of democracy depends on variables of a different sort, specifically the cultural or cognitive factors that shape early institutional choices and thus the likelihood, pace and sequence of democratic transitions. Critically at issue are the civic traditions, norms, beliefs and practices thought to help democratic prospects through their existence, or hinder democracy's chances by their absence. Chapter four opens with a consideration of political cultures and how they work, followed by a critical reflection on the role of cultural explanations more broadly. We then consider the importance of civil society in democratic transition and consolidation, noting the part it plays in birthing political opposition movements and parties, the avenues it presents for everyday participation in a political system and its watchdog functions that safeguard against abuses of state power. The latter portion of the chapter is devoted to a trio of case studies of civil society – set in Afghanistan, China and the United States – each of which faces different impediments to the onset or health of democracy.

Non-democratic regimes have grown increasingly diverse in recent decades, and the task of differentiating them from democracies has become more complex. 'Hybrid regimes' – that is, those which exhibit signs of being both democratic and non-democratic – are the focus of chapter five. In the past, many books on democratization did not devote much time or attention to hybrid regimes. This is because some scholars saw hybridity as a temporary thing. Some thought of hybrid regimes as unfinished transitions, or as snapshots taken at difficult points along a path that would ultimately lead to successful democratization. Today, however, hybrid regimes tend to be seen as a fixed category in their own right, with many such regimes appearing to be stable while straddling the authoritarian–democratic divide. Chapter five explores different sorts of hybrid regimes. 'Illiberal democracies' frequently have formal democratic procedures in place, such as elections, but are characterized by a range of illiberal practices, such as a corruption, patronage, intimidation and manipulation. Beyond the right to vote itself, the rights of citizens are thinly protected. By contrast, competitive authoritarian regimes tend to be better at protecting citizens' rights and upholding the rule of law. Elections are held, and may be free and open, but, crucially, are not fair. In competitive authoritarian systems, practices and structures remain in place that make it all but impossible for opposition candidates or parties to win, thereby preventing power transitions from taking place. We illustrate the concepts with reference to two case studies, the Philippines and Singapore, though there are plenty more we could well have chosen. As we note, countries that are not wholly authoritarian or democratic are now the most common type of regime worldwide.

Part II: Democratization from without: Considerations of the global age

While Part I was primarily concerned with elaborating the range of internal political, economic and social conditions that enable or constrain democratization, Part II draws attention to the external factors which exercise pressure for democratic reform from outside or beyond the state.

Whereas chapter five introduces the 'grey zone' between democracy and authoritarianism, chapter six explores a range of threats that are present even in well-consolidated democracies. For past generations of scholars, coups and counter-coups were probably the most serious threat to democracy, especially in newly transitional states where the military played a major role in politics. We would be remiss if we did not take this opportunity to discuss the role coups have played in transition processes historically. Our main focus, however, is the more contemporary trend in which democracies come under attack from their own elected civilian leaders. Unlike coups, which tend to wash away incumbent regimes quickly, sometimes overnight, the patterns we call attention to engender a slow, steady decline in democratic quality. Using the cases of India and the United States, the chapter shows how populist leaders wielding nativist rhetoric have contributed to serious democratic backsliding in countries once regarded as 'safely' democratic, and given rise to events more classically associated with illiberal democracies. We include a discussion of populism and illiberal democracies – both appear to be common challenges worldwide, with perhaps some demonstration or 'copycat' effects at work, particularly when we consider the rise and role of demagogues.

Chapter seven examines the broad issue of globalization, at the heart of which is the issue of states and their continuing relevance in world politics. In the aftermath of the Cold War, globalization was taken as synonymous with dissolving borders, a freer flow of people, goods and ideas and a concomitant rise in the importance of non-state actors such as multinational corporations. In chapter seven, we acknowledge the altered position of states in a globalized world, and focus our analysis primarily on two key events. First we call attention to global civil society, or transborder networks of non-state actors and the role they play in value diffusion. While we recognize that non-governmental organizations (NGOs) can perform internationally some of the democracy-supporting functions that domestic civil society groups carry out, we also note the power imbalances and 'uncivil' organizations that limit the democratic nature of global civil society itself. Taking these power differentials into account, we then consider the question of democracy's universalism or cultural boundedness in the context of globalization and the spread of ideas and norms to parts of the world far from their points of origin. The latter half of the chapter explores 'neighbourhood' effects, which refers to the apparent spill-over of democratization from one state into a neighbouring one and explains the tendency for democratization to occur in geographic clusters, as a result of information sharing and cross-border value diffusion. Our examples highlight that such 'snowballing' is not confined to any particular part of the world, but neither are democratic outcomes always guaranteed.

If peace is a desirable end, and one accepts the premise that democracies are more peace-prone than other types of regimes, then logically the creation of new democracies ought to lead to a more peaceful world. By launching international democracy assistance programmes – also known as 'democracy assistance' or 'political aid' – a range of consolidated democratic donor states have attempted to do just that. Chapter eight seeks first to define democracy promotion, and to address the motivations for its provision. It then delves into a detailed description of some of the more common types of assistance, including electoral support (including monitoring), political party aid, rule of law development and the support given to civil society organizations. At several points along the way, we note persistent problems with measuring the results of democracy assistance. Does it make any difference to the emergence or health of new democracies? If it did, how would we know? Because these measurement difficulties have provided ammunition to critics of international democracy promotion, we conclude the chapter with a brief assessment of changing donor attitudes and behaviours, most notably during the presidency of Donald Trump, when US assistance efforts were dramatically scaled back.

By way of conclusion, chapter nine considers what the future may hold for democracy and democratization. The foundational observation of the chapter is that the definition and practice of democracy is not historically stable, but has fluctuated and acquired new and different meanings over time and space. For example, the way democracy was practised in ancient Athens is very different from how it was practised in nation-states of the industrial age. Both differ from common understandings of democracy today. Elements of the democratic idea have retained their value across periods and from place to place, but have not stood still. Given this, why would we expect conceptions of democracy to stand still in the future?

Some have used this question to try to improve upon liberal democracy by experimenting with the nature and scope of political participation and representation. Discussion of these experiments, including sortition, deliberative polling and various forms of e-democracy, occupy the bulk of the chapter. The chapter then concludes with a discussion of a radically different political model emerging in China, one which adopts the epithet of 'democracy' but repudiates the liberal values commonly associated with it. Supporters argue for the superiority of China's model over liberal democracy. For them, China's developmental success in recent decades is evidence of the model's desirability and replicability elsewhere, raising the prospect that it may spread and further challenge democracy as we know it. This, we contend, is part of what drives fears of China's rise among liberal democratic governments. At precisely the moment when democracy in many of these places appears to be declining, and the number of illiberal democracies in the world is expanding, the argument that China's model may be more effective seems just as threatening as its military rise and economic power, and perhaps even more so. What if liberal democracy isn't the last phase of human political development? What happens after the end of history?

Questions for discussion

1 How do we measure democracy or democratization?
2 What is meant by 'the Third Wave'?
3 Do you think democracy in the world is advancing, retreating or standing still, relative to twenty-five years ago?
4 What are some of the most serious threats to democracy today? Can you think of others not explicitly mentioned in this chapter?
5 Why would scholars contend that the transition paradigm is no longer an effective framework for thinking about political change?

Further reading

Boix, Carles, 'Democracy, Development, and the International System', *American Political Science Review*, Vol. 105, No. 4 (2011): 809–28.
Boix, Carles, and Susan C. Stokes, 'Endogenous Democratization', *World Politics*, Vol. 55, No. 4 (2003): 517–49.

Carothers, Thomas, 'The End of the Transition Paradigm', *Journal of Democracy*, Vol. 13, No. 1 (2002): 5–21.

Crouch, Colin, *Post-Democracy* (Cambridge: Polity Press, 2004).

Diamond, Larry, and Marc F. Plattner, eds, *The Global Divergence of Democracies* (Baltimore, MD: Johns Hopkins University Press, 2001).

Geddes, Barbara, 'What Do We Know about Democratization after Twenty Years?' *Annual Review of Political Science*, Vol. 2 (1999): 115–44.

Grugel, Jean, 'Democratization Studies Globalization: The Coming of Age of a Paradigm', *British Journal of Politics and International Relations*, Vol. 5, No. 2 (May 2003): 258–83.

Slater, Dan, 'Democratic Careening', *World Politics*, Vol. 65, No. 4 (October 2013): 729–63.

Tilly, Charles, *Democracy* (Cambridge: Cambridge University Press, 2007).

Van Hanen, Tatu, *Democratization: A Comparative Analysis of 170 Countries* (London: Routledge, 2003).

Part I

Democratization from within

1

Modernization and its discontents: Economic development and democratization

Throughout this book, our task is to enumerate some of the key explanations as to why some countries are democratic and others are not. We begin here with one of the oldest and most well-studied premises in the social sciences – that democracy and capitalism support and reinforce one another. More specifically, we interrogate the notion that economic development fuels democratic transition and consolidation.

This postulate traces its intellectual lineage to what is known as 'modernization theory', a category that includes but is not strictly limited to economic development, and touches upon a range of cultural, historical and geographic factors. Rooted in the work of famed sociologists like Max Weber (1864–1920) and, later, Talcott Parsons (1902–79), modernization theory of the mid-twentieth century – a time of global optimism about democracy – was mainly preoccupied with understanding the causes of (or impediments to) social change, which was observed and interpreted by theorists of that era as movement from a pre-modern or 'traditional' society to a more 'modern' one. Traditional societies tended to organize themselves politically as chiefdoms, monarchies, tribal alliances or confederations of ethno-linguistic clans. They were also less well-off materially and lacked the trappings of 'modern life', having lower life expectancies, higher rates of preventable disease and reduced access to education. Individuals in 'pre-modern' societies also owned less: only an elite few drove cars, watched television, made long-distance phone calls or machine-washed their clothes, let alone held the deeds to their homes. By contrast, nearly all the inhabitants of 'modern' societies took these and many other conveniences for granted. Modern societies had different economic and social structures in place, ensured that children attended school and received vaccines en masse, and their governments were determined by results at the ballot box, not by heredity. Thus, there was a perverse progressivism to modernization theory that put capitalist democracies on a pedestal. Modern societies were regarded as advanced, superior and worthy of emulation, while traditional ones were seen as primitive, sick and in need of help if they were to reach their potential. Modernization was therefore also a prescriptive formula, pointing out those aspects of traditional society that were to be jettisoned if development was to ever occur.

As this chapter proceeds, it will be important to remember that both negative and more favourable views of modernization theory are often based on historical context – scholars form their assessments from their observations of what is happening in the world at a given point in time. Because of the dismissiveness with which traditional social structures are treated, the version of modernization theory outlined above is now very much out of fashion. In 2021, many of us are uncomfortable with the view that poorer societies are inherently less-than, or that wealthy democratic ones must be better. Rightly so. However, these *normative* (i.e. value-based) judgements of modernization theory are different from evaluations that we might make *empirically* (i.e. based on evidence gleaned through the observation of patterns). It is this latter orientation we are primarily concerned with in this chapter.

A glance at world history might lead one to infer that capitalism and democracy support one another. Many of the world's oldest democratic nation-states happen to be some of the wealthiest. The United States and France, which trace their origins as democracies to the late eighteenth and early nineteenth centuries, fall into this category, as does the UK, whose democratic roots extend back even further. Does this mean that there is something mutually reinforcing about the political and economic structures of these countries, or is the apparent alignment of wealth and democracy merely coincidence? Did democracy succeed in these places *because* of their rapid economic growth, or *despite* it?

More recent occurrences in world history also saw capitalism and democracy gain broad, global acceptance at approximately the same time. This too might suggest that the two are natural companions. The pivotal event was the collapse of communist systems in Europe, particularly the

Union of Soviet Socialist Republics (USSR) in 1991. Prior to that point, global politics had been defined by a condition known as bipolarity – an ideological and diplomatic splitting of the world into two primary factions, capitalist democracies, led by the United States and its allies, on the one hand, and communist authoritarian states, led by the USSR, on the other. The term 'Cold War' is commonly used to refer to this period of world history, since although the United States and USSR were bitter rivals that competed militarily, technologically, economically and politically, bipolarity had the surprising effect of 'balancing' each of these factions with the other, thereby forestalling an active, 'hot' war of mutually assured destruction. With the collapse of the USSR, however, liberal democracy's main rival had been vanquished. Thus, it appeared there were no longer any viable alternatives to capitalism or democracy. Humanity had reached the final phase of its political development, and its future would be defined jointly by complimentary economic and political systems.

Yet the question of how (and how well) democracy and capitalism support each other remains unsettled. Indeed, as we argue in the latter portion of this chapter, there are good reasons for believing that unchecked economic growth may be destructive of democracy in certain circumstances, or that it may be used to keep democratic transitions at bay. We begin below with a theoretically orientated discussion of capitalism and democracy which serves twin purposes. First, it is meant to highlight the depth of the connection between the two theories in the understanding of major thinkers of the last century. Second, it shows the inescapable tension that arises between liberty and equality in capitalist democracies. We therefore take the opportunity to explore how various democracies have sought to mitigate this tension – to varying degrees and with varied degrees of success. From the outset, we underscore that there are many variants in the relationship between capitalism and democracy present throughout the world. While there is no singular model, one common variant, known sometimes as 'social democracy' or the 'Third Way', seeks to mitigate the negative effects of unbridled capitalism with welfare state construction and intervention. Such interventionism points out the dynamic, flexible nature of both capitalism and democracy, and the broader range of institutional and policy options available to transitioning states.

We then move on to examine the trend of post-Second World War political science that treated economic development ('modernization') as one of the so-called structural preconditions for the onset of democracy, a trend that remains influential in the study of democratization to this day, though much of the literature emphasizes that economic development and its correlates, discussed below, are as important for democracy's post-transition maintenance as for its initial onset. The flipside of this argument is then taken up in the latter half of the chapter, where we discuss the role of economics in regime collapse before concluding with an examination of a particular set of economic-structural hypotheses known as the 'resource curse' – a paradoxical circumstance where state reliance on revenues from exploitation of a limited, often single resource is thought to undermine prospects for both development and democratization.

Capitalism and democracy: Are they compatible?

By now, some readers might be thinking, 'Why would anyone expect economic growth to encourage democracy?' Perhaps they would point out that growth drives inequality, leading to an over-concentration of power in the hands of the few at the expense of the many. They may even point to the mass movements and demonstrations within democracies that seem to suggest anger and frustration over the disproportionate influence of the '1 per cent', as in the famous 'Occupy Wall Street' demonstrations that began in New York and spread across the United States, and indeed the world, in 2011. For these people, capitalism is oligarchy in disguise, and the very antithesis of what genuine, inclusive democracy is or ought to be.

If you hold such a sceptical view of democracy and capitalism's compatibility – let alone their complementarity – you are not alone. Many scholars argue that the two systems are at best uncomfortable alongside each other (Merkel 2014: 1; Lindblom 1982, Beetham 1997). But if this incongruity is so widely acknowledged, why have democracy and capitalism come to be seen as mutually supportive? On what basis is this claim made? There are several interrelated reasons.

First, as suggested in the introduction to this chapter, one enabling factor was the demise of ideological rivals after 1990. Back in the 1940s and 1950s, the future of capitalism and democracy was less certain than it appears today. Even after the vanquishing of fascist regimes in Germany, Italy and Japan, communism presented itself as a viable means to organize societies and meet human needs. Communist countries of the Cold War era, such as the Soviet Union, China, Yugoslavia, Cuba, North Korea and many others, were said to have 'command' economies because they functioned through careful and centralized planning by the state, without citizen consultation, voluntary association or free markets. Communism was thus a practicable alternative to democracy and capitalism, one serious enough for its spread to be viewed as a threat in need of 'containment' by the United States and its allies. Moreover, communist revolutions justified themselves on grounds of moral superiority – the belief that capitalism did a poor job of meeting humanity's needs, that another system could do so more equitably and that violent insurrection was necessary to achieve this end. Yet in hindsight, just the opposite turned out to be true. With the collapse of the Soviet Union, communism and central planning fell into disrepute, leaving market-orientated democracy as the most workable alternative (Fukuyama 1992).

Second, communism itself proved sufficiently dynamic and modular for a related ideological variant, 'socialism', to soften the effects of capitalism and render it more compatible with democracy. In the early twentieth century, a split developed within the communist movement which led to the creation of new parties whose adherents called themselves 'social democrats'. Although clearly influenced by Marxist-Leninist thought, just as the communists were, they were (generally and to varying degrees) less antagonistic towards markets and more willing to embrace peaceful democratic means to advance their agenda. In the years between the world wars, social democracy emerged in force, particularly in Europe, as a possible means of reconciling capitalism and democracy by at once mitigating capitalism's exploitative and inequitable tendencies by redistributing wealth, and by eschewing the violent seizure of power in favour of electoral methods and non-violent grassroots political mobilization (Berman 2006). In the Western academy, the outlook for socialism was positive enough for prominent theorists to predict that it would outlast capitalism, as Austrian economist Joseph Schumpeter did in 1942's *Capitalism, Socialism, and Democracy*.

Due in large part to the influence of social democratic parties, capitalism also turned out to be more malleable than was originally envisioned, something that translated directly to its spread and durability over time. Capitalism may have triumphed over communism in the end, but it had vulnerabilities of its own, namely social instability bred by boom-and-bust cycles of 'creative destruction' and the polarized distribution of wealth. The solution to these problems was the development of welfare states. Democratic governments would raise revenues via taxation and redistribute material benefits to offset the uncomfortable tension between liberty and equality that was the product of democracy's marriage to capitalism. In other words, a measure of socialism was to be introduced to ensure that capitalism and democracy could co-exist and survive. Countries differed in how they went about this task and what specific benefits they provided to citizens, but interventionist 'mixed' economies became the norm among democracies in the latter half of the twentieth century (Esping-Andersen 1990; Offe 1984). As a result, we now have many subvariants of liberal democracy that maintain fidelity to markets but temper their less desirable effects with social spending (Hall and Soskice 2001; Ware 1992). For example, some countries in Northern Europe gained reputations as 'social democracies' for the high degree of state intervention in their economies and the extent of their welfare programmes. This term is still applied to the platforms of centre-left parties and candidates in many democratic states, such as Canada's New Democratic Party or Democratic presidential hopeful Bernie Sanders in the United States. 'Corporatism', which implies a similar type of state intervention to achieve equity and social justice without abolishing private property rights, was often used in places like France and Germany, though many distinct models exist (Katzenstein 2019; Molina and Rhodes 2002). In the UK, the term 'Third Way' was introduced by sociologist Anthony Giddens to denote a middle path between socialism and capitalism and was associated with the policies of the Labour Party under Prime Minister Tony Blair (Giddens 1998).

It can be tempting to view talk about democratic welfare states and the reform of capitalism as relics of another time. Bill Clinton famously declared back in his 1996 State of the Union Address that 'the era of big government is over', and many democracies have scaled back social programmes since its post-Second World War heyday (Starke 2008; Swank 2005; Clayton and Pontusson 1998). Yet in the early decades of the twenty-first century, the discussion retains its relevance, as significant trepidation remains over the durability of the capitalism–democracy nexus.

The Great Recession of 2007–9 triggered a worldwide banking crisis and brought the economies of several democracies, especially Greece, Iceland, Ireland and Spain, to the brink of ruin. Begun because of excessive high-risk lending and the bursting of the US real estate bubble, the event was later labelled by the International Monetary Fund (IMF) as the most severe crisis of capitalism since the Great Depression. It was capitalist democracies which mostly bore the brunt of the financial meltdown. By comparison, non-democratic states fared far better, particularly those in Asia. While the Western democratic world seemed to be in economic freefall, China's

Gross Domestic Product (GDP) grew by 13 per cent– a figure it achieved despite the effects of the downturn. As an official for DBE, the largest bank in Southeast Asia, explained, 'Fundamentally, there was broad-based growth across Asia … Whether that was in the auto sector, airlines, consumer goods, commodities, services – all of these things were actually growing because of middle-income growth in Asia' (Vaswani 2018). In part, the relative performance of Asian economies during this period is attributable to their turn to China at a time when Western markets were not as healthy, further suggesting that authoritarianism – not democracy – provided fertile soil for growth. Of course, this line of argument is not entirely new. In 1990, democratic theorist Robert Dahl contended that market economies were necessary but not sufficient conditions to produce democracy and noted that capitalism is quite conducive to authoritarian governance in many cases (Dahl 1990).

In recent years, probably no effort on the subject has attracted more international attention inside and outside the academy than *Capital in the Twenty-First Century* by French economist Thomas Piketty. Writing in 2013 after the Global Financial Crisis had ended, Piketty focused on the wealth and income inequality since the late eighteenth century in Europe and the United States, the temporal and geographic cradles of modern democracy as we know it. His argument therefore acknowledges a logical and analytically prior relationship between democracy and economic development.

In essence, Piketty contends that material inequality is a natural and inevitable feature of capitalism as practised in these places. When the rate of return on capital is greater than the rate of economic growth, the result is increasing concentrations of wealth, which in turn generates greater economic uncertainty and provokes social instability. Thus, the book provided a compelling and timely explanation of anti-capitalist movements like Occupy Wall Street, and the more general sense of malaise that many in the world's most prominent democracies felt towards their economic systems. As a testament to the currency of the book, it hit number one on the *New York Times* bestseller list (nonfiction) almost immediately upon its translation to English from the original French in May 2014. Piketty's book, however, was not merely explanatory but also prescriptive. He argued that without decisive corrections to the concentration of wealth at the heart of social unrest, democracy itself was in danger of collapse (Piketty 2014). The remedy, according to Piketty, is the effective implementation of a tax system targeting the wealthy in order to prevent a widening of the gap between rich and poor. However, some political scientists argued that it was not helpful to reduce inequality to a basic economic formula, and that the organization of political institutions held a huge but understated effect on the distribution of economic resources (Acemoglu and Robinson 2015).

Wherever one stands on Piketty's book or the more general theme of state intervention in the economy, it serves to highlight some critical questions – exactly what social conditions are required for democracy to take root, or to survive when it does emerge? Are all pre-transition social structures to be considered equal or are some more likely than others to produce democracy? If so, what are these and how do they work? Are there certain actors working in and through these structures which might shape democracy's prospects? If so, what are their incentives to encourage political change? These latter questions form the basis for our analysis in the next chapter, when we consider the choices and trade-offs faced by 'reformers' (i.e. those driving democratization forward), and 'stand-patters' (i.e. those who fight to retain the status quo), and the sometimes-uncomfortable bargains that must be struck from time to time for democratization to advance. However, the section below delves into the former question more deeply, examining some of the structural preconditions that historically animated much scholarship on democratization.

The structural preconditions for democratization

Political theorists may not agree that capitalism and democracy are uniquely or sustainably suited to support one another, but most concede that markets have historically provided fertile soil for democracy's development. Why might this be? One prominent current of thought is that the two systems are underpinned by common culture and values which, though potentially destructive to democracy when left unchecked or taken to extremes, provided a basis for their historically coincidental emergence (Almond 1991). Liberalism – a belief in individual liberties and equality before the law – provides the most fundamental common ground. The same values that support one's right to form a commercial enterprise and pursue private interests in competition with other firms support the formation and pursuit of interests in other aspects of life too. Just as markets need and encourage competition among many economic interests, individual liberties breed social and political pluralism, with many actors and viewpoints vying for influence within a broadly recognized and respected framework of rules. Thus, the logic of markets could be extended to the political sphere, producing interest aggregation, the formation of voting blocs and, ultimately, multiparty electoral competition. Of course, this overlap in values provides a sanitized and somewhat rosy picture of how early liberal democracies worked. The realities were far messier, but liberalism provides a kind of theoretical calculus that makes the early causal connection possible. On occasion, scholars have expounded on this line of thinking to suggest that the relationship of capitalism to early democracy not only required common values but also gave rise to new ones, helping to sustain democracy in the longer term. For example, Albert Hirschman argued in the 1980s that early capitalism had a 'gentling' effect on manners, implicitly suggesting a broader effect on social mores that disposed capitalist societies to the type of moderation and compromise democracies require (Hirschman 1986).

Beyond arguments of coincidental values, scholars of the mid and late twentieth century set about understanding precisely what it was about the organization and function of capitalism that seemed to produce democratic regimes. We term these efforts the 'structural preconditions' school of democratization. Barrington Moore's *Social Origins of Dictatorship and Democratization: Lord and Peasant in the Making of the Modern World*, written in 1966, was among the first to unpack these preconditions (and impediments) to democratization, and is still rated as one of the most influential political science books of all time. Twenty-first-century students of democratization might be surprised to learn that the book is considered 'Marxist', a seemingly odd label to apply to any study of political reform. In fact, the book is in no way an endorsement of the Marxist-Leninist regimes that pervaded at the time it was written, but follows a style of argument typical of the Marxist tradition in sociology, namely 'the conception of social class arising out of an historically specific set of economic relationships and of the class struggle as the basic stuff of politics' (Moore 1966: 116). Instead of emphasizing cultural values as a causal or inhibiting factor in modernization, Moore focused on social structures, and in particular how the formation and agency of different kinds of class actors led to democracy in some places and not in others.

Three pathways were described. The first, followed by the United States, France and Britain, saw a transformation from agrarian to largely industrial forms of capitalism beginning in the late eighteenth century, led by an increasingly well-heeled economic elite. As industrial capitalism blossomed, this new economic class began to seek protections for their gains. Initially these included private property rights, but later they expanded to include a fuller range of institutions that constitute democratic capitalism. Hence, Moore saw democracy in modern Europe and the United States as driven mainly by the upper economic class, an argument summarized neatly in his famous dictum 'no bourgeoisie, no democracy'. Social class remained at the forefront in the second and third types of transformations, but things panned out differently. Moore argued that in Germany and Japan, a landed aristocracy stifled the efforts of new commercial classes to carry democracy forward. One observer has called the result 'a system of capitalism encased in a feudal authoritarian framework' (Almond 1991: 468). In Japan's case, the new regime took the form of an authoritarian monarchy. In Germany, the result was a fascist, militarized aristocracy, scornful of both liberal democracy and Soviet-style socialism, and focused on racial superiority.

While Moore was concerned with the way social structures reproduced different types of 'modern' regimes, others took up the question of how and how much economic development was required to produce democracies. One of the first and consistently influential of such efforts was that of Seymour Martin Lipset, who in 1959 demonstrated a strong statistical correlation between Gross National Product and democracy. 'The more well-to-do a nation', he claimed, 'the greater the chances that it will *sustain* democracy [emphasis added]' (Lipset 1959: 75). What was innovative about Lipset's study was that he was able to break the concept of economic development down into indicators correlated with that development, including not only wealth, but levels of industrialization, urbanization and education, and suggest how each of these produced conditions needed for democracy. He found that economic development was positively correlated with important aspects of social development such as improvements in literacy and exposure to mass media, and with the emergence of social-psychological traits like the ability to think critically about the information received, and about the worth of participatory institutions – precisely the skills required for active, critical democratic citizenship. Thus education was considered to be the most important factor for sustaining democracy. In Lipset's own words, 'the higher one's education, the more likely one is to believe in democratic values and support democratic practices. All the relevant studies indicate that education is far more significant than income or occupation' (Lipset 1959: 75). This argument was bolstered by Lipset's quantitative approach, which enabled him to understand confounding cases of the day in the proper context. Germany, for example, stood out as deviant among the countries studied, having developed authoritarian political structures despite its vigorous education system, but could be written off as statistical white noise and the exception that proved the more general rule.

Lipset's work remains relevant, and made great strides in elaborating the connection between democracy and development, but a critical problem remained (Diamond 1992; Lipset 1994). His research established the link between economic advancement and democracy's durability, healthy function and sustainability over time. Countries that performed well economically, reaped the fruits of that development and established democratic institutions tended to enjoy higher levels of support from their citizens. This popular approval for the democratic status quo, or the sense that the way things are is the way they ought to be, is known as legitimacy (Gilley 2009; Beetham 1991). Simply put, countries that do better, or have a more established track record of governing well according to citizen expectations, are likely to be seen as more legitimate and are therefore more stable. This is why wealthy democracies, historically speaking, never fall (Przeworski and Limongi 1997: 165–6).

Yet the conditions that help to sustain a democracy in the long run may be different from those required for its emergence. Newer democracies are bound to have less legitimacy and might therefore be more likely to fail. And of course, many democracies do not begin from a position of good economic standing. This predicament leaves one wondering how democracies could ever hope to emerge from ex-communist countries where market logic was alien and even punished, or in other places that appear trapped in a generations-long cycle of poverty. More to the point, however, Lipset's framework is more suited to helping us understand politics at the post-consolidation phase than at transition. Therefore, the important questions that remain are 'What economic conditions need to be in place to initiate a democratic opening?', 'How many of these conditionalities are required for transitions to succeed?' and 'How exactly does development work to encourage that opening in the first place?'

Economic development and regime collapse

One possibility is that democratization does not arise from economic development per se, but rather materializes in the vacuum formed by authoritarian collapse. According to this theory, democratization is the endgame of a process that begins under conditions of non-democracy, and advances with authoritarian rot. 'Democracy is then secreted out of dictatorships by economic development', as one prominent study puts it, and is therefore considered 'endogenous' (i.e. driven from within). Przeworski and Limongi's elaboration of the process is so apt that it's worth quoting verbatim:

> A story told about country after country is that as they develop, social structure becomes complex, labour processes begin to require the active cooperation of employees, and new groups emerge and organize. As a result, the system can no longer be effectively run by command: the society is too complex, technological change endows the direct producers with some autonomy and private information, civil society emerges, and dictatorial forms of control lose their effectiveness. Various groups, whether the bourgeoisie, workers, or just the amorphous 'civil society', rise against the dictatorial regime, and it falls.
>
> (Przeworski and Limongi 1997: 157)

One key implication of this type of modernization hypothesis lies in its suggestion of a democracy-inducing level of development – a threshold at which the necessary breakdown of the incumbent regime is expected to occur.

There are any number of problems with this formulation, however. First, let us consider the predictive power of the threshold hypothesis. The underlying logic is that if democracy arises from economic development, we should expect to see authoritarian regimes die as levels of affluence increase. The higher development levels climb, the greater the pressure incumbent dictators come under to implement reform. Authoritarian regimes then either buckle outright under citizens' demands for change, or else implement a series of incremental half-measures to appease society which then snowball, setting in motion a process of more sweeping reforms that outstrips the autocrats' ability to rein in it. Traditionally, the level of development (measured in terms of GDP per capita) at which this scenario becomes increasingly likely is about US$6,000. Below this figure – that is, in the world's poorest dictatorships – there is a predictable amount of instability that either gives rise to a new and weak democracy or, more likely, successive dictatorships. Beyond this point, however, the effect of development appears to plateau, and authoritarian regimes become more durable as development rises (ibid.: 158–9). This may be a part of what explains the longevity of authoritarianism in places like Singapore, which has a level of affluence comparable to that of developed democracies, or

China, which has seen a rapid rise in mean levels of development. As Acemoglu and Robinson contend (2012), sound political and economic institutions are important – much more so than geographic or cultural factors – for preventing state collapse.

Case study 1.1: The Lee Hypothesis

Some have suggested that democracy hurts economic development and that authoritarian systems are more conducive to wealth-building. Named for the late Lee Kuan Yew, who served as Prime Minister of Singapore from 1959 to 1990, this proposition is known as the 'Lee Hypothesis'.

Authoritarian Singapore, with its strong, technologically advanced and internationally integrated free market system, has produced some of the highest standards of living in Asia. In 2019, it ranked ninth on the UN's Human Development Index, ahead of such highly developed democracies as Canada, Finland, New Zealand, Austria and Japan. Though these ratings were ostensibly achieved within a political framework of representative parliamentary democracy, multiparty competition is severely stifled, with the People's Action Party exercising power continuously since 1959. Freedoms of press, speech and assembly are also strictly curtailed. Lee Kuan Yew held that these aspects of 'benign' authoritarianism were essential to Singapore's economic progress.

Though it originated in reference to Singapore, the Lee Hypothesis has since been applied to a range of other countries too, especially in Asia. These include Taiwan under the Guomindang prior to 1996, South Korea before the election of Roh Tae-woo in 1987 and post-1978 mainland China, where it is sometimes known as 'neo-authoritarianism'. Various explanations have been put forward to explain the apparent prevalence of neo-authoritarianism in Asia, and why dictatorship might be more efficacious than democracy when it comes to encouraging growth. These include:

1. the presence of so-called 'Asian values' which predispose societies to authoritarian rule but promote hard work and economic progress;
2. a supposed history of 'developmentalist autocracy' in which party-based dictatorships in particular are more inclined towards growth-based economic policies;

3. the enhanced autonomy of authoritarian leaders, or the degree to which they can pursue growth-focused policies with limited interference from opposition parties or social factions;
4. the fact that non-democratic leaders are more able to encourage foreign investment.

Critics of the Lee Hypothesis charge that it is based on a limited and highly selective sample of countries, and that on aggregate, authoritarian countries are no more effective at promoting economic growth than democracies. Singapore is taken as an anomalous case within the wider pattern of democratization and development, and by itself it is insufficient to disprove or overturn the larger theory.

A second set of problems is more conceptual in nature. For one thing, the above formulation relies on a binary understanding of the nature of regimes. According to this rationale, a country is either democratic or it is not. Dictatorship and democracy are separated by a line in the sand and there exists no grey area between them, nor any wider continuum of more and less democratic regime types. As we will describe in detail at many points throughout this book, this is difficult to square with the array of countries that occupy the 'grey zone' having characteristics of both democracies and non-democracies and fitting into neither camp neatly (Carothers 2002). Secondly, the linear conception connecting the breakdown of dictatorship to a democratic endgame allows very little possibility, if any, of backsliding, or the reversion of new and weak democracies to either their authoritarian former selves or some new version of non-democratic rule (Svolik 2008: 153).

Finally, there is a related problem of attributing the breakdown of a political system to any single factor. There are many reasons that authoritarian regimes may fall, including not only a failure to develop but also, notably, a major military defeat that embarrasses incumbent leaders, or the structure of authoritarian party systems and patron–client relations (Levitsky and Way 2012; Schmitter 1975). In fact, in many cases so many interrelated factors are at play that in practice it becomes nearly impossible to tell precisely which factors are doing the heavy lifting, or whether any single factor may be more important than all the others. A similar challenge confronts the breakdown of new and weak democracies – many conditions besides development levels influence the failure to consolidate, especially the form of the executive, and authoritarian legacies (Svolik 2008).

It is for precisely this reason that many now consider the search for democracy's preconditions to be a wild goose chase. There are simply too many contingencies at too many points in time to be able to say what conditions were necessary for democratic transition to occur in any one country, let alone many countries worldwide. Even those conditions once thought to be necessary only hold for some places, some of the time. The structural preconditions school thus came to be criticized for its overly deterministic view of democracy's causes (i.e. hypotheses premised on an essential 'if x, then y' logic). Accordingly, the study of democratic transition shifted away from this tick-box approach towards more open-ended, probabilistic understandings based on the actions and choices of actors in key positions. These are explored in more detail in the next chapter. For now, we close out this chapter by considering one further twist on modernization theory: that not only can economic development fail to result in democracy, but sometimes works to keep it at bay.

Too much potential: The resource curse

One of the great and enduring mysteries of twenty-first-century global politics is why some countries that have a seeming abundance of natural resources build neither democracy nor material wealth. Sierra Leone and the Congo have diamonds, Kazakhstan and Azerbaijan have natural gas, Angola and Venezuela have enormous oil reserves, Bolivia has vast lithium deposits and Papua New Guinea has gold, silver, copper, nickel and a range of other rare earth minerals, yet none of these places have achieved wealth commensurate with developed-world standards. Most are not democracies, and those that are tend to be weak and unstable. What explains this situation? Is it possible that these and other states have too much of a good thing?

The term 'resource curse' was originally used by economic geographer Richard Auty to describe how some states with natural resource wealth were unable to capitalize on their advantages and, as a corollary, how others managed to develop despite being relatively resource-poor (Auty 1993). However, a range of other names have been given to the phenomenon. In economics, it is sometimes known as 'Dutch disease', though this usage often implies a lack of commodity diversification without necessarily having any consequences for democracy (Norway, with its reliance on North Sea oil, and the 1960s-era decline of manufacturing in the Netherlands, from which the problem takes its name, are two common examples). Sometimes, when the abundant resource in question is an agricultural product, such as cocoa or coffee, the afflicted country is called a 'banana republic'. This epithet, usually considered pejorative, has most often been applied to small, economically underdeveloped dictatorships in the Caribbean and Latin America.

In the study of politics, most of the scholarly attention has been focused on oil-producing states, which are commonly thought to face the greatest obstacles to establishing democracy (Ross 2015; Karl 1997). One prominent explanation is that reliance on oil revenues, particularly from international sales, decreases incentives for responsible, accountable government. This is known as the *rentier state* theory. Rentier states are those which derive most or all of their income from foreign sources, whether these are private corporations or other governments (Beblawi 1987; Mahdavy 1970). When the sale of their oil fetches a high price, political leaders may have less reason to rely on taxation to fund development (or, in the case of very poor or very small states, the tax base may be too limited to compete with international oil revenues). Because they are being only minimally taxed, if at all, citizens have less incentive to be watchful of how the government spends money. Consequently, citizens end up being poorly served by a government flush with cash from outside sources. If outcry arises, oil revenues can simply be used to buy critics' silence or, alternatively, to fund repression efforts. Corruption and clientelism creep in from multiple angles, compounding developmental and democratic difficulties still further.

Another hypothesis is that over-reliance on a single or limited range of commodities creates inherent volatility in state revenues, especially where the commodity in question is subject to fluctuations in demand beyond the control of the merchant government. Again, crude oil is a classic example, since it has been subject to periodic gluts in supply and demand, and hence a bobbing up and down of income for those selling it. When a given state is too invested in those revenues, the result is sometimes an inability to service debt. Reneging on financial commitments can produce a weakening of the rule of law and the collapse of social programmes, leading to an erosion of public confidence in democratic governance and, in extreme cases, a loss of social stability that causes weak democracies to implode.

Naturally, not everyone agrees that resource wealth encourages authoritarianism. After all, plenty of strong democracies have oil. And while public debates sometimes occur over ownership of resource revenues (i.e. 'Does North Sea oil belong to Scotland, or to Britain more broadly?' 'Does crude produced in the tar sands belong to the Canadian government, or to the province of Alberta?'), no one could reasonably claim that democracy in these places was in danger because of the economic importance of oil. Of course, democracy was not caused by resource wealth in these places either. Parliamentarism in Scotland long pre-dates the discovery of seabed oil and gas. Beef, wheat and a commitment to Westminster democracy existed long before oil in Alberta. By the time oil was discovered at Spindletop in 1901, Texas had been a US state for fifty-six years (having joined, seceded from and reintegrated into the Union in that time).

Thad Dunning, a political scientist with an economics background, argues that the relationship between resource wealth and regime type is more complicated than has commonly been supposed, since resource wealth, including oil reserves, can help or hinder democratic prospects. For Dunning, the key to understanding this relationship lies in disentangling precisely how revenues support differing institutional types. Basing his argument on a selection of resource-producing Latin American, African and Gulf states, he concludes that domestic structures, in particular the systems that regulate the distribution of wealth and, crucially, over-concentrations of that wealth, can enhance democracy's appeal. 'On the one hand, a resource boom may increase the incentives to control the distribution of resource rents and decrease the attractiveness of democracy to elites' [and hence promote authoritarianism], or 'a resource boom may also mitigate the redistribution of private income through taxation and thereby increase the attractiveness (or reduce the disutility) of democracy' (Dunning 2008: 11). Thus, some resource-rich states encouraged democracy, while in others its prospects were more limited. At a minimum, Dunning's work serves as a reminder that we ought not to chalk too much up to the causal force of resource wealth, and that we also need to bear in mind the effect of contextual conditions and omitted variables. To put it 'crudely', there are more compelling factors than petroleum to account for why procedural democracy has not emerged in Saudi Arabia, for example.

Conclusion

The purpose of this chapter has been to provide readers with a sense of the way in which scholars have assessed the relationship between economics and politics. It opened with a conceptual overview of the compatibility between democracy and capitalism, noting the points of tension and complementarity captured by scholars on what is perhaps one of the oldest debates in modern political thought – one that remains unresolved and, indeed, seems to have been reinvigorated in the early twenty-first century by a range of social and economic convulsions around the world, including the Global Financial Crisis of 2007–8, and the Occupy Wall Street movement of 2011.

Nevertheless, much twentieth-century social science took for granted that a positive empirical association existed between capitalism and democracy and, moreover, that economic development equated to political development. Economic take-off and development constituted a foundational precondition for democracy. Covariate conditions (i.e. those arising directly or indirectly from development, such as median education or income levels), may also be important for the durability of democracies over time.

Though highly influential in the study of democratization and in larger processes of social change, this formulation had run into a considerable problem by the twenty-first century. If democracy and economic development go hand in hand, what are we to make of wealthy countries that undergo rapid development but resist political change, or in some cases appear to legitimize authoritarian forms of government by their economic performance and thus limit democratic prospects? Many such places have gained prominence in global politics in recent years, most notably China, which just decades ago was among the world's poorest countries but as of this writing is the world's second-largest economy, with hundreds of millions being lifted out of poverty and into middle-income-hood in the process. Other non-democracies are wealthier still, boasting standards of living equal to or greater than the most economically developed in the world. As noted above, Singapore has achieved such a feat, and in the absence of liberal democracy (but with the pretence of some of its procedural trappings).

It is to be hoped this chapter has succeeded in reaching at least one pivotal, general conclusion about the relationship between development and democracy: it's complicated. At the very least, the relationship is made less clear by a massive range of contextual factors in any given case. As the subsection above on the resource curse demonstrates well, an abundance of a globally in-demand resource such as petroleum is no guarantee that democracy will emerge or endure (though it may), or indeed that a country will grow in prosperity or be stably, sustainably governed in any fashion. Often just the opposite occurs, hence the resource 'curse'. Diamond exploitation was at the root of civil strife in Sierra Leone in 2006, as was rubber more than a century earlier in the Congo. Difficulties with diversification have also given rise to narco-trafficking and, with it, various impediments to democracy in a long list of countries, from Bolivia to Afghanistan.

A final point bears mention here, which we have not yet touched upon: money can be corrosive of democracy where it is permitted to skew influence in representative processes and institutions. Indeed, this can happen even in the world's wealthiest and longest-standing democratic states. In the United States, for instance, a debate has long raged over the effects of 'soft money' in political campaigns. Some, including the US Supreme Court, have contended that 'money equals speech' and that in a country which guarantees free speech, anyone should be able to spend any amount they wish to support their preferred candidate or party. For them, a ban on 'soft money' contributions violates the First Amendment of the Constitution. On the other hand, opponents of soft money spending argue that it is tantamount to legalized bribery, in which the wealthy get to dominate political life simply because they can, and that those who accept such contributions are effectively engaging in influence-peddling. To 'vote with one's money' presupposes one has money to vote with in the first place, and obviously Americans vary widely in affluence levels. If democracy is about representation, and not just majority rule, where does this leave the United States' poor and middle classes? In the coming chapters, we consider in more detail the motivations and means available to various actors that animate democratic transition, or hold it back, including not only wealthy elites invested in the political status quo but also the economic classes, grassroots coalitions and mass movements that sometimes drive change from below.

Questions for discussion

1 Modernization theory emerged and developed in the post-Second World War era when optimism about democracy and capitalism was high. Do you think that a similar optimism would be found in the world today? Why or why not?

2 Do you think education levels are an important correlate of the prospects for democracy in the present day?

3 Do you think that too much economic development could be destructive of democracy, or limit the prospects for democracy's emergence? If so, why and how? If not, why not?

4 Is there something problematic about the term 'modernization' itself? Does it carry an implicature that people living in less economically developed or less educated societies are 'not modern' or 'backwards'?

5 What alternatives to capitalism exist? Are there any? Would democracy be more or less compatible with other forms of economic organization? Is there closer affinity between democracy and socialism than democracy and capitalism?

Further reading

Acemoglu, Daron, and James A. Robinson, *The Economic Origins of Dictatorship and Democracy* (Cambridge: Cambridge University Press, 2006).

Brooks, Sarah M., and Marcus J. Kurtz, 'Oil and Democracy: Endogenous Natural Resources and the Political "Resource Curse"', *International Organization*, Vol. 70, No. 2 (2016): 279–311.

Bunce, Valerie J., and Sharon L. Wolchik, *Defeating Authoritarian Leaders in Post-communist Countries* (Cambridge: Cambridge University Press, 2011).

Deutsch, Karl, 'Social Mobilization and Political Development', *American Political Science Review*, Vol. 55, No. 3 (September 1961): 493–514.

Foa, Roberto Stefan, 'Modernization and Authoritarianism', *Journal of Democracy*, Vol. 29, No. 3 (July 2018): 129–40.

Imai, Kunihiko, 'Internal Versus External Requisites of Democracy', *International Journal on World Peace*, Vol. 27, No. 3 (September 2010): 49–87.

Przeworski, Adam, Michael E. Alvarez, José Antonio Cheibub and Fernando Limongi, *Democracy and Development: Political Institutions and Well-being in the World, 1950–1990* (Cambridge: Cambridge University Press, 2000).

Rostow, Walt W., *The Five Stages of Economic Growth: A Non-Communist Manifesto*, 3rd edn (Cambridge: Cambridge University Press, 2012).

Snyder, Jack, 'The Modernization Trap', *Journal of Democracy*, Vol. 28, No. 2 (April 2017): 77–91.

Wright, Joseph, 'Do Authoritarian Institutions Constrain? How Legislatures Affect Economic Growth and Investment', *American Journal of Political Science*, Vol. 52, No. 2 (April 2008): 322–43.

2

Historical sociology and transition studies: Actors, interests and institutional change

As discussed in the previous chapter, certain types of social structures may be important for the emergence of democracy. These may include, for instance, the type of economic system a given society employs, as well as related levels of economic prosperity, education and mass literacy, among many other things. While there is broad agreement that structural preconditions can and often do matter for democratization, their presence invites as many questions as it answers. Where did these structures come from in the first place? Why and how were some structures adopted while others were not? Were there critical turning points at which alternative structures could have been chosen? What factors shape the way structures evolve over time?

Historical sociology is an approach that allows us to gain some perspective on these types of questions by drawing together many causal factors at work within and across complex, interlinked systems at various points in time. We might think of this approach as a sort of 'macro history' that reveals important clues regarding the background and development of social structures, enabling us to glimpse historic events, trends and trajectories towards or away from democratization, within singular societies and sometimes multiple societies too. In other words, historical sociology offers us a reasonably parsimonious means to explain complicated processes of institutional change.

Part of historical sociology's appeal lies in its long view of past events (Collins 1999: 1). Much of the rationale for its emergence came from the sense among scholars that a narrow emphasis on interests or conflicts between particular actors was ahistorical – too little attention had been paid to temporal aspects of social change, the roots of those interests or conflicts and perhaps even the conditions that precipitated the creation of rival interest groups in the first place (Aminzade 1992). At the very least, there was a belief that historical sociology could provide a necessary corrective to the 'short-termism' and perceived oversimplicity of modernization as an explanation for democracy's emergence.

As a method for studying democratization, historical sociology involves piecing together the way past occurrences interact, and assigning causal attribution to especially important structures at moments of occasion, often called 'critical junctures', or in less academic language, 'key turning points' (Capoccia and Kelemen 2007). Thus the practical application of historical sociology bears much resemblance to other qualitative approaches in the social sciences, such as process-tracing and path-dependence (Mahoney 2000; Bennett and Checkel 2014; Collier 2011; Pierson 2000). The goal is not merely to help us join past causes to contemporaneous effects, but to assess *how* history matters by paying attention to the intricacies of timing, including the pace, duration, trajectory or sequence of events in a chain. We can then use these findings to test hypotheses or establish new ones about when democratization takes place, as well as the nature of the causal relationships at play in that process. Is it necessary for prior conditions to unfold in specific order for democratization to happen? For example, do rudimentary markets need to exist in order to foster a certain level of affluence (such as is required by modernization theorists) before social pressure to democratize comes about, or can democratic change happen even without such market reforms? When is the best time to hold a first election? Should it precede and give legitimacy to other types of institutional reforms that may follow, such as establishing judicial independence, or are national elections best held after a range of other requirements for democracy are in place? Are there other steps in the sequence of events leading to democracy which, though seemingly important on the surface, turn out to be only incidental at most? Many ingredients may be required to produce a new democracy, but these may not all be of equal importance, and almost certainly will not happen all at once. These are the sorts of details historical sociology can shed light on.

Besides helping to sort out issues of sequence and timing, thinking carefully about processes can also be useful for providing us with some of the fine-grained contextual details about how structures work to produce outcomes in certain cases but not others. These details are valuable for two main reasons.

First, the sheer breadth and complexity of historical circumstances around the world means that one country's pathway to democracy may not look like that of another, and it is important for researchers of democratization to understand general patterns by which political changes proceed (or do not), as well as what occurs in places that do not conform to some of the more common transition pathways. Second, having rich contextual information is valuable because structures, considered in and of themselves, may not tell us enough about why democracy does or does not emerge in a given context. Much depends on the users of structures too – the actors and agents that operate within structural environments, and the configurations of interests they bring to bear on institutional development. In other words, we need to know not just about the parts that comprise human societies but also those which animate those parts, causing them to move and change (Rustow 1970).

Transition studies provides us with a further framework for thinking about who is acting, upon what and in what ways, for what reasons, and at what time to produce, capitalize on or limit democratic prospects. It works as a kind of zoom lens on historic processes, giving us an up-close look at democratic change by highlighting the interactions of key actors, such as democratic reform elements or incumbent authoritarians. The framework gives special consideration to the choices available to and made by strategically minded agents, in light of the structural opportunities and constraints they face and the information they have access to (Munck 1994). Depending on the situation, transition researchers might investigate many different kinds of structure–agent interactions. The actors involved may be very large sociological units, such as economic classes, ethno-cultural, religious or linguistic groups, or other types of social movements (Klandermans and Van Stralen 2015; Snyder 2000). In a classic study by Rueschemeyer, Stephens and Stephens, for example, democratization is depicted as a fundamentally class-based phenomenon, just as it was in the work of Barrington Moore from which they took inspiration. However, unlike Moore, who pinned democratic prospects on a propertied gentry – 'no bourgeoisie, no democracy' – the authors contend that democratic change is apt to come from the grassroots. When class antagonism reaches an unsustainable point, it boils over, resulting in popular pressure for egalitarianism and redistribution – a sentiment perhaps best captured in the slogan of France's revolutionaries: 'liberté, égalité, fraternité'. In other instances, the actors in question may be political parties, militaries (or elite units, juntas or prominent officers within them) or on occasion even well-placed and influential individuals, as happens in some highly personalistic dictatorships (Capoccia and Ziblatt 2010). Indeed, such individuals personify the well-known term 'autocrat', which means, literally, 'rule by one'.

This chapter opens with a typology of varied transition modes (i.e. the distinctive pathways democratization processes take). It then unpacks some of the common dynamics found within these processes, and some of the choices faced by incumbent dictatorships and democratic reformers. These include, among many other things, decisions of authoritarian leaders about the conditions under which they may cede power voluntarily to their political rivals (or dig in their heels to avoid having to do so); how to draw a line in the sand under the abuses of outgoing regimes in order to allow society to make peace with the past, heal and move on; whether to grant any concessions to ranking members of the old regime or hold them to account publicly; and when to hold a first election. Not all of these may be necessary or applicable in every case of democratization, but they do comprise some of the more common tasks to be carried out if a transition is to be successful and consolidation eventually reached. Because so many either failed to consolidate or backslid towards authoritarian rule, the final part of the chapter reverses the narrative to examine some of the common models of authoritarian survival, and the tools used by those wishing to forestall democratization processes.

What kinds of structures matter?

One of the central premises of historical sociology is that the structural features of a given society shape the course of large-scale changes. This is because different kinds of social structures create different kinds of pressures and needs, and therefore play a major role in the preferences of individuals and groups. As noted in the previous chapter, certain economic structures can be important. Modernization theorists, for example, see economic development as conducive to the emergence of democracy, or at least more conducive than 'pre-modern' systems based on feudal or tribal relations and the payment of tributes. For them, free markets lead to free people, and it follows that markets would need to be established and functional before pressures for democracy might emerge.

Beyond economics, forms of political organization matter too. The existence of a state might be the most fundamental structure to consider – because so much early work in historical sociology was focused on social forces, later theorists (i.e. from the late 1970s onwards) prioritized the state to a much greater degree, seeing it as a main locus of social interaction and competition (Evans, Rueschemeyer and Skocpol 1985). Indeed, democratization presupposes the existence of a state. If democracy is a set of institutions or rules by which a state is governed, then for democracy to exist, a state to govern must exist also. Ergo, the process of democratizing, of becoming democratic, usually refers to a change in the nature of governance in a continuously functioning state. Probably the most broadly recognized and often used definition of stateness is that coined by sociologist Max Weber, who understood them as having:

- an administrative and legal order subject to change by legislation;
- binding authority over its members (i.e. citizens);
- definitive territorial boundaries (i.e. the place where citizens live);
- a monopoly on the legitimate use of force to enact and enforce its will upon citizens (Weber 1964: 157).

Additionally, modern states are differentiated and autonomous from other organizations operating within a definite territory, and have divisions or parts that are coordinated with one another – meaning that they function as part of the same entity or system (Tilly 1975: 70). This latter criterion can be tricky, particularly in the context of presidential democracies, where a separation of powers is an entrenched part of the constitutional order, as in the United States (Linz 1990). There, it is completely normal for the House of Representatives and Senate to be at odds with each other, for one or either to be at odds with the President, or for any of these bodies to oppose the Supreme Court, making it appear as if the US government has no unity of purpose, or is in fact not cohesive at all. However, the division of the US government into three main parts – executive, legislative and judicial – is by design, not by accident, and was meant to prevent any single part of the government from becoming disproportionately powerful (recall the context in which the US constitution was written, after its framers waged a war of independence against what they felt was an unduly powerful British king).

A democratic state, then, is one in which popular sovereignty is meaningfully exercised. Citizens hold and exercise an ability to change those who wield state power, and therefore alter the course of decision-making on binding legislation. However, popularly elected governments that lack the ability to use legitimate force to ensure compliance with the law cannot fulfil the purpose for which citizens sent them to public office. If they are too lacking in cohesion or are too indistinct from other forms of social organization, they may have trouble making or enforcing any laws at all (Nordlinger 1981). The ability for a state to convert its preferences into authoritative actions is known as its *capacity*, or strength. Low-capacity states may support democratic governance, but only weakly. Extreme cases are often called *failed* or *collapsed* states (Rotberg 2003). These do not support democracy but do show heavy symptoms of lawlessness and chaos. Examples might include Somalia in the final decade of the twentieth century, or Afghanistan after the fall of the Taliban in 2001. In addition, some states may be deemed partially failed if certain bureaucratic functions become impossible or control is lost in certain parts of formerly controlled territory. For instance, the flourishing of drug cartels in Mexico during the early 2000s led to the virtual collapse of parts of the Mexican state. Assassination and bribery of judges, lawyers, anti-drug politicians and other officials soared, causing widespread dysfunction in the court system especially. Because the cartels could afford to pay better wages than state security forces, large numbers of police officers and even some whole military divisions defected. In turn, this meant that the cartels gained their own monopoly on force in some areas, effectively displacing the Mexican state and creating a new one in the cartel's image, without allegiance to the public interest, resulting in a deepening cycle of violence.

Prior regime types are also regarded as structures of special significance which exert a large influence on the course of democratization. For example, where the old regime takes the form of an absolutist monarchy, transitioning to democracy might involve not only the creation of new democratic institutions, but the establishment of a republic. Such was the case for the United States and France in the late eighteenth century, but similar processes have occurred elsewhere, such as Greece in the 1970s. These processes are seldom smooth – the United States permanently removed its ruling monarch, but both France and Greece experienced periodic reinstatements of theirs. In other countries, abolition of a monarchy may not be necessary, either because no meaningful tradition of monarchism was in place, or because a decision was made to incorporate monarchist traditions into newly created democratic ones. 'Constitutional monarchy' – in which monarchs are retained for largely ceremonial purposes but subjected to popular sovereignty – emerged in relatively new democracies such as post-Second World War Japan and Thailand, as well as in long-established ones like Canada, Sweden and New Zealand.

The importance of prior regimes and institutional legacies was a central theme of landmark research by US-based political scientists Juan Linz and

Alfred Stepan, who argued that non-democratic political systems vary widely in the forms and degrees of leadership, pluralism, ideology and social mobilization they exhibit or allow (Linz and Stepan 1996: 38). As such, they suggest a range of varied prospects and challenges for democracy.

Totalitarian regimes, exemplified by the Union of Soviet Socialist Republics (USSR) under Joseph Stalin or the Third Reich under Adolf Hitler, have the grimmest prospects for democratization because of the way they score on the Linz–Stepan metrics. By extension they would also have, therefore, the largest number of obstacles to overcome if democratization were to happen. In these kinds of places, political, social and economic pluralism (understood as differentiation of purpose, interest or opinion) is almost nil. There is usually an official and overarching or 'guiding' ideology – Marxism-Leninism and National Socialism respectively, in the examples above – which is treated as sacrosanct within the legal system and from which no deviation is possible. This applies to views expressed in public, but often also in private. Historically, many totalitarian regimes of both the left and right have employed secret police or other means to enforce rigid adherence to official narratives. Mobilization is not stifled but actively encouraged, provided it occurs within state-sanctioned bodies – for example the Hitler Youth or Communist Youth League –which likewise serve to reinforce ideological hygiene. Political leaders have no formally defined limits on their power, and certainly none that is publicly explicated or known.

Case study 2.1: Personality cults

Totalitarian regimes, known for extreme concentrations of power in the hands of political leadership, sometimes produce 'cults of personality' – a type of 'hero worship' in which images of a given leader are pervasive in both the public and private lives of citizens, and by which leaders acquire a vaunted and in some cases almost other-worldly or god-like status, cementing their hold on power further still.

One prominent example comes from China during the Great Proletarian Cultural Revolution (1966–76), when Mao Zedong launched a campaign to eradicate ideological enemies within the Chinese Communist Party and in Chinese society at large. The famous painting *Chairman Mao Goes to Anyuan* depicts a young, handsome Mao wearing scholastic robes and standing on a mountaintop, looking beatified, just as a saint might in a Renaissance-era work of Western art. The painting first appeared in 1967 and has been widely reproduced and displayed in China since then.

Another classic example is the Soviet Union's Joseph Stalin. Georgian by birth, Stalin's given name was Ioseb Besarionis dze Jughashvili. Stalin, the name he later gave himself, means 'man of steel' – superman – in Russian. Like Mao, works of propaganda commonly portrayed Stalin, who led the Soviet Union from 1927 until his death in 1953, in an almost all-powerful light. A famous 1951 print by Boris Belopol'skii is captioned 'Glory to Stalin, Great Architect of Communism!' and features Stalin posed commandingly in party dress in front of an adoring crowd and hydroelectric dam.

Since 1948, a mythic status has been accorded to members of the Kim family in North Korea, one of very few genuinely totalitarian regimes remaining in the world at the time of this writing. Statuary in Pyongyang poses Kim Il-sung against a backdrop of Baekdu Mountain, the 'sacred mountain of the revolution' from which Kim launched his resistance, later becoming founder and first President of the Democratic People's Republic of Korea. Though the country is currently run by his grandson, Kim Jong-un, the elder Kim formally retains the title of 'President for Life' despite having been deceased since 1994, giving the Kim family a sense of eternal, ethereal power.

A further, relatively recent example is captured by the 'Neutrality Monument' in Ashgabat, Turkmenistan, a former Soviet Central Asian republic. The statue depicts Saparmurat Niyazov, who led the country from 1985 until 2006. It stands atop a large pillar, which rotates 360 degrees, so that the golden Niyazov raises the sun over the Turkmen capital each morning, and puts it to bed each night.

By comparison with totalitarianism, regimes labelled as authoritarian by Linz and Stepan show signs of softening, or fewer or less encompassing traits with regard to leadership, ideology, mobilization or pluralism, and thus may have less distance to travel and fewer tasks to complete before democracy becomes possible. Official ideologies may be present, but cracks may have begun to appear in adherence to them such that they are paid lip service, but compliance is not widely enforced. Leaders are also typically much less powerful, perhaps operating with few formal constraints but within predictable and well-known limits. Tolerance for a greater level of pluralism may be present socially, economically and even politically where opposition forces are well organized, and civil society may be increasingly active, being more freely able to mobilize in pursuit of divergent interests. Egypt under the rule of Hosni Mubarak (1981–2011), the Indonesian 'New Order' administration of Suharto (1966–98) and present-day Belarus – where Alexander Lukashenko has served as President continuously since 1994 – are just three of many possible examples.

Linz and Stepan also include an intermediate category of structures, which they call post-totalitarianism. This type of system typically has fewer limits on leadership, broader adherence to ideology and lesser degrees of pluralism and social mobilization than do authoritarian ones, but does not carry any of these to the extremes found under totalitarianism. Instead, some economic and social pluralism may be recognized, but political pluralism is not, because an incumbent party still has a monopoly on power. Guiding ideology is still a meaningful part of everyday social reality, but visions of utopianism have faded from what they were in earlier times. There may be a loss of enthusiasm for mandatory mobilization in state-based organizations, but small cracks in the former power base may lead to the emergence of political opportunists concerned with advancing their own careers and power bases. Consequently, leaders may become increasingly concerned with personal security, and with maintaining social stability. Until the consolidation of power by Xi Jinping in 2012, post-1978 China might have been considered a ready example of post-totalitarianism, showing minimal but freer social mobilization, greater pluralism, relaxed ideology and more limits on paramount leaders than was the case previously under Mao Zedong.

Finally, the Linz and Stepan typology includes a category known as sultanism, which may hold authoritarian or (post)totalitarian characteristics but is distinguished by its highly personalistic style of rule. In sultanistic, or 'neopatrimonial' regimes, patron–client relationships run amok because virtually all governance is conducted according to the will of a single person, often in a very arbitrary manner and outside legal boundaries. Indeed, the law itself may be a construct of the leader's wishes (Bratton and Van de Walle 1994). Political leadership may comprise handpicked favourites of the 'sultan', regardless of their qualifications – it is common for family members and business associates of the leader to occupy key government posts. Some economic and social pluralism may exist, but it is subject to despotic intervention, and no groups operate outside the sultan's potential influence. Mobilization is therefore lopsided as well, tending to occur only when and where it is expedient for the leader that it does so, or where the sultan stirs up social fervour through the manipulation of groups or symbols. Examples of sultanistic regimes might include Muammar Gaddafi's Libya (1969–2011) or Saddam Hussein's Iraq (1979–2003). In the Hollywood film *The Last King of Scotland*, Forest Whitaker portrays Idi Amin Dada, the exceedingly personalistic and paranoid ruler of Uganda from 1971 to 1979.

The foregoing schematic of non-democratic regimes is helpful for thinking about the ways entrenched social structures and patterns may shape a country's democratic path. However, it does come with some liabilities. It presents different kinds of social structures and political transitions as if they were neat analytic classifications wholly distinct from one another. Not only are political realities in the non-democratic world far messier in reality, but there is a natural temptation for those who study democratization to attempt to shoehorn familiar cases into 'ill-fitting a priori categories' in order to identify systematic regularities more easily (Gerring 2001: 231). The Linz and Stepan scheme also does not recognize the middle ground of 'illiberal democracies' or 'hybrid regimes', a subject we turn to in more detail in chapter five.

Secondly, there is some confusion over the nature of the way differences in regime types were measured by Linz and Stepan, specifically whether they meant to make distinction by type or degree of non-democracy. This challenge is especially pronounced if one regards post-totalitarian and totalitarian regimes to be progressively extreme versions of authoritarianism, rather than qualitatively distinct from it. Moreover, the framework is not fine-grained enough to capture much within-category variation. For example, among authoritarian regimes there may be considerable differences in the behaviour of party-based dictatorships, as in the cases of Vietnam, Laos or China, and military dictatorships, as were common throughout Latin America in the 1970s and 1980s, with one still in place in Thailand (Brooker 2014).

Finally, and most critically, this classification of non-democratic regimes, with its seeming gradients in degrees of severity and repressiveness, gives an impression of linearity and directionality in democratic transitions. Authoritarian regimes are clearly distinct from democracies but thought to be much closer to the point where crossing the line in the sand becomes a possibility – much closer than is the case for totalitarian regimes. Movement from the totalitarian or post-totalitarian category to authoritarianism brings a country closer to that line. Ergo, movement away from the extremes of non-democracy is movement closer to democracy. The problem with this is that it obscures the potential for backsliding towards the totalitarian end of the scale once a move towards post-totalitarianism, authoritarianism or democracy has been initiated. Such was the fate of many countries which began an apparent transition but later stalled or reversed course, and came to occupy a 'grey zone' between regime types (Carothers 2002). Crossing the line demarcating authoritarianism from democracy once – by, say, holding inaugural elections – is no guarantee that a given country will maintain its progress towards consolidation. A related challenge is that the classification scheme above implies that the causes of regime liberalization are cumulative – that is, that gradual, step-by-step passage through each phase is required before a transitioning country can move on to the next. This is simply inconsistent with the historical experience of several countries (Romania, for instance) that have undergone radical, rapid transitions from totalitarianism to democracy, spending little if any time in the intervening categories. It is also even more reason to take process-tracing seriously, since as a tool for research it can help us to sort out what links in a causal chain are necessary for democratization, which are sufficient, and which are neither.

Transition modes

It should be clear at this point that the weight of history exercises great influence over the prospects for democracy, and that pre-existing structures can make the tasks associated with democratization easier in some places than others. Yet structures alone are not enough to explain when or why political change happens. The ways in which well-placed agents use and interact with these structures are also important. Structures can help us to understand how the actors that drive democratization understand their available options, and hence both are needed to arrive at a well-rounded understanding of the complexities at play.

In principle, democratization processes may assume almost innumerable permutations. In providing an overview such as this one, it is not possible to fully take stock or do appropriate justice to all of these. However, theorists have identified three common modes by which transitions occur. To reiterate a point made above and in previous chapters, it must be remembered that transition processes are distinct from consolidation. Not all transitions result in healthy, stable democracies, and authoritarian breakdown is no guarantee of a democratic endgame.

One common transition mode involves the implosion or overthrow of the authoritarian incumbent, and its replacement with an alternative set of institutions. In this scenario, opposition forces outside the authoritarian establishment are strong, while impetus for reform from within the regime is comparatively weak. Collapse occurs when the balance of power reaches its tipping point, and the government can no longer stand. Often, a battle then ensues between the opposition and powerless remnants of the old regime or, more frequently, between various wings or factions of the opposition over what happens next and what the future ought to look like. Samuel P. Huntington (1990) labels this transition mode 'replacement' (Linz calls it 'ruptura') and describes it as unfolding in three phases: the struggle to produce the initial collapse, the collapse itself and the subsequent struggle after the fall (Linz 1978: 35). He notes that this type of transition was relatively uncommon during the Third Wave, with just six occurring by 1990 (Huntington 1990: 121–42). This means, in turn, that most authoritarian regimes of this era did not crumble entirely of their own accord and that democratization, where it happened, took place by way of external social pressure but with some form of complicity from incumbents. Sultanistic dictatorships were slightly better represented within this type than were party-based or military regimes.

A second common type of transition involves just the opposite dynamic. Instead of a crumbling of authoritarianism, egged on by opposition forces, this involves the voluntary and deliberate reform of a non-democratic government from within itself – an endogenously driven process of 'transformation', or 'reforma' to use Linz's language (Linz 1978: 35). What distinguishes this kind of transition is that powerful authoritarian elites play a role in bringing that system down and replacing it with a more democratic one, sometimes voluntarily (Slater and Wong 2013). Roughly half of all third-wave transitions were of this kind – an estimated sixteen out of thirty-five cases. Because such transformations from within depend upon the government in power being stronger than its opposition, they tend to occur in military or party-based dictatorships and may be most likely to happen where the state has an unambiguous hold on the means of coercion (i.e. when ranking military officers are closely allied with incumbent office holders), and in states that are reasonably well-off materially. The question, then, is why a strong authoritarian leader would willingly share power with their political enemies, especially if these enemies are weak and not obviously in a position to form a stable new government themselves. In some (but not all) cases of transformation, cracks may appear within the façade of government unity because of some crisis, often an economic collapse or a devastating loss in war, as with Argentina's military regime in the 1980s. These crises cause an escalation in intra-party factionalism, either creating new rifts or deepening those that may already exist, perhaps for a long time. Under these conditions, elements of the old regime or its leadership may become emboldened to the cause of change and embrace democratization as a solution to the woes and inertia of the authoritarian system. Huntington refers to this face-off within ruling governments as a showdown between newly generated reformers, who wish to change the rules of politics, and stand-patters, who do not.

As with the classification of non-democratic regimes in the previous section, this breakdown of transition modes is simply a heuristic device. Many countries may show signs of both the transformation and replacement types. Moreover, circumstances in times of political upheaval can shift rapidly, sometimes without warning. Just because reformers are weak at one moment does not mean they will be so the next. Hence, a third transition mode, termed 'transplacement', reflects those situations in which democratization is the result of some combined effort by regime forces and outside opposition (Share and Mainwaring 1986: 177–9). If the implacability of stand-patters is fuel for authoritarian collapse, as in the replacement mode, then transplacement is about a balance of power within a government such that it may be willing to negotiate a change of regime at the behest of reformers, but is unwilling or unable to initiate the process of doing so and thus has to be dragged into democratization by opposition forces applying pressure from outside the regime. Likewise, the power of these outsiders is balanced – they are organized and resourceful enough to demand change, but not powerful enough to bring down the government on their own. Thus, the only viable path to democracy lies in the willingness of both sides to negotiate. About one-third of third-wave transitions moved ahead in this way – eleven out of thirty-five by Huntington's reckoning.

Negotiating for democracy: What's on the table?

Regardless of who makes the first moves, all these scenarios suggest a range of further challenges to be addressed if transition is to proceed and consolidation is to be eventually reached. As we've seen, these may be dependent on many of the macro-historical structures in place, or in some cases, their absence. For instance, if no viable state exists to, at a minimum, keep civil peace and provide a stable environment for longer-term political change, one will have to be created. At some later stage, an election will need to be held and broadly recognized as open, free and fair. Both statecraft and elections are primary tasks in the sense that they are widely recognized as essential for the democratic governance of a modern nation-state.

In this section we examine sets of common secondary tasks which can be similarly essential for democratization but are not necessarily present in all cases and are highly contingent on the needs of particular places and shaped by the experience of the outgoing regime. These conditionalities typically become important after an initial democratic opening has been made but before it can be completed. Incumbent dictatorships may have collapsed wholly or in part, or may be sufficiently weakened by societal opposition or challenges within their own ranks that they are ready to negotiate. Either way, the critical and inescapable question arises – what must be done for a country to move on from its past and make democratic aspirations into a reality?

The initial crumbling of authoritarianism commonly comes about through a defeat in war or some domestic crisis, frequently economic in nature. One example is the collapse of the Argentine military junta amid spiralling hyper-inflation and an ill-considered attempt to recover Las Malvinas (The Falkland Islands) from UK possession. The regime was deposed soon afterwards, when the attempt to salvage its dwindling legitimacy backfired amid the embarrassing defeat.

However, the scholarly literature on the topic also makes note of fate in determining the course and the needs of a democratic transition. Trivia, ephemera and the unforeseen can sometimes be the undoing of autocrats. Well known for graft and its brutality towards political opponents, the New Society regime of Ferdinand Marcos, which ruled the Philippines from 1965 to 1986, is a good example. Operating with near impunity under the protection of strict martial law, Marcos was ultimately brought down by public pressure in the 'People Power' revolution after the accidental discovery of fraudulent financial and war records. International scrutiny has also been an important source of authoritarian weakening in more recent times. Some scholars have suggested that pressure from the global public forced the de Klerk regime to begin talks that led to the unravelling of apartheid and the eventual democratization of South Africa, for example (Klotz 2002). The topic of transnational advocacy of regime change is examined more thoroughly in the later portion of this book.

Another big consideration in many transitioning democracies is how to come to terms with an authoritarian past, and how best to heal the wounds of history while leaving behind a stable, healthy environment in which democratic values and institutions can take root. There may be a strong desire in some countries to completely eradicate any and all vestiges of the *ancien régime*, bury the past and move on boldly into a new democratic future. Such desires may stem from fears of coup or counter-coup attempts from the old guard, or from a belief that the new regime will be contaminated by remnants of the previous one. Yet ignoring the past is not always practical, for a variety of reasons.

First, there may be a strong desire for retributive justice to be served against those formerly responsible for corruption, chaos, torture and death. In some instances, former dictators may be put on trial, either in their homelands or in international courts, and sentences passed for crimes against the populace. These may be lengthy or lifelong prison terms, or even execution. For instance, Saddam Hussein was executed on 30 December 2006, at an Iraqi military base known as Camp Justice. The sentence of death was handed down following a conviction of crimes against humanity by the Iraqi Special Tribunal in response to the Dujail massacre – the mass killing of 148 Iraqi Shi'ites in 1982 in retaliation for an assassination attempt against Hussein. The execution drew considerable international criticism, especially after a mobile-phone video of the hanging made its way onto YouTube. The grainy video showed Hussein being led to the gallows, then mocked by his countrymen, before falling through the trapdoor, his neck breaking immediately. However, defences of the execution emerged also. Some argued that it was important the sentence was imposed and carried out by an Iraqi court rather than a foreign intervention force (no Americans were present at the hanging, and in fact US forces had exerted pressure, unsuccessfully, to see it deferred), which underscored both the legitimacy and independence of Iraqi legal institutions. There was also a suggestion that the hanging sent an important message about accountability, since no one – not even Saddam – could escape justice in post-Ba'ath Iraq, and that this was a positive step forward for the rule of law. Finally, there were arguments made that the punishment fitted the crime and was therefore morally justified: some crimes are simply too great to be let go. In carrying out the sentence, victims of the old regime are also given a chance to heal. Of course, this claim implies that healing is best accomplished through corporal vengeance, and that the future of democracy is best served when physical embodiments of the outgoing regime are literally laid to rest forever. Alternatively, some dictators have been allowed passage out of their countries to live in exile abroad. For example, Idi Amin lived out his life in Saudi Arabia after the Ugandan capital, Kampala, was captured by Tanzanian forces in early 1979, bringing his regime to an end.

A further complication arises over how to reintegrate everyday members or adherents of the old regime into the new democratic society. Uncomfortable as it may sound, most members of Germany's National Socialist Party survived the Second World War and were not executed at Nuremberg. The latter was the fate of many who held prominent leadership roles and thus personified the Third Reich, of course, but most rank-and-file Nazis, even those who were ideologically committed, re-joined German society and became a part of the reconstruction effort in a newly divided Germany. The decision to reintegrate former ideological extremists did not happen immediately, but only after a lengthy process of denazification had been conducted. Similar circumstances arose in Iraq after the fall of Saddam. Ardent members of the Ba'ath Party did not simply disappear when the regime fell, but were reintroduced to Iraqi society after an extensive period of de-Ba'athization. However, Iraq and Afghanistan provide us with two cautionary tales about the urgency and delicacy of de-racialization efforts amid regime transition. In the former, the reintegration of former Ba'athists into Iraqi society has been a long and troubled process, with evidence emerging that former Ba'ath security officers played a role in the rise of the Islamic State (ISIS), their intelligence gathering and organizational experience abetting a new form of disruptive extremism (Sly 2015). In the latter case, efforts to eradicate and reintegrate extremists after the 2003 US-led invasion have obviously not been successful. A resurgent Taliban seized power in Afghanistan in August 2021, sparking mass evacuation of foreign nationals and worries for the safety of those remaining behind, particularly women, and other known opponents of the Taliban.

One way in which peace can be made with the past and reintegration facilitated is through truth commissions, sometimes also referred to as truth and reconciliation commissions. Rather than seeking justice through criminal proceedings, which conclude with an imposition of punishment, such commissions aim to promote public knowledge, dialogue and ultimately a measure of understanding about past national traumas. Memorializing what occurred is thought to be vital for drawing a line under the past and moving on, with a sense that what transpired must never be allowed to happen again. It may also be important for the establishment of public trust and, with time, the development of tolerance that sustains liberal democracies. Truth and reconciliation commissions have been held in former authoritarian regimes all over the world, including Rwanda, Sierra Leone, Cambodia, Argentina, Northern Ireland and territories comprising the former Yugoslavia. In some cases, these have occurred years after a regime transition took place. We have noted their role here, however, because they may appear on a menu of tasks to be completed in order to reach consolidation, and can be an important means of (re)building values such as tolerance and compromise which are so vital to democracy's long-term viability.

Lastly, fallen regimes leave behind not only people to be integrated or brought to justice, but symbols too, the effects of which can sometimes be subtler but are no less important to address. Depending on the nature and degree of repression experienced under authoritarian rule, many transitioning states choose to disband, or at least fundamentally rebrand formal institutions, especially those tasked with state security. Much research in the field of democratization from the 1970s and 1980s emphasized the need to subject militaries to civilian control. This sentiment was a direct response to the role of military dictatorships in perpetrating widespread human rights abuses in places like Argentina, Chile and Brazil. 'What is fundamentally at stake,' as one classic work put it, 'is the change of the armed forces messianic self-image as *the* institution ultimately interpreting and ensuring the highest interests of the nation – a conception, alas, even enshrined in the written constitutions of some countries' [emphasis in original] (O'Donnell, Schmitter and Whitehead 1986: 31). In some states, other bodies which are part of the security apparatus, including the (secret) police, may be most identified with the repression of the old regime and are in need of retirement. Headquartered in East Berlin, the Ministry of State Security, commonly referred to as the Stasi, was a powerful surveillance and law enforcement body that kept files on millions of civilians during the Cold War. Under the motto 'Sword and Shield of the Party', the organization was tasked with protecting the rule of the Socialist Unity Party of Germany and its relationships with the Soviet Union. When the communist German Democratic Republic fell in 1990, an agency called the Federal Commission for the Records of the State Security Service of the Former German Democratic Republic was established to gain access to the secret files, many of which had been destroyed. Ultimately many Stasi officers were prosecuted for their activities during the Cold War, and Stasi museums now exist in many German cities, including Berlin, Dresden, Hamburg, Leipzig, Potsdam and elsewhere. The Stasi's Soviet counterpart and close partner organization, the KGB, was similarly tasked with suppressing internal dissent and protecting the communist regime. While Moscow ostensibly restructured the KGB after the fall of the Soviet Union to limit its power and prevent its role in any reverse coup attempts, the changes are thought to have been largely cosmetic, and many ex-KGB agents remain active in Russia's extensive domestic intelligence system (Albini and Anderson 1998). In still other cases, the reformed institutions were practices rather than agencies. Nicolae Ceauşescu, who ran communist Romania from 1965 to 1989, and his wife Elena, were the last people to be executed in a country where the death penalty had long stood as a symbol of state terror. The Ceauşescus were arrested, convicted after a brief trial and shot by a contingent of soldiers. The execution was later shown on Romanian television, after which the death penalty was permanently abolished to shed the country's dictatorial past.

The decision to reform or abolish, to punish or reconcile, is never easy. The above is only a partial list of the tasks that may need to be negotiated for democratic transition to proceed. But it *is* usually a negotiation, one that takes place between particular agents or actors who have interests to protect and more. For outgoing authoritarians, it may be avoiding prosecution or securing a safe passage guarantee out of the country. For military officers, it may mean that ranks or titles are retained. Those who amassed vast amounts of wealth under the auspices of authoritarianism, even those who did so legally, may require assurances that transition to democracy will not engender a shake-down in which their wealth is stripped and radically redistributed. The bargaining process that takes place between well-placed elites of the old authoritarian regime and the new democratic one is referred to as a 'pact', the terms of which are not necessarily always made known to the public. When honoured, pacts can serve to placate elements of the outgoing regime and thus serve the new democracy. Equally, the terms, if known, may be unpalatable to the public, altering perceptions of the new regime and whose interests it really seeks to protect.

Choices for authoritarian resilience

One common criticism of transition studies is that it was too 'teleological' in its approach to democratization, the *telos* being a belief in the worth and inevitability of liberal democracy. Some scholars in the field had experienced life in non-democratic societies at some point in their lives, but most lived and worked in democratic countries and took advantage of the civil liberties afforded them in these places to think and write about how political systems change. Thus, liberal democracy came to be viewed as an idealized end, one towards which all change processes pointed. A problem arose in the 1990s, however, when many of the places that were thought to be on a path towards democracy never made it. Still others appeared never to have initiated any of the reforms expected. Since liberal democracy had vanquished communism and no viable alternatives were left, how could this be?

It turned out that democratization theorists had underestimated the dynamism of many authoritarian regimes, as well as the will and ability of their leaders to hang on to power. Consequently, scholars began to focus more on the mechanisms of authoritarian resilience in places that appeared to strongly resist democracy. While several ways and means suggest themselves, the one thing they all have in common is a tendency to confer legitimacy on authoritarian incumbents. Legitimacy means 'rightful rule' and is demonstrated by the consent of citizens for their government (Gilley 2009). Nearly all the world's governments care about having the support of their publics. Almost none but the most totalitarian rule with the naked use of force alone. In democracies, citizens give consent to their government, and thus confer legitimacy, at the ballot box. Authoritarian regimes often seek other means to win and retain public approval. But the basic objective of gaining and retaining power is something virtually all politicians share. In turn, this self-interest requires them to seek and maintain support from others (Bueno de Mesquita and Smith 2012).

One of the more common choices authoritarian incumbents make is to institute controlled, centrally mandated democratic reforms – ones that ease social tension and may even placate calls for greater openness, but that stop well short of a genuine power transition. What unites all such instances of controlled liberalization, however, is that they act like release valves which vent pressure on the regime to pursue bigger changes. Venting prevents explosions, and thus makes good, rational sense for many dictatorial leaders to pursue.

Experiments with electoral authoritarianism are a good example. Since elections are the *sine qua non* of democracy, holding them tends to create a façade of competitiveness and accountability to the public – a subject we return to in chapter five. But competitive or electoral authoritarianism is not about genuine multiparty competition, and the contests may be open, but not free or fair, thus ensuring the incumbent retains power while creating a much-needed air of legitimacy (Levitsky and Way 2010; Schedler 2002; Karl 1995). Examples are legion – Zimbabwe, Iran, Russia, Singapore, Malaysia, Venezuela, Egypt and Hungary all hold elections, but none are described as healthy democracies. Other countries have experimented with controlled openness in other ways. Beginning in the 2000s, China instituted a range of 'deliberative polling' exercises, the aim of which was to ascertain public opinion on certain policy matters, in order to help the Communist Party govern more responsively and thus retain popular approval (Fishkin et al. 2010). In other words, the façade of consultation assists autocrats in giving citizens what they expect from their governments, and therefore prevents challenges to their rule. If authoritarian leaders, like their democratic counterparts, are fundamentally most concerned with staying in office, and doing so depends in part on winning favour with others, authoritarian rulers face a relatively easy choice to listen to public sentiment and engage in pork-barrel spending as part of what might be termed the political economy of authoritarian survival (Pan 2020; Bueno de Mesquita et al. 2003). In fact, by helping out their citizens, they help themselves.

Conclusion

This chapter has summarized some of the key trends in transition scholarship of recent decades. We began with a discussion of historical sociology, an approach that helps us to gain an understanding of how certain kinds of pre-existing social structures may create opportunities and constraints for democracy. Such structures involve more than modes of economic exchange – forms of political organization matter too. For the last several hundred years, the state has been the most basic and fundamental structure, and it remains so. In practical terms, it is virtually impossible to speak of democratization without reference to change occurring within states. Statism may be a prerequisite for democratization, but states themselves vary widely in terms of form, size and capacity. Thus, scholars of democracy have come to consider the nature of prior institutional types in greater detail, creating detailed typologies based on the degree to which a given state deviates from accepted democratic standards. Often, these are imagined to form a kind of continuum, something like a thermometer, with the democratic ideal at one extreme and totalitarianism at the other, and milder grades of non-democracy positioned along the scale. States are scattered at various points along this 'freedom spectrum', but a clear line exists separating those which are democracies from those which are not, not unlike the way in which zero degrees marks the position on the thermometer at which liquids become solid. This conception, while useful for showing how states differ politically, carries with it a tendency to presume that political change occurs in a linear and progressive way. Since movement away from one extreme means movement towards the other, states abandoning more extreme forms of authoritarianism are assumed to be becoming more democratic. There is little allowance, conceptually speaking, for states that stall before reaching democracy, or for authoritarian reversion – that is, backsliding towards the more repressive end of the scale.

The latter portion of the chapter, based in the tradition known as transition studies, sought to call attention to the actors, interests and contingencies embedded within democratization – crucial points when the choices of influential people could either cement or derail democratic change. Part of this discussion necessarily involved the importance of timing (i.e. when certain actors inserted themselves with causal force into the reform timeline), as well as precisely what issues are at stake when one regime replaces another. Such factors may include the fates of authoritarian incumbents, the reform of powerful institutions, practices or symbols associated with the old regime in the popular consciousness and social healing processes that serve to reintegrate rank-and-file figures from the former authoritarian government, party or military, into civilian life such that democracy has a stable base in which to grow over time. Finally, because so many countries that were expected to undergo democratization either failed to initiate reform, experienced stalled transition or even reversals to authoritarian rule, special notice was taken of the choices non-democratic leaders sometimes make to avoid giving up power. Because of the numbers of authoritarian regimes that were expected to transition over the last few decades but did not, we also noted how some authoritarian elites made choices that allowed them to side-step broad-based calls for political reform. This opens the question of how well authoritarian regimes can govern in accordance with popular demands, both in absolute terms and relative to democracies. This is an unsettling thought to many in a field of study where democracy was, at least until recently, thought to be the pinnacle of human political development – what if some non-democracies can govern as well or better?

Obviously, there is more, much more, to the question of political change than the interests and choices of the elite few. In the next chapter, we examine some of the particular challenges associated with violent political pasts, especially in places with deep linguistic, ethnic, religious or cultural divisions. In chapter four, we consider grassroots pressure and the role of civil societies in the emergence and health of new democracies.

Questions for discussion

1 Consider the country in which you are currently living. If one were to adopt historical sociology as an approach, what kinds of structures would be identified as important for the way it has evolved politically?

2 Is it preferable for an emergent democracy to punish former dictators in order to heal and move on from past social wounds, or does doing so perpetuate a cycle of violence likely to undermine democracy?

3 What are the key differences between authoritarian and totalitarian regimes? Is totalitarianism simply an extreme degree of authoritarianism, or is it qualitatively different somehow?

4 What are some of the choices authoritarian rulers can make to bolster support for themselves, or forestall democracy? Are the same choices available to all authoritarian leaders?

5 What is political legitimacy? How is it conferred in democracies versus non-democracies? What can political leaders in either type of regime do to win or lose legitimacy?

Further reading

Beach, Derek, and Rasmus Brun Pedersen, *Process-tracing Methods: Foundations and Guidelines* (Ann Arbor, MI: University of Michigan Press, 2013).

Diamond, Larry, *Developing Democracy: Toward Consolidation* (Baltimore, MD: Johns Hopkins University Press, 1999).

Haggard, Stephan, and Robert R. Kaufman, 'The Political Economy of Democratic Transitions', *Comparative Politics*, Vol. 29, No. 3 (April 1997): 263–83.

Khachaturian, Rafael, 'Uncertain Knowledge and Democratic Transitions: Revising O'Donnell and Schmitter's Tentative Conclusions about Uncertain Democracies', *Polity*, Vol. 47, No. 1 (January 2015): 114–39.

Linz, Juan J., 'An Authoritarian Regime: The Case of Spain', in E. Allardt and Y. Littunen, eds, *Cleavages, Ideologies and Party Systems*, 291–341 (Helsinki: Transactions of the Westermarck Society, 1964).

Linz, Juan J., *Totalitarian and Authoritarian Regimes* (Boulder, CO: Lynne Rienner Publishers, 2000).

Migdal, Joel S., *Strong Societies, Weak States: State-Society Relations and State Capabilities in the Third World* (Princeton, NJ: Princeton University Press, 1988).

Stradiotto, Gary A., and Sujian Guo, 'Transitional Modes of Democratization and Democratic Outcomes', *International Journal on World Peace*, Vol. 27, No. 4 (December 2010): 5–40.

Waldner, David, 'Process Tracing and Causal Mechanisms', in H. Kincaid, ed., *The Oxford Handbook of Philosophy of Social Science*, 65–84 (Oxford: Oxford University Press, 2012).

Weller, Robert P., 'Responsive Authoritarianism and Blind-eye Governance in China', in N. Bandelj and D. J. Solinger, eds, *Socialism Vanquished, Socialism Challenged: Eastern Europe and China, 1989-2009*, 84–98 (Oxford: Oxford University Press, 2012).

3

Conflict and democracy: Politics in divided societies

Up to now, we have mostly been concerned with understanding the kinds of structural conditions thought to lay the groundwork for democracy, as well as some of the different forms democratic transitions may take and the choices faced in those processes. Yet there must be more to the story. If preconditions matter so much, why don't all states showing those conditions reach democratic consolidation? We noted the particular importance of capitalism and economic development in the classic democratization literature, but the prevalence of wealthy, rapidly developing authoritarian economies seems to undercut much of what we thought we knew.

With this chapter, we consider a further condition which afflicts many developmental and transitioning states: conflict. Why do so many new and emerging democracies descend into violence? Here, we regard violence both as a critical intervening variable that can affect the trajectory of democratization at many stages, and as an occasional outcome of these processes. As the scholarship in this area shows, violence is frequently a complication to democratization, but can be caused by it too.

Curiously, however, a hypothesized relationship between democracy and peace features prominently in international relations scholarship and, indeed, has gained wide acceptance in the foreign policies of many countries. As we explain in more detail in chapter eight, Democratic Peace Theory (DPT) – the premise that democracies do not go to war with one another – provides a key rationale for international democracy promotion initiatives. After all, if democracies are more peaceful than non-democracies, and no two modern democracies have ever gone to war, then bringing forth new democracies is only likely to expand the prospects for international peace and security. While not everyone agrees that democracies are more peaceful, most concede they are associated with a lower risk of international and domestic war. They are also less likely to experience civil war or other forms of political violence within their borders. There is less consensus on why this is so, however, and over whether autocracies also see a form of autocratic peace, with most violent conflict occurring in the grey area of countries having both democratic and authoritarian characteristics.

The chapter opens by discussing the evidence for the democratic peace both between and within states, exploring leading explanations for why democracy might reduce the risks of violent conflict. The chapter also highlights that while group violence might be less common in democracies, it is by no means entirely absent. We first consider the problem of 'dangerous transitions' and 'quasi-democracies', using a pair of case studies – Indonesia and Rwanda – to illustrate how the weaknesses of fragile democracies can cause deeply rooted social tensions to boil over. We then examine 'politics by other means' within already-democratic states, using the case of Rift Valley, Kenya, to show how political elites sometimes cause violence by manipulating both people and symbols for their own gain. The chapter introduces several explanations for how and why various forms of violence continue to occur in consolidated democracies. The final section examines leading approaches of electoral engineering seen as able to minimize the risks of violence in the political process. As we note, elites in some other cases, such as Gujarat, India, engage in a tactic known as 'ethnic outbidding', which erupts into violent riots. We conclude the chapter with a brief note on the leading approaches to institutional design for divided societies. These too form part of the essential tasks and choices facing states undergoing transitions to democracy.

The democratic peace

Jack S. Levy wrote that the 'absence of war between democratic states comes as close as anything we have to an empirical law in international relations' (Levy 1988: 661–2). The absence of war between democracies has continued in the post-Cold War period. One study found that the probability of pairs (or dyads) of democratic states going to war with each other was 57 per cent lower than pairs of mixed states (i.e. one autocracy and one democratic state) and 35 per cent lower than two non-democratic states (Raknerud and Hegre 1997). Such findings provide hope that as democracy spreads across the world, the risk of war declines. Democratic countries can still be warlike, of course, and the evidence that democracy makes states less likely to wage war is slim. Indeed, democracies participate in wars as much as non-democratic states, although these are normally conflicts initiated by autocracies (Gleditsch, Christiansen and Hegre 2007)

There are various potential explanations for the absence of war between democratic states, all of which find some support in the scholarly literature (Russett et al. 1995). Some scholars suggest that democracies are more likely than authoritarian states to make policy in ways which reflect a commitment to dialogue and the peaceful resolution of disputes. Executives in democratic states are constrained by parliaments and judiciaries in ways that warlike authoritarian leaders are not. Democracies also tend to have similar interests to each other and take similar positions on international issues (which also might explain the 'autocratic peace', the absence of war between authoritarian states). They are likely to be enmeshed in the same international organizations which constrain unregulated belligerent interaction between states, or in alliances such as the North Atlantic Treaty Organization (NATO) (Jervis 2002).

Even more important than democracy's correlation with an absence of interstate war has been its association with peace within states. Since the Second World War, civil war and other forms of collective violence within state borders have been more common, and deadly, than wars between states. Many studies have found that democracy has a negative association with violent conflict (Gleditsch and Ruggeri 2010). In other words, democracies are more peaceful. Some studies have concluded that the level of democracy has a direct correlation with the absence of conflict, meaning that the lower the level of democracy, the greater the chance of violent conflict. Bartusevicius and Skaaning divide regimes by their electoral practices, with five forms: non-electoral autocracies; single-party autocracies; multiparty autocracies; minimalist democracies; and polyarchies (2018: 626). They find that polyarchies with unconstrained political competition are the most peaceful, with minimalist democracies only marginally less peaceful. In turn, hybrid regimes with some type of elections are more peaceful than autocracies.

However, other studies of the relationship between conflict and democracy which take a simpler focus on three forms of regime – democracies, autocracies and semi-authoritarian regimes (with characteristics of both the former types) – find that civil war and other forms of political violence have an inverted U-shaped relationship to the level of democracy. They find that conflict is relatively low in both autocracies and democracies but is higher in the grey zone of so-called quasi-democracies or semi-authoritarian states which exhibit both democratic and authoritarian characteristics. Why this might be the case is discussed below.

Several studies find that when they do occur, internal wars within democratic states are also less deadly, partly because their governments are less likely to use heavy-handed repression and mass killings than autocracies, particularly against civilians (Colaresi and Carey 2008). Authoritarian states can use extensive repression, and mass killings, sometimes without worrying about losing support or legitimacy, and are more likely to do so because they have fewer alternative sources of authority.

There are several reasons for the relative absence of civil war or ethnic conflict in democratic states. Democracy allows groups to air grievances against the state (or other groups) publicly and peacefully, thereby reducing tension and the incentive to turn to non-institutionalized action (such as violence). Democracy also provides for the peaceful resolution of disputes, through, for example, courts and mediation. The costs associated with achieving group objectives are lowered in a democracy, and so more costly strategies, such as conflict, are forsaken.

Democracies are also better at dealing with some forms of crisis, such as economic or financial, than authoritarian states. Such crises are often incubators for societal conflict. As a way of avoiding challenges to their power, authoritarian leaders sometimes weaken the institutions (and leading officials within them) which might respond effectively to crisis. They instead rely on nepotism and the loyalty of family members and cronies, whom they often appoint to key roles despite their lack of expertise. This was a key factor in the failure of the Suharto regime in Indonesia to respond effectively to the 1997 Asian Financial Crisis, which in turn played a role in triggering separatist and communal conflict throughout the country.

Democracies are also more likely to allow some form of federalism or decentralization of political and financial authority to the regions than authoritarian states. As a way of maintaining dominance, autocracies are more likely to concentrate power in the capital. Although there is some debate about the conflict-reducing effects of regional autonomy, in general it reduces tension by allowing restive regions and groups some power over their own affairs, control over local resources and spending and freedom from impingement of cultural and political rights by state actors from outside the region. And as discussed above, executives and regimes within democracies are more likely to face institutional restraints on their behaviour, meaning they are less likely to engage in the abuse of liberties and rights, a key driver of conflict.

Another potential explanation for why democracies are less conflict-prone is that they often (but not always) display a higher quality of governance in ways which reduce the risk of collective violence. In particular, democracies are generally more responsive to societal demands and are therefore better at service delivery and exhibit lower levels of corruption than autocracies. High levels of corruption increase poverty, reduce per capita Gross Domestic Product (GDP), undermine service delivery, increase inequality and can increase environmental degradation, all of which can increase public anger and feed into conflict, both between groups and between state and society.

Other studies have found that autocracies may be just as successful at avoiding domestic war. Indeed, non-democratic states have a number of advantages in this area. Firstly, intergroup competition between classes, ethnic groups and regions is at the heart of democracy. Non-democracies can also avoid domestic war by pursuing divide-and-rule strategies, by targeting one group or small number of individuals, by crushing prospective rebels or by buying off opponents. This is one reason why hybrid regimes with both democratic and authoritarian characteristics are more prone to conflict: they provide the political space for rebels to mobilize free of repression, but may lack the democratic channels to address grievance. When regimes do decide to negotiate and compromise with rebels or aggrieved groups, they can do so without facing a potential backlash from the public as democratically elected leaders do.

Although there is a great deal of evidence that democracies are more peaceful, both internally and internationally, than non-democracies, it remains uncertain if it is democracy which *causes* peace. This doubt remains for two reasons. The first revolves around a chicken-or-egg problem: democracy is more likely to become established and sustain in conditions of peace and stability, meaning peace may in fact lead to democracy rather than vice versa. The second reason for doubt is that it is possible that both democracy and peace are caused by the same phenomena. High levels of economic development might both lead to democratization (as argued by modernization theory) and to peace. Conversely, greater economic and social inequality or a greater reliance on exporting primary commodities is associated with both conflict and low levels of democracy. In practice, it is likely that democracy acts in concert with other important state characteristics, such as level of economic development, to avoid conflict.

Dangerous transitions and 'quasi-democracies'

While democracy appears associated with peace, the transition from authoritarianism to democracy is often fraught with the risk of conflict. As highlighted above, many studies have found civil war and other forms of political violence to have an inverted U-shaped relationship to the level of democracy (Hegre 2014). Conflict is relatively low in both autocracies and democracies but is higher in the grey zone of so-called quasi-democracies or semi-authoritarian states which exhibit both democratic and authoritarian characteristics.

The democratization period is prone to conflict for several reasons. Regimes generally have less opportunity to repress rebellion or bring communal violence under control. Politicians in the capital are often distracted by the manoeuvring involved in creating a new government. And periods of democratization are also periods of great change, producing new opportunities and new fears. Ethnic and religious communities can perceive a dangerous future in which their security or wellbeing is not secure. The various ethnic and regional groups and factions of society compete over the nature of the new political system. It also takes time for democratic norms and institutions to become established.

According to Jack Snyder, 'Before democratization begins, nationalism is usually weak or absent among the broad masses of the population' (2000: 32). The level and form of nationalism – for example whether civic and inclusive or ethnically exclusive – which emerges during the democratization process depends on the form that transition takes. Perhaps most importantly, it depends on the sequence in which the main elements of the transition occur. The most dangerous period is in the first few years after the transition begins, when the political system is in flux, no longer authoritarian and not yet democratic (Mansfield and Snyder 2005: 54).

Ethnic nationalism and violent conflict are most likely when mass political participation is allowed yet the main institutions necessary for consolidated democracy have not yet been established. In particular, exclusionary nationalism is likely to be effective in the absence of the rule of law and an impartial bureaucracy, judiciary and media, when representative institutions and political parties are weak and when the democratizing country is poor and its citizens have no previous experience of democratic participation (Snyder 2000: 37, 41). When such institutions are strong, inflammatory rhetoric can be countered in the media or the legislature, but they can become vehicles for advancing a nationalist programme when they are weak.

Political elites can mobilize followers and assume power by pointing to the threat of domestic or international enemies. 'Nationalist elites commonly argue that ethnic minorities, the working class, rival elites, or other political opponents should be excluded from political participation' (ibid.: 37). They use that same threat to preclude full participatory democracy. Whether or not elites use the opportunity afforded by weak institutions to resort to exclusionary nationalism depends on the level of threat they perceive from democracy and whether their interests can be adapted to the new political system (ibid.). The weakness of government institutions also exacerbates this sense of insecurity. When institutions such as the rule of law are weak, elites can have no confidence that any assurances made to them during the transition will be honoured once they relinquish power.

Snyder identifies three forms of nationalism which can emerge in the context of threatened and unadaptable elites or weak state institutions or both. When elites are threatened by democracy and therefore refuse to adapt but have recourse to strong administrative institutions with which to protect their power – and no strong representative institutions to counter them – counter-revolutionary nationalism is likely to emerge (Mansfield and Snyder 2005: 171). Targeted groups are likely to be those seen as revolutionary threats to the nation (Snyder 2000: 37). When institutions have collapsed and a new opportunistic elite willing to adapt to obtain power emerges, a revolutionary form of nationalism results in which mobilization will be aimed at protecting the new order from threats at home and abroad (ibid.). When institutions had never been established and elites remain unadaptable, ethnic nationalism is most likely to emerge (Mansfield and Snyder 2005: 172). With no other institutions with which to overcome the collective action problem, elites must resort to loyalties based on 'traditional popular culture' (Snyder 2000: 38). As we discuss next, this form of nationalism appears most applicable to the case of Indonesia.

Case study 3.1: Indonesia 1998–2001

Indonesia's democratization process between 1998 and 2000 presents a most likely case study for Snyder and Mansfield's theory, explaining the onset of exclusionary ethnic nationalism. After thirty years of military-backed rule, President Suharto resigned in May 1998. Throughout his rule, Suharto and his regime hollowed out all state institutions, turning the Parliament, local governments and judiciary into conduits for patronage and loyalty.

In 1999, reformers not only faced widespread and strident demands for democracy but also held credible concerns over national disintegration because of simmering regional frustration after decades of centralized control. Their response was to hold elections almost immediately and to rapidly decentralize political and financial authority to the regions. Within a year of the President's resignation, the first national and local elections were held, which were considered largely free and fair by international observers and the Indonesian people. And local office was now of crucial importance in the transfer of extensive financial and political authority to the regions.

As a result, local office was suddenly both more enticing and far more competitive and democratic. And in the absence of democratic institutions and the rule of law, local politicians often turned to identity-related tensions to win power, intentionally or unintentionally causing violent conflict. Perhaps unsurprisingly, one scholar found that all the communal conflicts of this era involved 'local politics by other means' (van Klinken 2007: 138).

Nationalist violence erupted in numerous areas of the country over this period. While violence did not always emerge when electoral contests were in full swing, the question of who was to hold local power was never far from the minds of the main protagonists. Far more than for national-level elections, winning and losing local office held immense consequences for local elites and their followers. The public service is a crucial source of employment and access to state resources in Indonesia, particularly in areas with a limited private sector and high rates of urbanization (ibid.: 42). Employment in local government departments and the large offices of the governor and district heads is often the only stable career available. These positions also provide officials with the possibility of extracting further wealth through bribes and other forms of corruption, particularly in so-called 'wet' departments with large and difficult-to-monitor budgets. From late 1998, parties and politicians needed to compete for popular support to win seats in local legislatures. Contests over who would become the local executive became heated affairs, both in parliaments and among followers on the streets.

Local conflict in Indonesia during this transitional period was widespread. Ethnically based separatist insurgencies flared up in three provinces: Aceh, East Timor and Papua. Non-secessionist, but no less deadly, ethno-religious violence occurred in five provinces – West and Central Kalimantan, Central Sulawesi, Maluku and North Maluku – a marked change from the Suharto era, when almost no communal violence occurred. In all, almost 20,000 people died.

With many ethnic groups concentrated in remote, inaccessible and resource-rich substate regions, and with a long, sometimes brutal authoritarian history, the country had many conditions conducive to separatist conflict. Three such regions – East Timor (now Timor-Leste), Aceh and Papua – had waged rebellions of varying intensity for much of the period since they were incorporated into the country. Both East Timor and Papua were incorporated into modern Indonesia against their will and well after the country's independence. In each case, but particularly in Papua and Timor, a strong sense of national distinctiveness and a belief that the region had been incorporated illegally provided separatist movements with a powerful rationale of resistance. Yet there was nothing inevitable about rebellion in any of the regions, despite their forceful inclusion into the republic. Had Jakarta offered greater autonomy and a more inclusive, less abusive approach, this would likely have engendered a greater willingness to integrate into Indonesia (as can be seen in contemporary Aceh, discussed below). New Order repression simply strengthened distinct Acehnese, Papuan and Timorese identities in opposition to Indonesia. While revived by democratization, therefore, all three insurgencies had their roots in the pre-democratic era. With the resignation of President Suharto in May 1998 and the onset of democratization, many in each region again demanded greater self-determination or independence.

Even more violent than the secessionist struggles were a series of local wars between ethnic and religious communities, or at least their most militant members. Serious communal violence was confined to five provinces – Maluku, North Maluku, Central Sulawesi, West Kalimantan and Central Kalimantan – sometimes concentrated in particular districts within them. Communal clashes had started before Suharto's resignation, suggesting intergroup tension was already becoming endemic to the authoritarian era. Religion was central in the conflicts in the east of the country (in Maluku, North Maluku and Sulawesi), where large Christian communities make up a sizeable proportion of the local population. In West and Central Kalimantan, however, ethnic animosity was paramount. Some conflicts burned themselves out quickly, such as those in Kalimantan, where the Madurese were quickly expelled from the province. Others, such as that in Maluku, remained at a high intensity for several years.

The intensified political competition from 1999 cannot by itself explain the communal violence in five Indonesian provinces, of course. Electoral contests, decentralization and the division of districts took place elsewhere with no violence. And some of the worst clashes, such as those in Ambon in January 1999, occurred many months before elections were to be held. Ethnic and religious violence is rarely purely instrumental: emotion, status rivalries and contingency all also play their part. Political campaigning from late 1998 was sharpened not only by the rewards of political office, but by the fears some groups had of being dominated by an ethnic or religious other, a sense of injustice at loss of control in one's homeland and distrust of the security forces and intergroup animosities.

In the worst-affected areas, the consequences of conflict were extensive and took years to dissipate. By 2001, there were 1.4 million Internally Displaced Persons (IDPs) in Indonesia (Hedman 2008: 4). Approximately half that number remained displaced by 2004, many IDPs remaining in camps with security concerns hindering their return or because resettlement funds provided by the central government and international agencies had been corrupted by local government. In addition to the extensive loss of life and displacement, much of the infrastructure of affected provinces or districts was destroyed, compounding the effects of the Asian Financial Crisis. As protagonists took control of enemy territory, they destroyed schools, health clinics, markets and gardens. Poverty increased in conflict-affected areas more than other Indonesian provinces which had suffered the impact of the financial crisis but not experienced extensive collective violence. In Aceh, for example, the poverty rate increased from 14.8 per cent of the population in 1998 to 28.4 per cent in 2004 (Barron and Burke 2008: 2). The violence undermined trust in neighbouring communities and in state security institutions suspected of provocation and failing to defend victims from attacks.

Given this sequence of events, Indonesia from Suharto's resignation in May 1998 until it achieved economic, political and institutional stability in around 2005 appears to closely follow Mansfield and Snyder's theory on the onset of exclusionary ethnic nationalism. A further point emphasizes this connection between transition and conflict in Indonesia. The last time there was a change in regime, between 1965 and 1966, even worse violence occurred. As the increasingly leftist regime of President Sukarno was shunted aside by the military-led and highly authoritarian regime of Suharto, massacres intended to eradicate the Indonesian Left killed over half a million people.

Case study 3.2: Rwanda 1994

In 1994, Hutu extremists killed approximately 500,000 people, predominantly Tutsis, in Rwanda in what is sometimes referred to as the fastest mass killing in history. The trigger for the genocide was the shooting down of a plane carrying the Hutu President, Juvenal Habyarimana. The genocide also came after almost four years of civil war between the Hutu-dominated Rwandan Army and the Tutsi rebel army the Rwandan Patriotic Front (RPF), led by Paul Kagame.

Civilian political figures – most notably from the Hutu hard-line political party the MRND (the Revolutionary Movement for National Development) – were heavily involved in planning and coordinating the genocide. But it is inconceivable that the scale, speed and efficiency of the tragedy could have been realized without a leading role by the Rwandan military and other security forces. Alison Des Forges writes that 'Soldiers, National Police (gendarmes), former soldiers and communal police played a larger part in the slaughter than is generally realized' (Des Forges 1999: 11). In the first days of the genocide, senior army officials broadcasted a call to all soldiers and other Rwandans to 'unite against the enemy ... who wants to reinstate the feudal monarchy' (Straus 2006: 50). Like the man recognized as the leading exponent and coordinator of the genocide, Col. Theoneste Bagosora, most leaders of the genocide were largely 'retired officers-cum-politicians' or commanders of elite units (Des Forges 1999: 12). Bagosora coordinated the formation of numerous civilian paramilitary groups, and his office served as the genocide's headquarters. Only after soldiers and police initiated the mass slaughter did civilians join in with the killings (ibid.).

The genocide's roots lay in colonial policies which reified ethnic identities and difference, and in past violence between the groups. And racist ideology flourished in the years leading up to the genocide, with Hutu nationalists claiming that Tutsi were foreign invaders from the north who had long believed themselves superior to, and sought to dominate, Hutu. The two ethnic groups had fought in the past, notably with the coming of independence in 1962, when the Hutu majority overthrew a Tutsi-dominated government, sending thousands of Tutsi into exile. This heralded the start of several decades of authoritarian Hutu rule and the exclusion of Tutsis (McDoom 2012: 132). After seizing power as Rwanda's most senior army official in 1973, Habyarimana held a series of façade elections which he won with almost 100 per cent support.

Yet the genocide's immediate causes stemmed from a period of political liberalization and uncertainty beginning in 1990. This period brought to an end several decades of unopposed authoritarian rule by the MRND. Economic decline and domestic and international pressure forced the President to accept multiparty democracy in 1991. The demands of opposition politicians and the mobilization of their supporters threatened the power of the MRND, while the streets became increasingly volatile as party youth wings attacked rival supporters.

Civil war, and the advance of the RPF from Uganda, compounded the sense of political anxiety in the capital. In the face of the potential fall of Kigali, the country's political parties divided into hard-line Hutu and moderate Hutu and Tutsi factions. Yet it was an internationally sponsored peace agreement to end the war, the Arusha Accords, which really amplified the tension in the capital. At stake was the division of power in post-conflict Rwanda. The Rwandan military was to be a key loser from this agreement.

When the terms of the accords were announced, the RPF had won substantial power. Aside from inclusion in a transitional government, the RPF was to provide 40 per cent of army troops and 50 per cent of officers. Moderate Hutus had also been allocated key government positions (Straus 2006: 43). The Arusha Accords specified that the new army would be made up of 19,000 soldiers and 6,000 police, meaning both the Rwandan Army and the RPF would need to be substantially reduced. Many rank-and-file soldiers in the Rwandan Army therefore feared demobilization, meaning there were numerous willing participants in genocide. By the time of the accords, the national army itself had swelled to 30,000 soldiers, all of whom had become accustomed to the comparative comfort of military life and feared a return to a stagnant economy and high unemployment (Des Forges 1999: 48). This was particularly the case for older and more senior officers, who would be the first to face forced retirement (ibid.: 96). As a result, throughout the negotiations during 1993, hardliners acted as spoilers in attempting to destabilize the agreement. In February, just after a key power-sharing provision was signed, Hutus killed 300 Tutsis in Gisenyi prefecture (Lemarchand 2009: 84). Military opposition to the agreement was so strong that it pushed Habyarimana to publicly disavow it (Des Forges 1999: 49).

A sense of fear among senior Ministry of Defence and military leaders and among rank-and-file soldiers was therefore a key cause of the genocide. As Straus puts it, 'The hardliners pursued radical and violent measures from a position of eroded power' (Straus 2006: 49). Filip Reyntjens writes that for the 'political-military-mercantile network, the democratization process and the redistribution of the cards as a result of the Arusha peace accord constituted a vital threat to interests and activities of a mafia-like nature' (1996: 243). The importance of these concerns in triggering the genocide was shown by the perpetrators' first targets. Within a day of Habyarimana's plane being shot down, hardliners had eliminated all those about to assume key positions in the new civilian-led government dictated by the Arusha Accord, including the Prime Minister and the President's likely replacement (Des Forges 1999: 150).

Violent conflict in democracies

Although democracy is strongly associated with peace, this does not mean that democracies have been free from violent conflict. Many democracies with both advanced and developing economies, in the West and elsewhere, have experienced violent riots, insurgencies and civil war, from separatist rebellion in Northern Ireland to riots in India and civil war in Sri Lanka. This section explores some of the reasons for violent conflict in democracies.

Politics by other means

In many cases, political elites in democracies have caused violent conflict by using ethnonationalism and manipulating ethnic and religious grievances and tensions as a way of maintaining, gaining or augmenting their own power. Whether or not they intend to cause the carnage that they do, that has often been the result. In a very influential study of the role of such manipulation in causing conflict, Jack Snyder argued that Slobodan Miloševic played a key role in triggering the war in Yugoslavia as a way of retaining power in the shift from communism to democracy. Finding he could no longer rely on communism to hold power, he turned to ethnonationalism, playing on animosity and fears between Serbs and Croats.

Elections, while a key part of democracy, are also an important trigger for a great deal of violent conflict. Violent clashes claimed the lives of hundreds, in some cases more than a thousand, in Nigeria in 2007, 2015 and 2017, in Cote D'Ivoire in 2010 and 2020 and in Kenya in 2007 (discussed below). Elections in other locations have led to violent coups (such as in Thailand and Fiji), low-level street violence or massacres of candidates, supporters and media. Elections in the Philippines often involve violence. In 2004 alone, there were 148 election-related killings (not attacks: killings) and in 2007 there were 121. Part of the reason there is so much violence is because of the stakes which are provided by the extent of patronage and corruption, the wealth that can be gained by holding public office. Filipino politics is characterized by local warlords or bosses with a great deal of influence in each province or other region, who collectively control politics and patronage. In one of the worst cases of election-related violence, a militia associated with a local warlord murdered fifty-seven people in what is known as the Maguindanao massacre. The victims comprised a convoy of journalists and female relatives of a gubernatorial candidate, Esmael Mangudadatu, travelling to file the papers for his candidacy for the governorship election. One study has found that electoral violence is becoming more common globally. In 2020, 58 per cent of national elections held that year (thirty-three national elections) saw violence (Besaw 2021).

There are many reasons why violent conflict often occurs during election campaigns, during the vote itself or in the often drawn-out process after the election. Elections are times of both high emotion and mobilization. As discussed in the case of Indonesia above, there is much at stake for both ethnic elites and their constituents. Electoral victory often carries with it the promise of financial reward or employment in the public service. In societies dominated by patron–client links between politicians and their ethnic kin, whether your leader wins an election can have direct material consequences for many.

Closely contested elections are particularly likely to trigger rioting or clashes between supporters or, in some cases, civil war. In a context of high emotion with much at stake, expectations are raised and lost as the lead changes hands several times as results come in. Competitive elections and changing results also pose the risk of suspicion of rivals of stealing the election.

Case study 3.3: Rift Valley, Kenya 2007–8

Ethnic fighting erupted in Kenya, particularly in the Rift Valley region, following the announcement of the results of the general election of late December 2007. The presidential election between the incumbent Mwai Kibaki and challenger Raila Odinga had been forecast as very close. Tension had risen as the incoming results of the election favoured one candidate and then the other. As results came in from certain districts, supporters of Odinga believed he was on his way to victory. When the results were declared and Kibaki had won, Odinga's supporters claimed that the results were fraudulent. Indeed, there was very quickly evidence of irregularities and fraudulent behaviour on all sides.

Violence broke out immediately. In the Rift Valley, Odinga's supporters from the Kalenjin ethnic group attacked Kikuyu supporters of Kibaki. In other towns Kikuyu launched retaliatory attacks against Kalenjin and Luo. The police sometimes acted effectively but often made little effort to stop violence or acted over-forcefully, violating human rights. By the end of February 2008, more than 1,200 people were dead and over 500,000 displaced.

Analysts pointed to a number of irregularities in the tallying stage, in which Kibaki overtook Odinga, and international observers said the process had not been free and fair. The results of the presidential election were completely different to the results of the parliamentary elections, which the opposition won. Kibaki moved quickly to be sworn in, arousing further suspicion; within hours, violence broke out.

Although the election results acted as a precipitating factor for the violence, there had been clashes before the election, with perhaps 600 people killed in the three months before. By April 2007, eight months before the election, there were 380,000 IDPs. Most analysts point to the failure of government land reform policies over previous decades as a central source of tension between ethnic groups in Kenya. In the Rift Valley many Kalenjin believed they had been deprived of their traditional land by distribution policies which provided Kikuyu migrants with land. These tensions were exacerbated by growing populations and pressure on resources.

Yet these tensions were inflamed and utilized by politicians on all sides during the 2007 campaign. Ethnic issues and the ethnic differences between the candidates were a main talking point during the campaign. Odinga and his supporters demanded the revival of an ethnically based federal system known as Majimbo, in which Indigenous groups control their own regions. In effect, the policy would involve the expulsion of migrants from local regions. This rhetoric found support among many native Kalenjin in the Rift Valley who believed they had been deprived of land by government programmes. The tactic had been used successfully in past elections and referenda to win votes and support. Yet the emotive policy carried extensive risks of ethnic violence, as was seen between the end of 2007 and the beginning of 2008.

Riots and ethnic outbidding

A key mechanism by which elite manipulation of ethnic tensions can lead to group violence is known as 'ethnic outbidding'. Although a great deal of ethnic conflict in divided societies appears to be the result of tensions between the two antagonists, in many cases it stems more from internal tensions within the majority community. When two main political parties compete for the support of a single ethnic community, one party sometimes calculates that taking a more nationalistic position on issues related to the minority community is the most likely path to power. By playing on fears and tensions, the party and its politicians can present themselves as the real defenders of the community against the depredations of the ethnic other which seeks to 'take our land, steal our jobs and threaten our safety'. Through pointing to this threat, holding parades and reaffirming the in-group identity (thereby stimulating rising intergroup tension), and pointing to the weakness of their moderate opponents, these nationalistic elites seek to unify the communal vote behind them.

In his highly influential book *Votes and Violence: Electoral Competition and Ethnic Riots in India*, Steven Wilkinson finds that Hindu–Muslim riots are more likely in situations of greater political competition (2004). While such violence has its source at the local level, the most important factor influencing whether it becomes 'bloody or ends quickly' is the response of the political party in power at the state level, which, under the Indian Constitution, controls the security forces (ibid.: 5). This decision, in turn, depends on the party's electoral relationship with the minority community. If the party dominating the state government relies on the electoral support of minorities, or one of its coalition partners does so, then it will provide meaningful protection to that community (ibid.: 6).

Wilkinson finds that minorities are safest in situations of political fractionalization, where three or more political parties play a substantial role in state politics (ibid.: 138). In such situations, politicians need the political support of minorities and those in power will offer security in return for votes, ordering the security forces to take action to prevent riots. They are most at risk in situations of political bipolarity, where just two parties vie for power and attract the vast majority of votes. This risk is heightened if the party in power at the state level 'owns the antiminority issue', as it is likely to use ethnic wedge issues, such as the slaughter of cows or Muslim use of 'Hindu' land, to win votes, and subsequently fail to prevent provocation and violence (ibid.: 23, 139). Yet even potentially antiminority parties may under certain circumstances seek the support of minorities, particularly when there are serious economic or ideological cleavages within the majority community (ibid.: 141). They are more likely to do so if the minority community provides a substantial number of votes but demands little in return for their support aside from security from militants (ibid.). Wilkinson contends that anti-Muslim violence is now rare in most Indian states for these reasons; Muslims, always wary of oppression by Hindu militants, have demanded few social or economic rewards in return for supporting Hindu-led parties (ibid.: 146). In addition, in very few states do Muslims present what can be portrayed as a challenge to Hindu dominance, through numerical strength, over-representation in the security forces or supporting Muslim political parties, for example.

Case study 3.4: Gujarat, India 2002

In 2002, large-scale anti-Muslim rioting in the Indian State of Gujarat killed approximately 2,000 people, displaced 140,000 and destroyed thousands of Muslim-owned businesses. The trigger for the months-long onslaught was the burning of a train in the town of Godhra in which fifty-nine Hindu pilgrim activists had died. Yet analysts have concluded that the rioting was closely connected to impending state elections rather than simply a spontaneous reaction to that event (Spodek 2010). The incumbent Bharatiya Janata Party (BJP) in power in Gujarat was facing a potential electoral loss due to dissatisfaction over several governance failures. The riots proved an effective means of uniting the Hindu vote. Immediately after the violence, the government called an election and won with more than 50 per cent of the vote. The BJP did best in wards affected by rioting, faring less well where violence did not occur. While a belief that Muslims had been involved in setting fire to the train in Godhra no doubt motivated many participants in the riot, the coordination of political actors such as the Vishwa Hindu Parishad and BJP was conducted with the purpose of convincing Hindu voters to give political support to the latter.

Avoiding political violence in democracies

Given the role of political competition and elections in violent conflict in democracies, reducing the incentive for political elites to manipulate ethnic tensions is a key mechanism for reducing the risk of conflict. There are two key approaches to designing electoral systems to reduce conflict. Broadly speaking, the first, known as consociationalism and most associated with Arend Lijphart (1977), attempts to create moderate power-sharing coalitions of ethnically based political parties. The second, known as centripetalism, best associated with Donald Horowitz, involves a set of approaches designed to depoliticize ethnicity, with the goal of forming multiethnic parties (1985).

Consociationalism often involves a mixture of several approaches to conflict management. National constitutions may mandate proportional representation in Parliament, cabinet and government as a whole, requiring that all communities are represented according to their proportion of society. They might also specify that ethnic communities have veto powers over all policies of relevance to them or have some form of regional or other autonomy. Power sharing can also be achieved by ensuring that the two running mates in elections for mayor, president or other executive position be from different communities. In principle, this motivates them to try and gain broader support and hence not take extremist positions. A candidate is unlikely to make inflammatory speeches about a particular ethnic group if (s)he and a running mate are trying to win support from that group.

The alternative approach is centripetalism, so called because of the intention to pull political parties and candidates into the centre, encourage cooperation and integration and thereby dilute the power of ethnicity. Centripetalism seeks not just to replicate society's ethnic divisions in government but to depoliticize ethnicity and create incentives to reach across ethnic lines. Rather than allowing for equal representation of ethnically based parties, the approach seeks to create multiethnic parties. Potential means of achieving this goal include making it necessary that parties receive a certain proportion of their support from each community, for example at least 40 per cent from each of ethnicity A and ethnicity B. This is seen as likely to make political parties and candidates take more moderate positions on ethnic issues and to soon lead to multiethnic political parties with candidates from both ethnicities. The use of preferential voting is another way of getting politicians to moderate their rhetoric. Centripetalism is therefore a type of majoritarian first-past-the-post electoral system, but with specific mechanisms to encourage moderation. Politicians need to show voters that they will govern in the interests of society as a whole rather than just in the interests of one group. Parties will move to the middle on issues of importance to ethnic relations. Advocates of the policy see the creation of moderate multiethnic coalitions before elections as inherently more stable than power-sharing coalitions before elections.

Conclusion

That democracies seldom go to war with one another, and that democracies face a lower risk of political violence, finds supporting evidence in a range of quantitative and comparative studies. Most agree that a combination of executive restraint, transparent and effective governance, public participation and institutionalized mechanisms for reducing and addressing grievances act in concert to reduce the chances of mass violence. There is also substantial evidence that semi-authoritarian regimes, those with a mix of authoritarian and democratic characteristics, experience the highest proportion of violent conflicts. In this chapter, we have suggested a range of reasons why, drawing from the DPT framework that is commonly applied in international relations, but which holds deep relevance for the study of domestic political transition as well.

Drawing on case studies from Africa to Asia, we noted how the expansion of political participation can pour gasoline on existing inter-communal tensions, deepening divisiveness and giving an institutional platform for identity to act on historical grievances. Democratization, it seems, can carry considerable risks in cases where these kinds of divisions are an entrenched and salient political reality. We also showed how post-transition states can become vulnerable to violent outbreaks, especially when prominent political elites are incentivized to manipulate identities and enflame social divisions for their own gain, a phenomenon known as 'ethnic outbidding'. The example given above, that of Kenya's Rift Valley, is all the more troubling because it is a fairly common, rather than atypical, scenario worldwide. Indeed, politicians in many democracies use outbidding strategies, often because they pay electoral dividends. Even well-consolidated countries are not immune. Donald Trump's persistent calls to build a wall along the Mexican border followed this logic. Trump openly played on fears of illegal immigration and the supposed criminality of Mexican migrants, alleging that many were rapists or drug dealers ('bad ombres') in order to unite his support base and paint his opponents as soft on both immigration and crime. From an electoral standpoint, at least, it worked. As both the Rift Valley and Trump instances suggest, outbidding is not just bad for the integrity of democracy, threatening liberal values of tolerance and accommodation, but is actually made possible by democratic processes. This makes the apparent rise of anti-immigrant, populist rhetoric in many democracies all the more dangerous, as we suggest in chapter six.

This chapter concluded with a brief overview of the main approaches to preventing violence and building a civil, democracy-sustaining peace in divided societies. Though consociationalism and centripetalism are usually presented as competing theories, the reality of forging new democracies that bridge significant linguistic, cultural or religious divides is more often a grab bag of tools, tailored to circumstances, drawn from both approaches. The challenges are huge. Old enmities die hard, and even harder where these have been perpetuated by institutionalized practices or policies, sometimes inherited from a colonial authority that privileged some groups over others.

Yet history and demography are not always destiny. Some countries do manage to overcome significant divisions. Canada has built lasting peace and stability by means of federal structures that grant autonomy to geographically clustered minorities, and through omnibus political parties. Northern Ireland has seen major improvements in Catholic–Protestant relations since the 'Troubles' of the 1970s, mostly thanks to an electoral formula designed to reduce religious alienation as generations pass. At the same time, however, the fact that a country experiences unity and stability at one moment is not necessarily a guarantee that it always will, or that it has suitable institutions for managing deep differences when these arise. The United States is now perhaps more divided, politically and ideologically, than it has been at any point since the civil war. At times, these divisions flare up into violence over issues such as policing, race relations, abortion or gun control, to say nothing of the role and size of government itself. How well US institutions are able to mitigate or represent the many currents of opinion on deeply divisive issues is very much an open question.

Questions for discussion

1 Are democracies less likely to go to war? Or are they just less likely to go to war with another democracy?
2 Does democracy reduce the chance of civil war and other forms of internal war? If so, why?
3 Why does violent conflict so often occur in the period between authoritarianism and democracy?
4 Why does violent conflict often happen around elections?
5 What are the best approaches for preventing violent conflict connected to the political process in democracies?

Further reading

Birnir, Jóhanna Kristín, *Ethnicity and Electoral Politics* (Cambridge: Cambridge University Press, 2006).

Brass, Paul, *Ethnicity and Nationalism: Theory and Comparison* (Newbury Park, CA: SAGE Publications, 1991).

Cavallar, Georg, 'Kantian Perspectives on Democratic Peace: Alternatives to Doyle', *Review of International Studies*, Vol. 27 (2001): 229–48.

Doyle, Michael W., 'Three Pillars of the Liberal Peace', *American Political Science Review*, Vol. 99, No. 3 (August 2005): 463–6.

Esman, Milton J., *Ethnic Politics* (Ithaca, NY: Cornell University Press, 1994).

Gurr, Ted R., *Minorities at Risk: A Global View of Ethnopolitical Conflicts* (Washington, DC: United States Institute of Peace Press, 1993).

Horowitz, Donald L., *A Democratic South Africa: Constitutional Engineering in a Divided Society* (Berkeley and Los Angeles: University of California Press, 1991).

Horowitz, Donald L., *The Deadly Ethnic Riot* (Berkeley and Los Angeles: University of California Press, 2001).

Lake, David A., 'Powerful Pacifists: Democratic States and War', *American Political Science Review*, Vol. 86, No. 1 (March 1992): 24–37.

Lijphart, Arend, 'Constitutional Design for Divided Societies', *Journal of Democracy*, Vol. 15, No. 2 (April 2004): 96–109.

McGarry John, and Brendan O'Leary, 'Consociational Theory, Northern Ireland's Conflict, and Its Agreement 2: What Critics of Consociation Can Learn from Northern Ireland', *Government and Opposition*, Vol. 41, No. 2 (Spring 2006): 249–77.

Rabushka, Alvin, and Kenneth A. Shepsle, *Politics in Plural Societies: A Theory of Democratic Instability* (Columbus, OH: Charles E. Merrill Publishing Company, 1972).

Reilly, Benjamin, *Democracy in Divided Societies: Electoral Engineering for Conflict Management* (Cambridge: Cambridge University Press, 2001).

Rosato, Sebastian, 'The Flawed Logic of Democratic Peace Theory', *American Political Science Review*, Vol. 97, No. 4 (November 2003): 585–602.

Shepsle, Kenneth A., *Models of Multiparty Electoral Competition* (New York and Abingdon: Routledge, 1991).

Sisk, Timothy D., *Power Sharing and International Mediation in Ethnic Conflicts* (Washington, DC: United States Institute of Peace Press, 1996).

4

Democratization from below: Civic culture and civil society

Up to this point, we have been primarily concerned with the way certain structures – i.e. education systems, levels of economic development and inequality – constrain or enable democratic prospects, as well as the motivations of actors inhabiting these structural environments. Much of the scholarship produced over the last several decades has emphasized the role of political, social and economic elites in either fighting for or against democratization, and with good reason. Some actors are more influential than others in processes of political change, usually because they are more resourceful or uniquely placed within a given political system to affect outcomes.

However, there is much more at play in these processes than actors and their interests. Democracies are more likely to emerge and survive when they are supported by the proper values. But which values? When and how are these values introduced, institutionalized and used to strengthen democracies?

This chapter examines the role of 'civic cultures' – shared ideas, identities and beliefs – that provide fertile soil in which democracies can flourish. It calls attention to the ways in which certain democracy-reinforcing traits are practised and replicated within social organizations. We refer to such organizations collectively as 'civil society'. However, it is important to note at the outset that clearly not all social organizations support democratic values, and even those that do may not do so all the time. Accordingly, we emphasize the relevance of civic *behaviours* that prioritize public over private interests and may contribute to the emergence and consolidation of democracy in myriad ways.

The chapter consists of three main parts. In the section that follows, we first explore the broad notion of political culture. Of particular concern is the way cultural explanations of regime type and regime change have traditionally been applied in studies of democratization. This discussion also serves as a useful means of highlighting the definitions, uses and misuses of culture as an explanatory variable in social science research.

A second section then unpacks literature on civil society and its role in supporting transitions to democracy and ensuring the long-term health and survival of democratic regimes after consolidation. Much of our discussion centres on what exactly civil society is, but we are also concerned with what it is not. We call particular attention to the part civil society plays in birthing political opposition movements and parties, the avenues it presents for everyday participation in a political system, and its watchdog functions that safeguard against abuses of state power.

The final portion of the chapter is then subdivided into a range of case studies that illustrate the variation in civic (or uncivic) cultures and their relationships to political institutions. We emphasize the role of civil society groups in a failed, slowly recovering state (Afghanistan) and in an authoritarian one with a Leninist legacy and institutions not designed to cope with autonomous social organizations (China), and we discuss one case of consolidation in which changes to political culture and associational life over time actually coincide with a perceived drop in the quality of democracy (the United States). Comparisons among the three cases reflect extremes in the nature and degree of civic culture and civil societies cross-nationally, but not necessarily the complete range of national experiences.

Political cultures: What are they and how do they work?

The term 'political culture' refers to 'the collective orientation of people towards the basic elements in their political system' (Rosenbaum 1972: 4). Two aspects of this definition require further elaboration. First, political culture, like cultures more broadly, involves making meaning out of the symbolic aspects of life (Geertz 1973: 89). Political actors experience and interpret the world around them, and through immersion in a cultural environment are inculcated with values, ideas and beliefs that shape political activities and even the political system itself. This process of interpreting and internalizing life experiences in turn means that political cultures operate cognitively. They exist in people's heads, often to such a degree that their workings seem to be second nature, rather than a deliberate or rehearsed attempt to adhere to a given cultural narrative. Put another way, they become habits, routine patterns of interaction that are 'institutionalized' (March and Olsen 2009).

Second, the experiences and attitudes that make up political cultures are, to some degree, shared. For culture to exercise influence over politics, usually it must emanate from a collective. Seldom is a political culture the result of a single individual, though there are rare exceptions. Shared ideas, experiences and values aggregate to form identities and attitudes, which in turn affect mass behaviours. Thus, political culture has a permeating depth and breadth that affects the way politics works. We normally think of politics as playing out in formal institutions enforced by states, such as legislatures, presidencies or courts, but political culture also affects informal institutions, defined as 'socially shared rules, usually unwritten, that are created, communicated and enforced outside officially sanctioned channels' (Helmke and Levitsky 2006: 5). An expectation among your peer group that you cast a ballot in a local mayoral race, for example, or that you discharge your obligations when called upon for jury duty, may be as much a reflection of political culture as the way elected representatives behave in a televised debate.

The notion that cultures affect political and social institutions is hardly new. In 1831, French thinker Alexis de Tocqueville travelled to the United States and observed the essence of nineteenth-century democracy in the 'New England Town Hall'– a form of direct democracy based on community residents' participation in collective decision-making. For Tocqueville, this participation both requires and reinforces the sense of commitment and, ultimately, duty that Americans of the period felt towards the places they lived, providing a sound basis for democratic practice and strengthening support for it (Tocqueville 1835). A century later, Max Weber's *The Protestant Ethic and the Spirit of Capitalism* ascribed US institutions to attitudes predominant in the American labour force, which derived in myriad ways from the teachings of Protestant denominations that settled in the United States. These, he argued, distinguished America from the more predominantly Catholic societies found in Europe. Weber wrote mostly about economic institutions rather than political ones, of course, but his work provides another influential example of a cultural explanation for the habits and practices with which American society is identified, and as we have seen in previous chapters, there is a long intellectual lineage of associating markets and democracy.

In the early 1960s, political scientists wrote of a 'civic culture' – broadly held social norms and mores borne out of tradition and experiential history that lent themselves to the establishment of democracy in some places but not others. The most enduringly influential such book was *The Civic Culture: Political Attitudes and Democracy in Five Nations*, by Gabriel Almond and Sidney Verba. Based on sample interviews conducted in the United States, the UK, Germany, Mexico and Italy, the book identified three kinds of political culture, each exemplified by an archetypal persona: parochial, subject and citizen. Those in parochial cultures had little or no awareness of politics or the relationship of people to it. Subjects, meanwhile, had developed greater awareness of political structures but viewed themselves as living under these and obeying the state instead of contributing to it. Citizens, on the other hand, had detailed awareness of their political surroundings, and granted legitimacy to state structures while also feeling an obligation to contribute to public life. The authors observed that, where it was found to be present, a 'civicness', or democracy-supporting character, was reflected in 'a pluralistic culture based on communication and persuasion, a culture of consensus and diversity, culture that permitted change but moderated it' (Almond and Verba 1963: 8). While the book met with some criticism for its methodological approach (can a collection of interviews really capture the nature of a whole culture?), it did offer a compelling explanation for the relative strength and longevity of democracy in the United States and the UK relative to the other countries, and still stands as the pioneering work on political culture in democratization studies.

Almond and Verba's focus on culture was somewhat atypical for the period in which it was produced. As we saw in chapters one and two, much of the scholarly literature that developed during the 1950s and 1960s downplayed the significance of cultural factors in shaping regimes and regime transitions in favour of 'structural' or 'macro-historical' considerations. Moreover, disciplinary pressures within the social sciences created conditions less favourable to exploring the role of culture in democratization. During the latter half of the twentieth century, for example, political science underwent what has become known as the 'behavioural revolution' – a transition from a primarily descriptive way of studying politics to one focused more on providing explanations for political phenomena. Instead of simply describing *what* politicians, legislatures, courts or militaries did, or the way in which they were organized, there came to be an increasing emphasis on *why* political actors acted as they did, i.e. what accounted for behaviours (Easton 1953; Grigsby 2004: 15). Though it was always less cohesive as an approach to the study of politics than it appeared to be, behaviouralism came to be identified with the movement to make the study of politics more 'scientific' (Dahl 1961). As such, it embraced objectivity, value-neutrality and reliance on empirical evidence to support hypotheses, and rejected the more deductive application of grand theoretical paradigms based on *a priori* assumptions instead of observation, a practice that became known as 'traditionalism'. Within this context, rationality – an approach in which human actors fundamentally act to maximize utility and minimize risks – came to dominate the study of politics, especially in the United States. While it was considered more scientific and therefore more defensible to understand political actors in terms of their material interests, explanations based on culture were viewed as more emotive (i.e. not rationalistic) and were more at home within cognate disciplines such as anthropology than the study of politics.

So, what changed? How did political culture come to be recognized as so important in forging the fates of transitional states?

The collapse and subsequent fracturing of several states in post-communist Europe proved to be pivotal for initiating what political scientists have come to call the 'cultural turn' in their discipline (Berman 2001). For one thing, the rationality-based approaches that predominated during the Cold War failed to satisfactorily account for its outcomes, creating an opportunity for new and potentially fruitful approaches to emerge and subject themselves to empirical scrutiny. But it was the role of subnational culture and identity that ultimately was responsible for the break-up of the Soviet Union and many of its client states. Seemingly overnight, the map of Europe was redrawn, with many new sovereign territories appearing where multinational and multicultural states had previously been. The Soviet Union, once a vast continental empire, birthed no less than fifteen new countries. Each of these, as well as ex-satellites such as Bulgaria, Hungary, Romania and Poland, asserted new identities that distinguished them culturally from Russia. Cultural undercurrents also caused rifts that subdivided some of these new states: Czechoslovakia was dissolved into Slovakia and the Czech Republic in the 'velvet divorce' of 1993, and eastern Moldova has been administered autonomously by the internationally unrecognized breakaway territory of Transnistria since 1990. In Southern Europe, Yugoslavia dissolved in 1993, giving rise to the new independent states of Serbia, Slovenia, Croatia, Macedonia, Bosnia and Herzegovina and, after years of bloody civil war, Kosovo.

As it turned out, ethno-national identities (i.e. cultures) were a core cause of these dissolutions. In their official ideology, communist countries subordinated cultural as well as other forms of collective identities to those of labour. Class consciousness and class struggle provided the basis for national identities in the Soviet Union, its satellites, Yugoslavia and many other communist states, and these identities were rigidly enforced by dictatorships with strong coercive capabilities. When these dictatorships softened or changed, subnational identities which had been in abeyance throughout the Cold War began to assert themselves, resulting ultimately in the splintering of the Soviet Union into many new and independent countries (when applied to the former Yugoslavia, this was known as 'balkanization') (Beissinger 2002). In other words, cultures mattered much more to these political reform processes than had been previously thought.

The limits of cultural arguments

Any consideration of culture as a factor affecting democratization must come with a few caveats. This is important because it can be dangerous to reduce the thoughts, beliefs and behaviours of whole groups of people to their culture. The contention that all who live within a culture must therefore think, speak or act similarly or in culturally proscribed ways is sometimes referred to by scholars as *essentialism*, but closely resembles stereotyping. Often, essentialist arguments take the form of if/then statements, such as 'if a person is *x*, then they must believe *y*', or 'all people from region *a* behave like *b*'. Among social scientists who prefer to use the more technical language of statistics, the assumption that a subgroup of a population must carry the characteristics of that population is known as the *ecological fallacy*.

Handling culture carefully also matters, because cultures are not static, but constantly in flux. This is as true for democracies as for every other regime type. Twenty years ago, the right to marry whomever one chose was a non-starter in many places that have since legalized gay marriage, including the United States, with its 5–4 Supreme Court decision in 2015. The cultural change that made this decision possible is all the more startling when contrasted with US values in the 1950s, when Black and white Americans could not sit together on public transport or use the same drinking fountain, let alone marry. Attitudes, beliefs and, ultimately, social structures and laws shifted over time.

In studies of democratization, it is sometimes claimed that democracy fails to develop in certain places where the 'culture' is not disposed to it. Often, we hear this argument with reference to places such as Iran or China, whose own leaders draw sharp distinctions between the cultures of Western democracies and their own. Yet these distinctions are themselves essentialist, and do not allow for the contested, differentiated nature of Iranian, Chinese or other national cultures such that compatibility with democracy becomes a possibility. The basic problem is that claims of incompatibility or a mismatch between culture and democratic values adhere too closely to a static definition of culture, giving an overly deterministic impression of political destiny. For example, Francis Fukuyama has written of a 'Confucian ethic' which many suppose make China inhospitable to democracy. However, as he points out, 'the fact is that there are fewer points of incompatibility between Confucianism and democracy than many people in both Asia and the West believe' (Fukuyama 1995: 21). The Dalai Lama similarly warns against the presumption that democracy and 'Asian values' do not mix (1999). Indeed, his analysis invites debate over what constitutes 'Asian' values and who sets the parameters of such a construct, an important conversation to have, since plainly not all Asian cultures reject democracy. There are also long-standing claims over the incompatibility of democracy and Islam, with some arguing that these too are overdrawn, in part because of the diversity of cultures, histories and attitudes present across the Muslim world (Khatab and Bouma 2007; Filali-Ansary 1999).

Moreover, while it may be that China or Iran have political cultures very different from those of France or the UK, the presumption that these are unchangeable, and that democracy therefore is impossible, is not well supported by comparative evidence. Thirty years ago, the political cultures of many ex-communist states were thought to be unsuitable soil for democracy. Some failed to reach consolidation (Belarus) or backslid towards authoritarianism (Hungary), but others experienced a change in their political cultures and now support healthy democratic regimes (the former East Germany, Czech Republic). Four decades earlier, democracy's prospects in Japan, Italy and Germany seemed tenuous, owing to radically different political cultures there, but all have undergone radical cultural shifts and rate among the most stable democracies in the world.

A further challenge in the study of political culture concerns how individuals interact with their cultural environments. At one extreme, cultures could be thought to function like 'scripts', which individuals follow throughout their lives. As Goddard puts it, 'the term "cultural script" refers to a technique for articulating culture-specific norms, values and practices in terms which are clear, precise, and accessible to cultural insiders and outsiders alike' (2009: 68). In this view, traditions, beliefs, values and mores provide a kind of blueprint that shapes the choices actors make, and when considered on aggregate, the way a society functions. At the other extreme is the view that actors make the culture, not the other way around. This view rests on the assumption that individuals pursue self-interest rationally – that is, that they seek the greatest benefit at the lowest cost – and that it is this self-interest that mainly motivates their decisions. Cultural beliefs and values factor into those decisions only when individuals are unsure of what actions serve their interests best. In such a situation, cultural values and ideas can provide a sort of referent to broadly recognized rules that make certain choices safer than others. This rationalist ethos is perhaps best captured by the words of Arnold Vinick, a fictional candidate for the US presidency from television's *The West Wing*: 'When in doubt, do the right thing. The rest of the time, get away with whatever you can' (2005).

The main problem with the 'scripts' view of culture is that it leaves too little room for personal agency. Humans are not automatons, robotically moving through their lives as if their every choice were predetermined by their cultures. Often, they chafe, push back, buck or outright rebel against cultural values in order to change them, and sometimes they succeed. By not allowing space for agency, cultural 'scripts' also foreclose on possibilities for cultural change. The challenge with the more rationalist version, which relegates culture to a set of loose rules that can be pushed aside by self-interest, is that it is too agency-centred, and does not do justice to the persistence or 'stickiness' of cultural values, even in the face of long-running efforts to alter or overturn them.

What has all of this got to do with transitions to democracy? Plenty. Political cultures matter because they can shape the range of options or tactics reformers of regimes see as being available to them. But if cultures are also pliable, this means they can be moulded by a variety of actors in a variety of ways, slowly or quickly, with big and small consequences, for good or ill. As we explore in the next section, domestic civil society actors can be a force for democratization where they serve as carriers and spreaders of democracy-strengthening values. However, not all societies experiencing political transitions have functional civil societies capable of supporting the cultural changes needed for a healthy democracy. Many authoritarian countries show signs of vibrant organizational and associational life, yet democracy remains in a stunted state because the values required to strengthen it are weak or not present. Indeed, a key challenge of many transitions concerns how to create a civic, democracy-promoting culture from scratch where no prior one exists. Many authoritarian regimes, especially those of Marxist-Leninist stock, have historically sought to limit or eliminate civil liberties precisely because the freedom of citizens to associate and form organizations could become a source of political opposition (Hough and Fainsod 1979). And while we address the topic in greater detail in chapter seven, it's worth stating here that pressures for cultural change can come from outside a society too. A US occupation force, for example, was instrumental in demilitarizing and remaking Japanese political culture after the Second World War. As technological advancement allows for the shrinking of time and space, bringing societies into closer contact under conditions of globalization, we anticipate that exogenous pressures for domestic cultural change are likely to accelerate, with positive and negative implications for democracy.

Civil society: A conceptual overview

The term 'civil society' is not synonymous with 'society' in general. It is those elements of social life that contribute to democracy's emergence and survival that we call 'civil societies'. Sometimes this is referred to as 'liberal' civil society, since it captures and imparts liberal values, including (but not necessarily limited to) toleration, secularism, pluralism, diversity, inclusion, participation and representation, equity (of genders, sexualities, ethnicities, religions or other aspects of personal identity) and an emphasis on individual liberty and self-actualization.

This understanding is not the only nor even the original definition of civil society. The concept traces its origins to the works of Italian Marxist thinker Antonio Gramsci, founder and leader of the Italian Communist Party during the rise of Benito Mussolini in the 1920s and early 1930s. Gramsci was primarily occupied by a particular problem in Marx's thought – if capitalist exploitation led to workers' revolutions, then insurrection should logically come to those places where exploitation is greatest, and class divides the most severe. Britain, Europe's most advanced capitalist country, should face revolution first. Yet it was Russia, the most underdeveloped part of Europe, that held the world's first socialist revolution in October 1918, and forged the Union of Soviet Socialist Republics (USSR) shortly thereafter. Gramsci wondered why. His conclusion was that workers in advanced capitalist countries were too unaware of their exploitation to overthrow the economic order – a phenomenon known as 'false consciousness'. What was required, Gramsci thought, was a guiding force to educate the masses about the causes of their exploitation and lead them towards revolution (known to Marxist thought as a revolutionary 'vanguard'). He called this vanguard force that would destroy false consciousness and provoke an uprising to bring down capitalism 'civil society'. It was a place for the formation of a counter-hegemony, where opposition to the dominant order might coalesce (Fonseca 2016; Buttigieg 1995).

More than three decades after the fall of communism in Europe, the original Gramscian notion of civil society is seldom discussed, and almost never invoked in international policy or development aid circles. When scholars, governments and practitioners now talk of civil society, they primarily refer to 'an area, separate from the state, the market and the individual household, in which people organize themselves and act together to promote their common interests' (Swedish International Development Cooperation Agency 2007: 4). US-based democratization scholar Larry Diamond has carried this definition further still, characterizing civil society as a 'realm of organized social life that is voluntary, self-generating, at least partially self-supporting, autonomous from the state, and bound by a legal order or shared set of rules' (Diamond 1999: 221).

Voluntarism is an essential part of a democratic civil society, since it ensures citizens can freely pursue non-state interests. In some twentieth-century totalitarian political systems, such as Germany under the Third Reich or the Soviet Union under Joseph Stalin, participation in social organizations was compulsory, or practically so, under state laws. The non-voluntary nature of social organization in these states also meant that their interests or missions could not be distinguished from those of the state itself. Think of the Hitler Youth or Communist Youth League – their purpose was to bolster the connection between social organizations and the state, and in so doing they served to strengthen the authoritarian order by inhibiting the formation of political opposition.

For civil society to support democracy or democratization, membership must also be autonomous, or separate from the state. This means civil society organizations cannot be functionally dependent on the state if they exist to support genuinely democratic aims. Yet even in fully consolidated democracies, many civil society organizations receive state funding (often indirectly through tax subsidies), a trend that would seemingly violate their claim to autonomy. In practice, the line separating civil society from the state is often blurrier than one may suppose (Davis 2019). It is perhaps best, then, to speak of civil society's degree of autonomy from the state, defining civil society as more authentically liberal the greater the degree of that autonomy. Understanding autonomy in this way allows for the practical reality that social organizations often partner with states to deliver important public services such as healthcare or education.

Separateness from the state also means that civil society is distinct from political parties, whose main goal is to vie for and gain control of state power. While there may be a close relationship between civil society and particular political parties – and indeed many parties began as civil society organizations – once a group crosses the boundary to competing for state power it loses its separability from the state, and with it its function as an arena for giving voice to interests not aligned with the state's objectives.

Further, our definition of civil society refers to groups that act for the public interest. Although many civil society organizations work with private firms in myriad ways, the criterion of autonomy (from the market as well as the state) implies that democracy-strengthening civil society organizations prioritize public interests over private profit. The distinction is a tricky one, since many organizations, both public and private, blur the line between the two in practice. A corporation may contribute to the public interest when it undertakes a corporate social responsibility campaign, join with other firms to lobby governments for intellectual property laws that benefit whole segments of society or hold a charity car wash or fun run. When Bill Gates acts as founder and CEO of Microsoft, he is not working as part of civil society. However, the Bill and Melinda Gates Foundation, a separate philanthropic organization, is part of civil society when it raises funds to help with vaccine distribution, for instance. Because certain privately motivated actors sometimes work in the public interest, it is important to acknowledge the difference between civic groups and civic behaviours, both of which can contribute to democracy in meaningful ways.

Advocating in the public interest means that groups in civil society operate for a nearly infinite number of reasons on a diverse array of issues and causes – political, social, economic and cultural. Advocacy is an attempt to exert influence on others, whether state actors directly responsible for official policy or members of society at large. Either way, the goal is to win others over to their perspective. Thus, civil society organizations are competitive interest-maximizers, and this character becomes more pronounced in more economically advanced and internationally integrated societies (Cooley and Ron 2002; Lecy, Mitchell and Schmitz 2010). They seek to exert influence by appealing to the state for concessions, benefits, policy changes, relief, redress of grievances or enhancing accountability, or by aligning with others who share their point of view. Simply put, advocacy is a central, essential part of what a democracy-supporting civil society does. A lack of advocacy, or advocacy only in pursuit of private interests, falls outside the scope of civil society. Therefore, sporting teams, hobby clubs, yoga classes, church youth groups or any other entities not engaging in public-interest advocacy fall outside the scope of civil society, even if they contribute to associational life in other ways.

The requirement that civil society groups act in the public interest also means that groups which seek to limit or exclude the political participation of others are not a part of civil society and are certainly not democracy-promoting. Such groups might include criminal gangs or syndicates, armed insurgencies, revolutionary movements, terrorist cells, ethnic chauvinists or hate groups such as the Ku Klux Klan or other white power organizations. Such groups are sometimes referred to as part of 'illiberal civil society' or 'uncivil society' (Bob 2011; Chambers and Kopstein 2011).

How does civil society support democracy?

Civil society is both a prerequisite for and an essential component of any healthy democracy. A lack of civil society, or the absence of laws permitting individuals to associate freely in groups not aligned with the state, means that a key ingredient for the onset of democracy is also absent. Civil society can also prove decisive in democracy's consolidation, helping to build support and legitimacy for democratic institutions by ensuring, for example, the fairness of elections, the efficacy of political parties, the openness of political participation, the accessibility of public offices (including the ability to run for office), the assurance of political equality and the effectiveness and accountability of government.

One way civil societies support democracy is by enabling the effective and balanced representation of viewpoints within a political system. It is a means by which citizens participate in politics and is even more valuable because that participation is open-ended. Elections also offer a chance to directly participate in politics, but elections are often determined by term limits, and may come around only once every few years. In the United States, term limits for the presidency occur every four years, making it possible to calculate to the day when future elections will occur. In Westminster-type parliamentary democracies, where executive and legislative powers are fused rather than separated (as in presidential systems), election dates are free-floating and often set with some degree of political opportunism by the incumbent government. (In Canada, for example, a 'writ' is dropped and an election called within a prescribed time frame, but not according to a fixed date, making it possible for a government to drop the writ at a time most politically advantageous for itself and for strategizing over the coming election.)

By contrast, one could participate in politics every day by joining a civic organization and taking up public-interest advocacy. Because it brings together citizens who share viewpoints on issues of common concern, civil society also supplements the aggregation of societal preferences articulated by large blocks of voters. Indeed, civil society is the component of a democracy that works to ensure the other elements function effectively – including the fairness of elections, the degree to which parties and leaders are bound by the rule of law, the ability of candidates to run for and hold office, the efficiency of government processes and so on. By broadening avenues for citizen participation in public affairs, civil society also facilitates citizen interaction with different levels of government. It provides an especially strong foundation for democracy, stimulating participation in politics at the local level, where connections between officials and the public are deeper, and where average citizens have a more direct stake in decision-making.

By drawing on and enhancing interpersonal ties among members of a given community – known as 'social capital' – civil society can enhance the accountability and sense of trust citizens have in local political institutions (Putnam 1993). Of course, some conditions do apply. Theorists point out a key difference between two types of social capital: bridging and bonding. Bridging social capital is helpful for building and strengthening interpersonal trust when it encourages connections among individuals and groups across different segments of society, i.e. between strangers. Imagine you are sitting in a crowded café reading this book on a laptop or tablet, surrounded by other people whom you don't know, and need to use the restroom or place another coffee order. Do you pack up your laptop and take it with you for the few moments it may be out of your line of sight, or do you trust that the others in the café will not steal your computer and run out the door? Maybe you even ask someone sitting nearby, 'Would you mind watching my laptop a second while I go get a muffin?' If you chose to leave your device on the table where you were sitting, you demonstrated a high degree of interpersonal trust. If you were worried enough about that stranger stealing your computer that you kept it with you at all times, that level of trust is lower. For those that demonstrated trust, it may be because you would do the same for them and watch their laptop if asked. Such norms of reciprocity – the expectation that what one does for another they would do for you – help to solidify ties between those who might otherwise have little in common, and contribute to healthy democracy by encouraging people from different walks of life to recognize their common interest in cooperating. It also encourages a broader sense of trustworthiness. If someone behaves accountably in a café, they might also behave accountably in public office. By contrast, bonding forms of social capital typically refer to social ties within communities rather than across them. This is not necessarily a bad thing, but it is less useful for encouraging a broad type of trust that is healthy for democracy – those who already are known to each other, who share identities, might be expected to trust or help one another more readily. Sometimes, bonds forged within groups are strengthened at the expense of extra-communal ties, encouraging myopic and self-serving views of the world over the kind of trust in others that is needed for strong, stable democracies. In extreme instances, intra-communal bonds can run so deep that extra-communal bonds break down. Mistrustful, even hateful views of outsiders emerge that discourage acceptance of others and the political processes that put them in power, thus inhibiting democracy's emergence or leading to its decline.

As a corollary, civil society also operates as an 'antidote to the state', or a watchdog that exercises some countervailing power on behalf of citizens, in keeping with the democratic principle of popular sovereignty – i.e. that a state exercises authority only with the approval of its citizens (Van Rooy 1990: 11–12; Mlambo, Zubane and Mlambo 2020). Groups in civil society can be whistle blowers, exposing corruption or power abuses by public officials, an important function in authoritarian and democratic countries alike. In some authoritarian contexts, this may have the effect of delegitimizing a dictatorial ruler or party, and give fuel to a broader movement towards regime breakdown. In new democracies, the ability to exercise watchdog functions can be a critical test of fresh institutions and norms of accountability essential to the rule of law. Indeed, even in long-established, consolidated democracies, the ability for citizens to hold leaders to account is vital, though it usually occurs within a broadly recognized procedural framework. Journalists may also play a key role in civil society's democratic function by distributing accurate, timely, trustworthy information. This is why it is troubling to read about how little confidence the average US citizen has in 'mainstream media'. In late 2020, a Gallup poll revealed a full third of Americans had no trust at all in their mass media (Brenan 2020).

At formative and advanced stages of democracy, civil society can be a 'large free school', broadening awareness of the rights and responsibilities of citizens, providing a training ground for future political leaders and building the skills necessary to sustain democracy in the long term. While the inoperability of a democratic political culture is a major challenge in transitioning societies, particularly those lacking experience with democratic institutions, civil society may help to develop democratic norms of behaviour, like tolerance, respect for alternative viewpoints, moderation and a willingness to compromise. Over time, the internalization of such attributes in both citizens and their leaders may lead to the broad acceptance of the new 'rules of the game' and enhanced stewardship for democratic institutions. Relatedly, civil society may be a source of expertise for developing best practices of democratic governance. For example, universities, research institutes and think-tanks can all advocate for and advise on programmes of action for the reform of legislatures, judiciaries or electoral law.

Thus, civil society in most democracies plays a multifunctional role, from mobilization and consciousness-raising to providing inputs and pressures to legislatures, to pushing for the realization of essential rights. However, civil society may be destructive of democracy in some instances. At times, civil society groups may perpetuate inequalities, social conflict or political corruption, something that is far more likely to occur in countries that are deeply divided along cultural, linguistic, ethnic or religious lines, or where experience with democratic norms is limited. In such cases, extending rights of democratic participation can sometimes be a double-edged sword – democratic principles hold broad participation to be a virtue, and democracies are supposed to be more inclusive than non-democracies. Yet the drive towards greater inclusion can open the door for some groups with divisive or socially destructive agendas, especially where these groups are able to hide behind free speech protections.

This outline of the functions of civil society yields two important questions for those who would see new democracies brought forth. The first concerns the pace and sequencing of the steps taken towards dismantling an authoritarian political system and building a new democratic one in its place. Is it preferable to hold new elections quickly, gaining the consent of people voting in a free, fair and open contest, perhaps for the very first time, before building an independent court system, deciding upon formulas for executive power sharing or redrafting a constitution that puts into place the sorts of laws that will allow for a flourishing civil society? Or does the rush to a vote overlook the role of civil society in organizing political opposition, aggregating societal interests or forming political parties, and therefore stunt long-term prospects for democratic civil society (Carothers 2007)? Is it advisable or even possible to encourage civil society in a deeply divided society, or one where no legal basis exists to preserve its democratic function? Does the order in which these things emerge make a difference to democratization processes?

A second question then addresses how to create those values that preserve democracy where there exists weak or no civic traditions. If, as we suggested at the outset of this chapter, institutions are culturally embedded and support democracy where they capture values alive in a citizenry, what hope does this leave for political systems designed to suppress those values and limit political opposition from forming within civil society? Are countries with no civic tradition doomed to weakly democratic or undemocratic futures? In the final section below, we explore three different cases of embattled civil societies, to get a sense of the challenges present in a variety of national settings.

Political culture at work: Three civil societies compared

Civil society in a weak state: Afghanistan

Afghan civil society is best described as 'still emerging'. On the one hand, the country has a relatively rich tradition of community engagement and associational life, largely comprising grassroots Islamic organizations, and to some degree ethno-linguistic groups as well. These are complemented by many international and domestic non-government entities now working in a wide assortment of areas, such as education, public health, poverty alleviation, disaster relief, child services, gender equity, human rights protection and many others. On the other hand, Afghan civil society is prevented from fully realizing its democratic potential by an untenable security situation in many parts of the country. These conditions often hamper organizational involvement in public goods delivery and effective advocacy. Additionally, civil society in Afghanistan has been slow to emerge due to decades of civil strife, foreign occupation, sectarian violence, international military incursions and, not least, state-sponsored terror at the hands of the Taliban.

Development of the sector in recent decades can be broken into distinct phases. During the Soviet era (1979–98), an influx of non-governmental organizations (NGOs) was concerned with addressing shortages of food and shelter, as well as concerns related to refugee camps in neighbouring Pakistan. Agricultural and infrastructure development projects were the focus, aiming to provide Afghans with necessities of life that would allow them to remain in Afghanistan rather than flee to cross-border shelters. This occurred alongside an effort to raise consciousness of the plight of Afghans, especially refugee populations, within and among foreign governments. After the Soviet presence ended, this emergency assistance focus shifted towards ongoing development needs, and the number of active NGOs in the country grew, as did foreign support. With more resources for NGOs came new efforts to increase the capacity of Afghan organizations, leading to some progress in standardization, professionalization and cooperation across the sector.

In many respects, political restrictions under Taliban rule (1996–2001) hampered further sectoral development, and certainly precluded democratic civil society from taking shape. However, the harshness of the regime did introduce a measure of social stability which had often been lacking in the past. This allowed for some Afghan organizations to continue their work and even to cooperate with international agencies in some cases (this was not true of NGOs focused on gender equity goals, which could not operate). Between 1998 and the Taliban's ouster in 2001, Afghanistan experienced a severe drought leading to food shortages and internal displacement, shifting the sector back towards emergency relief, including cross-border coordination efforts with Pakistan to serve a resurgent refugee population there.

The fall of the Taliban in 2001, subsequent US-led NATO invasion and 2002 election of the transitional administration of Hamid Karzai substantially altered the working environment for civil society groups in Afghanistan (Ali 2009). Large numbers of internally displaced refugees, along with returnees from Pakistan, required a ramp-up of emergency services, combined with longer-term infrastructure, social, economic and political development projects to rebuild the shattered Afghan state and protect a bare modicum of social stability. These new needs, coupled with a now internationally recognized Afghan government, drove an expansion in the number of service-orientated NGOs, and brought new resources for enhanced capabilities. A policy and legal framework for NGOs in civil society was established in 2005, referred to as the Law on Social Organizations. Civil society groups have been involved in all major conferences on Afghan reconstruction since that time, including the Bonn Conference on Afghanistan (December 2011), the Chicago NATO Summit (May 2012) and the Tokyo Conference (July 2012). The Second Bonn conference highlighted a need for 'the further promotion of civil society participation, including both traditional civil society structures and modern manifestations of civic action, including the role of youth, in the country's democratic process' (Safi 2012).

While these may be interpreted as generally positive signs, sectoral expansion since 2001 has brought challenges of its own. First, professionalization of many civil society groups and better funding meant that NGO employees could be paid better wages – better wages than the Afghan government could provide for its workers. In turn, this wage gap has exacerbated enmity between civil society groups and the government. 'NGOs are as damaging for Afghanistan as are warlords', declared Minister of Planning Ramazan Bashar Dost in 2005 (Asian Development Bank 2009: 5). Official mistrust has also been fuelled by perceptions that some social organizations exist to do the bidding of the international community in Afghanistan, leading to their input at international gatherings ultimately being ignored when it comes to policy-making. At times, objections to civil society's role in public life are driven by a sense that the international community, which gave NGOs their voice, knows little about the needs of Afghanistan or how to solve its most pressing problems. This latter issue betrays a common belief that civil society is a narrow concept not designed for or suited to the Afghan context, a view shared by some international observers (Harpviken, Strand and Ask 2002). This supposed mismatch in understandings of civil society as applied to Afghanistan has given rise to a catch-22: civil society could be a tonic that spreads liberal values to support democracy and move the country towards a peaceful future, but is limited by ongoing instability and may in fact depend upon the participation of some entities engaged in inter-communal violence. Considering these constraints, it is not surprising that civil society in Afghanistan remains a work in progress.

Civil society under state control: China

In contrast to the Afghan case, in which civil society's development has been hampered by social instability and weak structures, China's civil society confronts just the opposite problem – too much state. Like most communist states, China's political system was not designed to be hospitable to autonomous and voluntary social organizations. Despite several decades of reform and the emergence of many foreign and domestic NGOs, state supervision of the sector remains extremely high.

While a small number of state-based service organizations did exist in communist China throughout the totalitarian period (1949–76), it was the economic reform and opening under the leadership of Deng Xiaoping, which began in the late 1970s, that paved the way for the expansion of civil society groups that followed. The main driver behind the expansion was the privatization of many state-owned enterprises (SOEs) in the early 1990s. The selling-off of SOEs at this time meant that the delivery of key social services was left untended, creating an opening for new kinds of organizations to fill the void. Thus, some of China's earliest NGOs were welcomed by the state and were seen as reducing the government's burden of public goods provision. Also, during the 1990s, foreign organizations and funding poured into China as its economy and society became more internationally integrated. (Some environmental organizations had made early inroads when access became possible in the late 1970s. The World Wildlife Fund, for example, developed a close relationship with Chinese authorities and eventually adopted the giant panda as its official logo.)

Even as the number of service organizations in China expanded, the working environment remained inhospitable. In the aftermath of the Tiananmen Square demonstrations of 1989, all social organizations were required to formally register with the Ministry of Civil Affairs' Bureau of NGO management. Registration in turn required organizations to have the sponsorship of a supervising government or Communist Party agency, creating what is now called the 'dual management system' and effectively rendering the autonomy of Chinese civil society groups an impossibility. Amendments and additions to this system in 1998 and 2004 emerged as the number of Chinese social organizations continued to expand.

However, the halting patchwork of laws and regulations has left its mark on the development of civil society in China in several interrelated ways. First and foremost, the long-time lack of an overarching and enabling policy framework has bred confusion among Chinese organizations over state requirements, leading to widespread flouting of regulations. In turn, this has deepened official mistrust of social organizations and a lack of understanding about their purpose and role. This is perhaps the most enduring challenge of Chinese civil society groups: coping with the ambiguities of a system that was never designed to handle autonomous associations and harbours deep suspicions about them. Having come of age in such an environment, NGOs and other social organizations often find themselves resource-poor, and struggle to professionalize. Weak and lacking organizational capacity, many organizations, even those working in the same developmental area, struggle to connect and collaborate. While this means that it is very difficult for groups in China to form nationwide networks that could improve service delivery, it is advantageous for a hegemonic party state that wishes to keep cohesive opposition movements from taking shape (Teets 2014; Hsu, Hsu and Hasmath 2017; Hildebrandt 2013).

Space for Chinese civic groups has contracted considerably under the leadership of Xi Jinping. The first sign that this would be the case came in 2013 with the 'Communique on the Current State of the Ideological Sphere'. Commonly called Document Number 9, it explicitly warns against civil society as a vehicle for democratic values and insidious external influences that could undermine China's constitutional order. Since tabling this document, Xi has set about creating new ways to monitor and limit the role of foreign funding and actors in China's non-state sector, most notably with the 2016 'Foreign NGO Law' and 'Charity Law'. While these do hamper the ability of international actors to provide aid to Chinese organizations, they may have the effect of making Chinese groups less dependent on foreign donors and more self-sufficient. Of course, this also leaves the Chinese state as the single largest partner and benefactor for the time being. In the end, this adds up to a situation in which civil society's democratic functions are co-opted and would-be civic organizations are redeployed in the state's service. In other words, under the present conditions, civil society in China is more apt to strengthen the authoritarian regime than to be an agent of democratization.

Civil society amid declining public connectivity and trust: The United States

When compared to the cases of Afghanistan and China, the United States has a strong tradition of civic engagement and participation that both gave rise to and reinforce democratic institutions. Yet even here, there are reasons to be sceptical that civil society is as healthy as it once was. US political scientist Robert Putnam has explored what he regards as the decay of social connectivity among Americans, and a concomitant drop in civic participation and trust in government. The explanation, according to Putnam, is that in recent decades Americans have become couch potatoes, and are now far more likely to spend time at home watching television than they are to join a softball team, girl guides/boy scouts, the Freemasons, Lions, Elks or other community service groups, or a bowling league, than they were earlier in the post-Second World War period (the book, called *Bowling Alone* and released in 2000, referred to the relatively solitary existence many Americans now lead, and the malaise they feel towards public officials, institutions and processes). In a nutshell, the breakdown of social connections has meant a decline in US associational life, at a considerable cost to democratic participation and legitimacy in many Americans' eyes (Putnam 2000).

Twenty-plus years on, we could say that Putnam was partially correct. Certainly, Americans still watch a great deal of television. By using streaming services instead of conventional cable, many can tailor what they consume to their individual tastes without hearing contrary points of view, and there is plenty to suggest the popularity of such patterns of consumption, especially during the Covid-19 pandemic, when many were already cut off from their neighbours with little else to occupy their minds. It may be that Americans are less likely to join civic organizations than they were a generation or two ago. It is also true that at the time Putnam wrote, voter turnout in national elections was approaching an all-time low. However, the November 2020 presidential contest, which sent Joe Biden to the White House, garnered the highest turnout in American history. Thus, it could be claimed that participation has rebounded, as, apparently, has faith in the democratic process itself – what else but a belief in the importance and effectiveness of voting could explain such a marked uptick in turnout?

However, the ongoing danger is not that participation is declining, but that Americans have grown further apart. Social connectivity is no closer to being repaired than it was at Putnam's writing and in fact may be worse. As Trump's presidency highlighted, the United States is a deeply divided society, with pitched and virtually unbridgeable opinion gaps on critical matters such as abortion, gun control, policing, the trustworthiness of news media, party affiliation and many others. Such ideological divides are thought to negatively affect the way Americans view their political system (Dionne 2013). Indeed, the gravity of the current cultural divide was made clear on 6 January 2021, when the US Capitol was stormed by rioters attempting to prevent Congress's ratification of Joe Biden's Electoral College victory and secure another term for Trump. It is difficult to imagine, considering the chaos of that day, how Americans might be reconciled and a sense of unity restored. But then again, it was also difficult to fathom how the degradation of civic life described by Putnam would lead to a direct assault on US democracy just twenty years later.

Conclusion

No civil society is perfect, just as no democracy is perfect. The three cases explored above demonstrate that civil society confronts a number of practical and developmental challenges in a vast array of circumstances, including within political systems not designed to accommodate autonomous actors, and even some which were. Yet this chapter has also shown how civil society can, under the right conditions, provide fertile soil for a democratic culture to grow and thrive.

In some cases, civil society actors may be important to democratization even before legal space for civil society exists. Underground activism by opposition forces has played a key role in fomenting the destruction of dictatorships in the past, performing some of the same watchdog functions that civil society does in more advanced democracies, exposing abuses and spreading information that undermines authoritarian rule. Sometimes these forces are able to coalesce into coherent opposition movements that ultimately become political parties and contest elections. Civic groups can also be important following authoritarian breakdown and in the initial transitions to democracy, providing citizens with regular avenues for political engagement or providing grassroots education about the requisites of democratic citizenship. Even in the oldest and most well-consolidated democracies, civic organizations are an important check on state power, working to preserve the accountability and effectiveness of government and thus maintain popular support for democratic political systems.

However, this chapter has repeatedly emphasized that the democracy-serving character of civil society is by no means a given. Indeed, civil society can pre-empt democracy in many ways, such as when the state is too weak or violence-ridden to function (as in Afghanistan), when would-be autonomous organizations are co-opted and redeployed in the service of the state (as in China) or where the connective tissues that bind democracies together have frayed, resulting in broad-based disaffection with democratic institutions, waning civic engagement and possibly even contempt for fellow citizens, especially when they hold differing political views (as in the United States).

In this chapter, we have been mostly concerned with civil society as an expression of grassroots political participation. There is a good reason for this. An essential feature of the Tocquevillian picture of democracy we began from is that colonial-era New Englanders were directly invested in the lives of their towns, as well as responsible for and impacted by the collective decisions they helped to make. However, the reality of civil societies – and, indeed, democratic transitions – in the twenty-first century is that they are influenced more than ever before by external actors, whether ideologically or through provision of money or other types of technical support. To fully understand how civil societies affect democratization, we therefore need to explore how they operate under globalization. This is a subject we will turn to in Part II of this book.

Questions for discussion

1   How is 'civil society' distinguished from other forms of social activity? Do the organizations that you belong to, or the activities you participate in, meet the definition of 'civil society'? Why or why not?
2   Can democracy-supporting values be built in a place that has little or no prior experience with democracy?
3   What are some of the benefits, perils and pitfalls that might accompany external support for civil society in a democratizing country?
4   What threats currently confront civil society in your country, state, province, city or town? Why might you label them as problematic?
5   What informal institutions can you think of that support democracy where you live, work or study? Can you think of an example of a time when you or someone you know demonstrated interpersonal trust or contributed to social capital?

Further reading

Dunn, Elizabeth, and Chris Hann, eds, *Civil Society: Challenging Western Models* (London and New York: Routledge, 1996).

Edwards, Michael, *Civil Society*, 2nd edn (Cambridge: Polity Press, 2009).

Eulau, Heinz, 'The Behavioural Movement in Political Science: A Personal Document', *Social Research*, Vol. 35, No. 1 (Spring 1968): 1–29.

Karl, Barry D., *Charles E. Merriam and the Study of Politics* (Chicago, IL: University of Chicago Press, 1974).

Kopecký, Petr, and Cas Mudde, 'Rethinking Civil Society', *Democratization*, Vol. 10, No. 3 (2003): 1–14.

Monroe, Kristen Renwick, ed., *Perestroika! The Raucous Rebellion in Political Science* (New Haven, CT: Yale University Press, 2005).

Rose, Richard, 'Rethinking Civil Society: Postcommunism and the Problem of Trust', *Journal of Democracy*, Vol. 5, No. 3 (July 1994): 18–30.

Ross, Marc Howard, 'Culture in Comparative Political Analysis', in M. I. Lichbach and A. S. Zuckerman, eds, *Comparative Politics: Rationality, Culture, and Structure*, 2nd edn, 134–61 (Cambridge: Cambridge University Press, 2009).

Seligman, Adam B., *The Idea of Civil Society* (Princeton, NJ: Princeton University Press, 1992).

5

Illiberal democracy and competitive authoritarianism

While many countries hold elections, and are classified as and claim to be democracies, many of their governance practices are quite dissimilar to those of 'liberal' democracies. Many exhibit central roles for corruption, patronage, nepotism and the use of violence in politics. While they hold regular elections, the playing ground is often unequal, with many benefits afforded to incumbents; in some cases, the same regime has remained in power for many decades. These democracies are often referred to as 'hybrid regimes' or democracies qualified with adjectives: 'illiberal democracy', 'patronage democracies' or 'quasi-democracies'.

This chapter discusses hybrid regimes, and in particular two types of such 'incomplete' democracies. Both claim to be democracies. The first is captured by the term 'illiberal democracy'. Such governments are often elected via a very competitive political system and governments and leaders are regularly ousted by popular vote. However, they have a number of characteristics which are illiberal in nature, including a great deal of corruption, vote buying, patronage, intimidation and interference in electoral systems, and a failure to maintain the rule of law. In short, they often fail to protect the rights of their citizens beyond the right to vote. The second type of regime is known as 'competitive authoritarian'; in these systems, elections, parliaments and the formal system of democracy exist, but certain political practices and structures are such that it is extremely unlikely, even impossible, that the ruling regime will be ousted from power through elections. Unlike illiberal democracies, however, competitive authoritarian governments often focus on maintaining the rule of law and the rights of their citizens.

Hybrid regimes

In democracies, executives and parliaments are chosen through free, fair and open elections, and universal adult suffrage. Elected authorities are able to govern without undue pressure from the military or from religious or other civil society organizations. Civil liberties such as a free press and rights of association are protected. While there are sometimes violations, they are not systematic, and there remains a level playing field between government and opposition.

In the post-Cold War era, however, there has been a proliferation of hybrid regimes – those governments which exhibit the processes of democracy alongside many undemocratic attributes, and even some features of autocracy. These regimes were generally seen as swimming against the tide, resisting what is an inexorable move towards democracy. For a long time, most observers saw these regimes as incomplete democratic transitions, and simply political states halfway through their transition to more complete (liberal) democracy. In some cases, regimes were classified as going through a 'protracted transition'.

But rather than transitioning towards democracy, many countries instead settled almost permanently on a type of third way, a place between democracy and authoritarianism. Now, most observers have come to see such regimes as a different form of political system. In fact, hybrid regimes are the most common form of regime around the world. Those agencies focused on monitoring and measuring democracy often refer to this type of regime as anocratic, semi-democratic or partly free. Yet the category of anocracy masks quite substantial differences in regime type.

In addition to considering whether such regimes have 'stalled' in a long period of transition, it is also important to consider whether they *should* be transitioning to liberal democracy. In some cases at least (such as the case of Singapore, discussed below), hybrid regimes have proven highly effective at establishing economic growth and political stability, and provided extensive rights for their citizens, even as one political party has remained in power.

The rest of this chapter examines two main types of hybrid regime: competitive authoritarian and illiberal democracies. The key difference between them revolves around the competitiveness of their elections. While illiberal democracies often involve highly competitive elections and see regular turnover of governments, competitive authoritarian regimes manipulate the advantages of incumbency to ensure they cannot be removed from power through popular vote.

Illiberal democracy

The term illiberal democracy is now commonly used to refer to those regimes in which governments are chosen through popular elections, but which fail to protect the civil, religious, economic and other rights of their people. The term was coined by Fareed Zakaria in 1997, and has become widely used, even by some illiberal leaders themselves, such as Hungary's Viktor Orbán.

The concept of illiberal democracy centres on a distinction between liberalism and democracy. Liberalism most often refers to the separation of powers and other constraints on the executive, the rule of law, the protection of human rights and private property, and religious and other freedoms. Democracy is characterized by universal (or near universal) suffrage and the regular choice (and expulsion) of governments by popular vote. Zakaria argued that while democracy and liberalism often appear naturally aligned, each can and has existed independently of the other. Most Western states developed constitutional liberalism well before they enacted mass or universal suffrage. He writes that while the 'Western model' is often equated with liberal democracy, it is in fact 'best symbolized not by the mass plebiscite but the impartial judge'. In other words, it is liberalism, not democracy, which most closely characterizes Western democracy. He argues that elections are an important indication of a virtuous regime, but democracy without civil, religious and economic rights is no consolation.

Zakaria points out that many new democracies, by contrast, have emphasized the holding of elections while paying little attention to ensuring rights. They are, in other words, democratic without being liberal. Many democratically elected governments have been so convinced that they represent the popular will that they have centralized power and restricted the individual rights of many citizens. In other words, the growth and sustainability of democracy has outperformed the spread of liberalism.

Because illiberal democracies are not fully free, but also not fully repressive, and many involve corruption and other poor governance practices, some observers have defined them as inherently unstable. Zakaria also wrote that the democratic process of elections, and political competition and suffrage, is also not naturally associated with peace and harmony. While established democracies are often effective at resolving ethnic tensions through peaceful means, newer democracies often see violence, even separatism, civil war or interstate war, as politicians seek to exploit ethnic tensions and nationalism to win and retain power. As will be discussed below, many democracies see high levels of (often deadly) violence as part of the political process (Zakaria 1997).

Larry Diamond points out that the Third Wave of democratization was characterized by the emergence of many more illiberal than liberal democracies (Diamond 2021: 4). While 83 per cent of democracies were 'liberal' in 1974, by 1984 that figure had declined to 74 per cent, dropping further to 40 per cent in 1994. While hopeful observers expected that new illiberal democracies would transition to liberal democracy, it soon became apparent that this progression was far from certain. Zakaria wrote that 'Far from being a temporary or transitional stage, it appears than many countries are settling onto a form of government that mixes a substantial degree of democracy with a substantial degree of illiberalism' (Zakaria 1997: 24).

The Latin American region demonstrated the prevalence of illiberal democracy. In a study of regimes in the region between 1978 and 2004, spanning the Third Wave period, most (40 per cent of country years) were found to be illiberal democracies (Smith and Ziegler 2008: 31). Competitive elections have been coupled with some degree of abuse of citizens' rights. By 2004, more than 310 million people were living under an illiberal democratic regime. Most transitions to democracy were to the illiberal variant. For example, Brazil moved from military rule to illiberal democracy, while some regimes moved in the opposite direction, from liberal to illiberal democracy in a process known as democratic backsliding, something we discuss further in chapter six. Many illiberal democracies were also long-lived, demonstrating they were not merely a step towards liberal democracy.

Corruption

Many illiberal democracies are characterized by a high degree of patronage, corruption and nepotism. These practices have an important effect on democratic processes, through vote buying, a decline in government effectiveness and legitimacy, and a lack of transparency. In turn, declining democracy and government accountability can exacerbate corruption.

Patronage, sometimes referred to as patron–client relationships, is an informal political relationship in which a politician acts as a patron to members of society and represents their interests to the elite. They promise to pursue a particular policy or to provide jobs, contracts or funding in return for the support of these constituents. Government officials thereby make decisions and policies in a manner which will benefit loyal groups rather than in the national or broader community interest. Many states in Southeast and Northeast Asia are characterized by patron–client relations; these are what Weber would call patrimonial states. In such systems, access to the state, or to those with official positions in the state, is extremely important. In other contexts, politicians purchase the votes of voters with public money. This is often referred to as 'vote buying', 'money politics' or 'clientelism'. Patronage is therefore a particular form of corruption. Some perspectives see patronage (or patron–client relations) as caused by particular local cultures of gift giving and reciprocity. This was particularly the case for modernization theorists, who saw such practices as the lingering effects of backward social and political structures. More materialist perspectives focused more on socio-economic conditions such as inequality, scarcity and the lack of responsiveness of impartial government agencies.

Corruption is 'the misuse of public power for private or political gain'. The United Nations Development Programme defines it as 'the misuse of public power, office or authority for private benefit – through bribery, extortion, influence peddling, nepotism, fraud, speed money or embezzlement'. In most definitions, therefore, the focus is on those holding some form of public office. Corruption comes in 'petty' and 'grand' forms. Petty corruption involves everyday extortion, such as that during interactions between ordinary civilians and police officers or bureaucrats, like when a utility official requires a payment to connect power or other service for a family. Grand corruption involves the payment of much larger amounts to government officials or the theft of large amounts from investors, for example. Grand corruption often involves those who are supposed to be monitoring and preventing corruption and is more likely to have an influence on the political process. Because corruption is almost always about the bribing of those with power by those without power, it generally involves the transfer of funds from the poor to the rich. It must therefore be seen as a crucial contributor to inequality.

One important way that politicians steal public funds is through the handing out of contracts for public construction projects for bridges, roads, ports, etc. In some cases, local politicians, contractors and police have created a complex system whereby the tender process for contracts appeared to be open and transparent, but in fact the successful contractor was decided behind closed doors. Each politician or other stakeholder receives a share of the fund that is supposedly set aside for this public project, right down to the thugs on the ground who protect the project from disgruntled landowners or neighbouring communities. Politicians take this money and use some of it to get themselves re-elected, and contractors commit to helping them do this in the future. In some cases, perhaps 50 per cent of the project budget is lost to corruption even before construction starts. In others, so little money is left for such construction that roads wash away with the first rains, or bridges collapse. Corruption therefore has a direct negative impact on society and perceptions of government, creating frustration and disillusionment and undermining democracy.

Whether or not corruption flourishes has a great deal to do with the capacity of the institutions tasked with monitoring and punishing corruption. Weak or complicit anti-corruption bodies are often a hallmark of illiberal democracies. If anti-corruption bodies are weak or unsupported, or if punishment for corruption is minimal, then politicians are rarely deterred. And when the media is weak or cowed by the regime, it is far less likely to investigate government corruption. Corruption often flourishes when the wages of public servants (such as bureaucrats or police) are too low. In the first years of Indonesia's democracy, a public servant's wage was estimated as enough to cover a third of their family's household needs. As such, many often request bribes in order to carry out routine tasks such as registering a birth or providing an identity card. In the Philippines, too, many public servants have second jobs, sell goods out of their offices or engage in corruption. In some cases, public servants' wages have been slashed as a means of balancing the budget.

Corruption can have a direct impact on the most important indicators of development, such as the environment, health, education and gender equality. The World Bank estimates that around 3 per cent of global Gross Domestic Product (GDP) is lost through bribes alone each year. In developing areas, the figure is much higher: the African Union, for example, estimates that more than US$148 billion is lost to its countries' economies each year through corruption. This equals 25 per cent of Africa's GDP, and is estimated to increase the cost of goods in Africa by up to 20 per cent. The use of corruption and patronage to gain political office also has a major detrimental impact on the quality of governance. If a candidate has bought their way into office, they have little reason to act accountably towards their citizens, and they often have to recoup the amounts that they spent to gain office and to prepare for their next campaign. And coalitions or political networks based on pyramids of patronage can quickly disintegrate.

These impacts of corruption can directly erode the legitimacy of government. Trust in government and the judiciary plummets. By increasing inequality between the rich and poor and giving greater access to services and assistance to those with money, corruption can cause powerful currents of resentment towards the regime in society. In the long run, this can destabilize the nation through protests. The collapse of many non-democratic and democratic regimes has involved widespread anger and demonstrations over corruption. Cases include President Suharto's resignation in Indonesia (and the subsequent democratization of the country) in 1998, the military coup against Nawaz Sharif in Pakistan and many others.

Political violence and intimidation

Illiberal democracies often have high rates of political violence and intimidation in their political system. Politicians often form alliances with thugs, paramilitary groups or militias, which use force as a way of winning or retaining power. Political elites provide incentives to these groups in the form of cash payments, contracts, employment or immunity from prosecution for illegal activities. Politicians use 'muscle' in this way not only to influence voters, but to intimidate or even kill opponents and supporters, and to threaten and influence electoral commissions, courts and other institutions and their personnel, all of which can influence the outcome of an election. Intimidation and violence are most concentrated around elections, and can continue throughout the campaign, on polling day, and in the weeks and months afterwards as votes are tallied, results are announced and victors are inaugurated. Violent actors connected to the regime might use violence to seek retribution after an election loss or against protesters after a victory.

These paramilitary groups often have a murky and indirect relationship to the regime, leader or senior politicians. Using civilian 'proxy' groups in this way can provide the elite with plausible deniability. In other contexts, lower-level politicians themselves can act as leaders of violent organizations. In illiberal democracies, the formal security services, such as the police, are often complicit in this intimidation, or choose not to intervene to arrest or hinder political thuggery because they are aware of the connections of these groups to the elite. Most studies of violence in the electoral process find that clashes are most common in the most tightly fought areas (Hafner-Burton, Hyde and Jablonski 2013). Incumbent politicians more concerned about losing their electorate seat, or governments about losing power, have more incentive to use coercion and violence to ensure they do not lose.

In many areas of India, 'muscle power' is considered necessary to win elections, particularly when political competition is tight. Thugs often became political players in their own right, leading to a criminalization of politics. One study found that a quarter of all MPs in the Indian Parliament's Lower House had criminal cases against them. This was particularly the case for small parties and those in northern India. In other cases, this form of patronage relationship between political elites and violent groups has 'gone wrong', leading to a sudden fracturing of the relationship and an increase in different forms of violence. Wisdom Iyekekpolo has argued that the emergence of the terrorist group Boko Haram in northeast Nigeria occurred as a previously mutually beneficial relationship between the group and local politicians descended into antagonism (2021).

In a broader sense, high or increasing rates of political violence are an indicator of a faulty or illiberal democracy. A key element of liberal democracy is the absence of the threat or use of violence and the pursuit of political outcomes through peaceful means. If political violence is common, then a democracy is not liberal. This might include violence not only by groups connected to the regime but also by civil society opponents of the government and its policies. The violence associated with the Black Lives Matter protests, for example, demonstrated the unresponsiveness of the state to demands for racial equality. In other circumstances, political violence can be in response to a flawed system, or a claim of electoral fraud or other injustice.

In some cases, however, political violence is not targeted at politicians, voters or opponents of the regime, but instead at a scapegoat community as a way of gaining support. As will be seen in the case of the Philippines discussed below, the regime targeted drug dealers and criminals in a campaign of terror which generated widespread support. Sometimes, political thuggery can be a remnant of a more authoritarian, even colonial, era. In Indonesia, for example, the use of political gangsters became common under President Suharto's military-dominated New Order regime and continued into the democratic era. In other cases, the use of political violence has increased as states have moved from authoritarian system to illiberal democracy, as politics became more hotly contested and more freedoms opened up.

Competitive authoritarianism

Another form of hybrid regime – not fully democratic but also not fully autocratic – is known as a competitive authoritarianism. In such systems, incumbent governments take extensive steps to ensure that they retain power. While elections are held and are often competitive to some degree, the regime ensures that there is no level playing field between incumbents and the political opposition. Levitsky and Way define competitive authoritarian regimes as 'civilian regimes in which formal democratic institutions exist and are widely viewed as the primary means of gaining power, but in which incumbents' abuse of the state places them at a significant advantage vis-a-vis their opponents' (2010). They found that thirty-three regimes were competitive authoritarian in 1995 (several years after the end of the Soviet Union), meaning there were more such regimes than there were full democracies (ibid.: 3).

Even in full liberal democracies, there are some advantages for incumbents seeking to win an election, including greater access to state resources and the ability to channel these resources into areas or parts of society which might generate much-needed votes. They have power over when the election will be held, better connection to many important institutions through political appointments and better access to media. Yet in true democracies, these advantages do not undermine the opposition's capacity to win an election (ibid.: 6).

In competitive authoritarian regimes, manipulation of these and other advantages are extensive enough to create an uneven playing field during elections. This system makes it very difficult for the political opposition, while still retaining some measure of (and the façade of) true competition. Competitive authoritarian regimes have much greater access to state resources, and use these to retain power; they also exercise influence and control over media and democratic institutions and use repressive measures.

Such regimes use public funds to stay in power, whether spending these funds directly during the electoral process or providing lucrative contracts to favoured cronies in the private sector who then, in turn, fund the regime and party. While formally there exists a separation of powers between the executive and the judiciary, in competitive authoritarian systems regimes often have direct control over courts through appointments and other means. The same control is held over electoral commissions and other important democratic institutions. Competitive authoritarian regimes exercise direct and implied control over the media, and thereby control the political narrative delivered in the media. In many cases, such as with the ruling *Barisan Nasional* in Malaysia, the state owns many private media channels. Those in power possess and use draconian laws and harass opposition candidates and their supporters, often using the courts and the police. They change electoral rules or electorate boundaries to ensure they win, and manipulate results when they are unfavourable. Opposition parties or individual candidates are often disqualified from running in elections, all through legal processes. Opposition candidates and media engage in self-censorship, knowing that they may be faced with repressive measures through the justice system.

In a good summary of how competitive authoritarianism often looks for oppositions, Levitsky and Way write that 'Opposition parties are legal, operate aboveground, and compete seriously in elections. However, they are subject to surveillance, harassment, and occasional violence; their access to media and finance is limited; electoral and judicial institutions are politicized and deployed against them; and elections are often marred by fraud, intimidation, and other abuse' (ibid.: 12).

Yet these regimes are also not fully authoritarian. Levitsky and Way define authoritarianism as a system 'in which no viable channels exist for opposition to contest legally for executive power' (ibid.: 6–7). In competitive authoritarian systems, elections are held regularly and involve open campaigning by the opposition. Elections are not simply a façade in which opponents of the regime have no chance. Opponents do have opportunities to win seats in legislatures (although winning power is unlikely). These regimes must take elections seriously, because if they perform poorly, they will lose popular legitimacy. They can use authoritarian repressive measures, but they cannot use them too heavy-handedly because then they will lose domestic and international legitimacy and may face massive protest. Opposition candidates are sometimes harassed or even imprisoned. When this is done, however, it must be done through legal processes, although competitive authoritarian regimes vary in their repressiveness. Outside elections, opposition and civil society are able to exert some pressure on government, even if it doesn't win the vote.

In the first two decades of the post-Cold War era, it was difficult for regimes to remain fully and overtly authoritarian. Elections became a central way for non-democratic regimes to legitimize their rule to domestic and international audiences. Authoritarianism is also hard work. Purely authoritarian regimes must eliminate or control all domestic opposition and maintain strong security apparatus. It is often necessary and easier, therefore, to have some measure of political competition or freedom to avoid constant criticism from overseas, retain some level of domestic legitimacy and avoid protest.

Levitsky and Way assert that the key driver of whether hybrid regimes transitioned to democracy or settled on a stable form of competitive authoritarianism depended to a large extent on their linkage to the West. Where there was a strong connection to the West, competitive authoritarian regimes democratized. Where the connection was weak, the outcome depended on how organized and cohesive the regime was. Where regimes were strong, cohesive and organized, they most often settled on competitive authoritarianism.

Case study 5.1: The Philippines

The 'People Power' revolution in 1986 against the authoritarian rule of President Ferdinand Marcos (in power from 1966 to 1986) generated hope about democracy in the nation. However, the Philippines remains a key case of illiberal democracy, with high levels of both corruption and violence in the political process. As one scholar puts it, 'Illiberal democracy in the Philippines rests on strong foundations' (Linantud 2005: 81). Illiberal characteristics in the politics of the Philippines were established during the colonial era and have been maintained by various regimes since. Yet at the same time, the country has extensive experience with democratic institutions, and neither these institutions nor the people of the Philippines will easily give up the vestiges of democracy.

A 2007 survey of businesspeople and expatriates in Asia found the Philippines was perceived to be the most corrupt in the region. Transparency International ranked the country 117th out of 159. The United Nations estimates that US$1.8 billion or 13 per cent of the nation's GDP is lost every year. It is probably not a coincidence that the Philippines also received the least amount of foreign investment in Asia around that time. Interference in the democratic process is also often rife, despite mass discontent. Paul Hutchcroft writes that 'several key aspects of Philippines democracy can be traced to the US-colonial era. The first is patronage-infested political parties that rely heavily on pork-barrel public works projects run through national legislators' (2008: 142). The United States nurtured an oligarchy as a way of gaining elite collaboration; this oligarchy established its rule and control over the population, a dynamic which has continued throughout the independence era. The United States also established a strong presidency, with links to powerful provincial elites. The subordination of weak state institutions to powerful national and local strongmen was also established around this time.

Yet leaders have at times stepped beyond what was acceptable to the Filipino people. Several presidents have been driven from office because of corruption scandals. Most notoriously, the former President, Ferdinand Marcos, and his wife Imelda stole billions in public funds and deposited them in the United States, Switzerland and elsewhere. The most widespread image representing this corruption was the two thousand pairs of shoes belonging to Imelda Marcos while much of the country remained trapped in poverty.

Corruption is still closely tied to the democratic process in the Philippines. Candidates regularly pay large sums of money to political parties or local strongmen for their support in running for office, knowing they will recoup it. This dynamic runs to the very top of politics. After President Gloria Macapagal Arroyo won her 2004 election by 1 million votes, a secret tape was released which recorded her saying to the commissioner of elections, 'So I will still win by a million overall?' In addition to corruption and deliberate undermining of the political process, elections often involve violence. In 2004 alone there were 148 election-related killings and in 2007 there were 121. The presence of violence in elections is not new, however, with much higher numbers of election-related violence in 1971 and subsequent decades. The extent of violence is partly because elections are high-stakes situations due to the extent of patronage and corruption, and a great deal of wealth can be gained by holding public office.

Filipino politics is characterized by the substantial political influence held by local warlords or bosses in each province or region. These figures and their clans often control politics and patronage in the region. Local politicians often also possess a security force, allowed under legislation permitting civilian defence units. Unsurprisingly, this leads to frequent and often large-scale violence in the political process. Also important and detrimental to democracy in the country is the role of family dynasties in politics. By their very nature, such dynasties confer advantages on some candidates over others, particularly when family members are in office, and allow political families to circumvent the term limits (limits on time in office) designed to ensure one leader cannot monopolize power over the long term.

The Maguindanao massacre

A recent and particularly infamous case of political violence in Filipino politics was the killing of fifty-seven men and women in Maguindanao in the country's south in November 2009. The victims were travelling to file candidacy papers for a candidate for the governorship of the province. The massacre shocked the world and involved the single highest death toll for journalists from one incident. The candidate, Esmael Mangudadatu, sought to challenge the long-standing control of Maguindanao Province held by the Ampatuan clan. Both the Marcos and Arroyo administrations had courted and supported the clan in return for votes from the region. Clans are a particularly effective vehicle for generating political support during elections. Some cities in the clan's province had had zero votes for the President's rival, others just a handful. Turnout in the region for the candidates for the President's party would often be around 95 per cent (as opposed to 60 per cent elsewhere).

Under the legislation allowing civil defence units mentioned previously, these warlord families can hold heavily armed paramilitary-style armies under legislation that allows for civilian defence units. The Ampatuan clan had previously been armed by the government to fight the Muslim insurgency in Mindanao. The intimidation of heavily armed visible military units also increases the clan's effectiveness as a political machine. The militia used the clan's wealth from its local political dominance to buy weaponry from Singapore and Israel that was more sophisticated than that of the Philippines military. The clan was also able to exercise some control over the military battalion stationed in the area, and was in phone contact with the President regarding the transfer of particular officers out of the region. While this is civilian control over the military of sorts, it is a non-democratic version. Mangudadatu's candidacy had infuriated the clan's leader.

When Mangudadatu decided to file to run for governor, there were clear signs and rumours that the Ampatuan clan would try and prevent his candidacy and that they were in fact planning an attack against him. He requested military protection, but this was denied: he was told by the military that election security needed to go through the police and election commission. Instead, the candidate and his advisers decided to send female members of the family and thirty journalists, believing this would surely deter an attack. The convoy was stopped by a group of armed men, and all fifty-eight members of the convoy were executed.

Duterte

The era of President Rodrigo Duterte has seen the Philippines move even further in an illiberal direction. Elected (in free elections) in 2016 on a populist 'strongman' platform based on his tenure as mayor of Davao City, Duterte promised that his presidency would be 'bloody because we will order the killing of all criminals'. He cursed the pope, and claimed to have several mistresses and as many undeclared bank accounts (Curato 2017: 146). Ninety-four per cent of Filipinos have access to the internet, and Duterte was the ultimate populist performer. He campaigned for months across the country while telling his supporters he would not run for the presidency. This teasing of the population kept him in the media spotlight.

During his campaign, Duterte emphasized the threats posed to the Philippines by drugs and illegality, and presented himself as the only one who could save the country from these. Drugs and crime soon became the key issues in the election, despite the use of drugs being lower in the Philippines than in many other countries, such as the United States. Soon after coming to power, Duterte launched a violent anti-drug campaign which involved the extrajudicial execution of suspected drug dealers. In the first six months of his term alone, over 6,000 people were killed in the campaign. The Office of the High Commissioner for Human Rights (OHCHR) described the campaign as involving 'summary executions, corruption, and abuse of power'. While most victims of the campaign have been from the poor underclass, there have also been more high-profile executions of elites. Since he took office, at least a dozen mayors and seven vice mayors have been assassinated, including several mayors who Duterte himself accused of being involved in the drug trade.

Dressel writes that in his second term, Duterte has placed substantial pressure on democracy in the Philippines. 'Incremental changes already made to critical oversight and accountability institutions, not to mention the shrinking of democratic space, suggest an underlying plan to replace the liberal political settlement with an illiberal, even authoritarian, order' (Dressel and Bonoan 2019: 135). Duterte has used the legal system to attack political opponents and critical media outlets. His administration has threatened or brought impeachment charges against a number of high-ranking public officials, including the head of the national election authority and the ombudsman after she suggested an inquiry into the Duterte family's assets, and successfully removed a chief justice who Duterte accused of plotting to oust him (ibid.: 138). The administration has also threatened media outlets and arrested the high-profile journalist Maria Ressa.

Over and above his campaign of extrajudicial killings as part of the war on drugs, human rights in general have been a key target of the Duterte administration. Duterte has regularly attacked the OHCHR for its criticism of his human rights violations. He has also undermined the legitimacy of the commission and of human rights in general, by linking it to Western imperialism. 'Human rights cannot be used as a shield or an excuse to destroy the nation,' he said in his first State of the Nation address (Curato 2017: 151).

Halfway through his second term, Duterte enjoyed an approval rating of 80 per cent. In midterm elections in May 2019, no opposition candidates were able to win any of the contested seats. Much of his support comes from the new middle class, who believe they obey the law and pay their taxes, but see little of the wealth that goes to the elite. They also worry about crime and disorder, and the theft of public money through corruption. Yet despite Duterte's rhetoric about fighting corruption and his war on crime and drugs, few improvements can be seen in either area. Transparency International's corruption perception score for the Philippines reached in 2021, a year in which corruption worsened in most Asia-Pacific countries. At the time of writing (February 2022), Duterte's daughter was in the running for the presidency.

Case study 5.2: Singapore

Singapore provides an important, and perhaps the most successful, case study of a competitive authoritarian system. The People's Action Party (PAP) has remained in power since 1959, not long after the formation of independent Singapore and its separation from Malaysia. Levitsky and Way contended in 2002 that Singapore is not a competitive authoritarian regime, but instead should be classified as a 'full-scale authoritarian' system. However, we believe that Singapore has many of the characteristics of competitive authoritarianism. While Singapore has been a one-party state since its inception, there remains a possibility that the opposition may win power at some point in the future; however, the playing field is heavily tilted towards the incumbent.

The PAP-led government has maintained civilian control over the military throughout independence. Undermining the notion associated with modernization theory that influence from the outside is likely to democratize a regime, Singapore has always been very open to contact and communication with the outside world. However, there are a number of characteristics of Singapore's political economy which do not represent liberal, pluralistic democracy as most observers would understand it.

The state has held regular elections since the creation of Singapore and the PAP has won each, becoming one of the longest-running parties in power worldwide. It has done so through a combination of co-optation and weakening of the opposition, through legitimacy derived from efficient economic and political management, and targeted repression. The state has also maintained strong control over the national economy, rather than opening up to the free workings of the market.

Singapore is a very small island state in the middle of much larger and more imposing states in the Southeast Asian region. The tiny country is one of very few to have not only moved from the Third World to the First World but also to have become one of the richest countries in the world. Despite its small size, Singapore's location between Southeast Asia and East Asia, and its deep port, meant it was in an ideal position to assume a role as a successful and thriving entrepôt. Singapore was an early and important case in undermining the argument that economic development and modernization automatically leads to democratization. Singapore developed economically to become wealthier than many Western democracies but did little to liberalize its political system.

So how can we explain the stability and durability of Singapore's political system? Singapore was a British colony, and was part of Malaya until expelled in 1965. Slater argues that political stability at the elite level has its source in early instability at the mass level. That is, the elite became stable and unified and the regime durable because of the threat of instability within society, particularly ethnic instability and organized leftist movements. Singapore (and the larger neighbouring country of Malaysia) had a large leftist movement in the years after Word War Two. Radical trade unions proliferated and strikes broke out across the colony, and a communist insurgency targeted colonial economic infrastructure. This turmoil and serious ethnic divisions caused tension between Chinese and Malay communities, leading to deadly riots. The leaders who took over independent Singapore had a fear of organized dissent, particularly leftist dissent. They also had the tools for repressing it, which they inherited from the British, most notably via the Internal Security Act (ISA).

When the PAP assumed power in 1959, the party's leader, Lee Kuan Yew, used the security apparatus to decimate the left. During what was known as Operation Cold Store, the Special Branch of the police arrested hundreds of leaders and activists. The leaders explained the need for such extreme actions and the centralization of power in terms of the fragility of the new state, the threat from neighbours and the need for economic development.

Since those years, the PAP has created a strong national ideology of the competence and well-meaning paternalism of the party and the state. The party's ongoing rule relies in part on fears that it has cultivated over what would happen if it were no longer in power. In essence, the party regularly makes clear that it does not believe the opposition is capable of managing the country or its economy, or maintaining its international and domestic security. The party has claimed that 'Western-style democracy' would lead to chaos and instability and destroy economic progress. The party has emphasized the importance of meritocracy in public service. Singapore's leaders and leading academics and diplomats have been some of the main proponents of what have sometimes been termed 'Asian Values', the idea that Asian societies value order and economic rights more highly than political freedoms.

Yet the PAP has worked hard to remove any credible opposition to its continuing power. This has had two main elements: making it very difficult for the opposition, and co-opting civil society to the regime and its goals. The party manages elections in a way that gives it an advantage over the opposition. It often redraws electoral boundaries, and does not announce electoral districts until quite late, so opposition parties don't know which areas they should be contesting and cannot begin campaigning (Ortmann 2011: 159). It draws electoral boundaries in ways that ensure it has the best chance of getting MPs.

The regime also uses more coercive measures. For the first two decades of its rule, the PAP relied primarily on the ISA left behind by the British to detain, inter and charge dissidents, social activists and political opponents without trial. Singapore had the dubious record of detaining one of the longest-serving political prisoners, Chia Thye Poh, an accused communist who was detained without trial for 23 years. The ISA was used until the late 1980s. In 1987, 22 people were detained without trial because of a suspected Marxist conspiracy to overthrow the state. The suspects were members of Christian organizations. Human rights organizations claimed the government had forced confessions from those arrested. The PAP now rarely uses the ISA for political purposes (mostly for terrorism suspects), recognizing that if it relies on blunt coercion, it could face losing legitimacy.

The main way of deterring and effectively scuttling opposition is through the courts and legislation. Some observers claim that the country does not enjoy the rule of law but is subjected to rule *by* law. The Supreme Court has frequently been filled with political appointments, but many appointments have been temporary and can be removed at the will of the government, thereby leaving a great deal of scope for political influence over the courts. One scholar argued that the actions of the judiciary exhibit a balance between the 'need for a reputable judiciary [and] the requirement by the political executive for the judicial system to assist with the control of political opposition' (Worthington 2001: 490). A main way PAP politicians have used the courts against opponents has been through defamation suits. This is often the case whenever accusations of nepotism are made against the regime, a common accusation with the ascension of Lee Kuan Yew's son, Lee Hsien Loong, to the prime ministership. Lee Kuan Yew and other PAP officials have used the courts to sue political opponents and critics.

The media in Singapore is also tightly controlled by the party: all media outlets are owned by a company connected to the regime. Lee Kuan Yew stated that 'Freedom of the press, freedom of the news media, must be subordinated to the overriding needs of Singapore, and to the primacy of purpose of an elected government'. Since the mid-1980s, the international media and foreign reporters have become a major target of court action for making criticisms of the regime. Many well-known news magazines such as *The Economist*, the *Far Eastern Economic Review* and others have had their circulation limited because they were critical of the regime. One *International Herald Tribune* journalist was taken to court for referring to an unspecified state in Southeast Asia which uses a compliant judiciary to silence opposition. International media outlets have successfully been deterred from being too critical of the regime or its officials, afraid of losing their circulation in Singapore and the comfortable operating environment of a country with great infrastructure that functions as a centre for the entire region.

One of the features of the success of the PAP has been its willingness and ability to alter its system of governance and change course slightly as a way of meeting new challenges and keeping up with changes in society or internationally. For example, over time the PAP came to see the allowance of some level of dissent as necessary, but it has channelled this dissent through the regime rather than allowing strong opposition parties or other sites of opposition to develop. The Prime Minister recently even suggested splitting the PAP into two parties so they could compete against each other, but this was rejected by the party and probably would not have created true competition either.

The PAP also survives because it enjoys widespread legitimacy, or at least appears to, within the Singaporean population. Along with economic and political management, elections have also bolstered the party's legitimacy, as many Singaporeans no doubt consider them a free exercise of the population's political will. While there is a great deal of unease over the most authoritarian of the PAP regime's policies and statements, it appears that the regime still has a great deal of support. It seems very likely that even if the political system in Singapore were more open and free, and opposition parties were given more space and the media were less controlled, the PAP would probably still be elected by the majority of the island's population.

This is the product mainly of the economic success of the country under the party's rule. The party realized early on that it needed to improve the lot of Singaporeans if it was to remain in power. And, as has been discussed, it has achieved impressive economic advances. Part of the reason the Singaporean middle class has not seriously challenged the PAP regime is that the government has always tried to connect the island with the world economy. Another way in which the PAP has managed to shore up its legitimacy has been through its successes in eradicating corruption. Transparency International and other corruption watchdogs regularly rank Singapore as one of the least corrupt countries in the world and the best for doing business. This success is not just contributed to legitimacy but also to the nation's growth.

From the 2011 election to now

The 2011 elections were a turning point for Singapore, with a large swing against the PAP. The Workers' Party gained six seats, the most any opposition party had held until then. Opposition parties won 40 per cent of the popular vote. But because Singapore has a first-past-the-post majoritarian electoral system, the PAP still dominates the Parliament, with eighty-one out of eighty-seven seats.

The 2011 results could partly be explained by the use of new media, which is far more difficult for the government to control. The regime allowed more extensive use of social and other media and greater coverage of opposition parties than it had in the past. Opposition parties also coordinated among each other so as not to cut the opposition vote. However, the PAP also restricted the holding of public rallies at Speakers' Corner, the location designated for such meetings. Restrictions on these meetings had been relaxed in 2008 but were reinstated in 2011. The government also redrafted electoral boundaries so as to give itself the best chance of winning seats, and only announced the new boundaries just before the election, which did not give opposition candidates much chance to react.

Following the 2011 election, the PAP took a number of steps in response to public criticisms or concerns with the regime. Party leaders have acknowledged making mistakes, cabinet has been reshuffled, former prime ministers Lee Kuan Yew and Goh Chok Tong stepped down from cabinet, and steps were taken to reduce ministerial salaries. The government also offered apologies and wider discussions regarding popular concerns over high rates of immigration into the island.

The 2015 election was far more successful for the PAP, with the party winning approximately 70 per cent of the vote. The election was held in the year of the death of Lee Kuan Yew, the nation's founder and revered leader. This gave the party substantial political capital which allowed it to take steps to reaffirm its control. Over the following years, at least two pieces of legislation were introduced by the government and passed by Parliament which enhanced the government's ability to suppress the opposition. The Administration of Justice (Protection) Act 2016 and the Protection from Online Falsehoods and Manipulation Bill 2019 disallowed criticism of the courts and the government respectively. The government has used this legislation against opponents since these were passed (Abdullah 2020: 1129). The government has also criticized academics and criticized and in some cases charged activists for speaking out against the regime or organizing protests. Despite its declining vote share over the past decade, the Singapore city state therefore remains a competitive authoritarian regime.

Conclusion

The political systems of most countries are now neither fully democratic nor fully authoritarian. In the decade after the Cold War, observers often referred to these regimes as 'incomplete' democracies which had stalled on their transition to full democracy. Yet as these regimes persisted, and in some cases became successful, scholars came to recognize them as a separate type of 'hybrid regime' which was not stuck on a protracted transition to democracy. As this chapter has shown, there is substantial variation within the category of hybrid regime. The two main types are illiberal democracies and competitive authoritarian regimes. The key difference between them revolves around the competitiveness of their elections.

Illiberal democracies often have elections which are highly competitive and open, and see the regular ousting of governments via popular vote. However, they are characterized by a high degree of illiberal practice in governance, most notably corruption (including patronage and vote buying) and violence. Competitive authoritarian regimes, by contrast, hold regular and formal elections, but the incumbent regime manipulates the advantages it holds in office to such an extent that the political opposition has little chance of winning power. Although these regimes can be repressive when it comes to retaining power, in some cases they are efficient technocracies, allowing for impressive economic growth and the protection of a broad range of rights.

Neither of these types of regime can be called fully democratic. While there is uncertainty in the outcome of elections in illiberal democracies, the lack of liberalism in the political process and the inability to participate politically without fear or favour, means that the rights of citizens and the democratic process are undermined. And although competitive authoritarian regimes hold regular elections and their governments often protect the civil, religious and economic liberties of citizens, these regimes often take a range of measures to ensure that they are not removed by popular vote. Such hybrid regimes are likely to represent the majority of regimes worldwide for some time to come.

Questions for discussion

1 What are the key differences between liberal democracy, illiberal democracy and competitive authoritarianism?
2 Why do regimes maintain democratic elections when so much else of their governance is authoritarian in character?
3 Are hybrid regimes eventually transitioning to full democracy? Should they do so?
4 How does corruption undermine the process of democracy?
5 What is the relationship between illiberal democracy and populism?

Further reading

Abdullah, Walid Jumblatt, '"New Normal" No More: Democratic Backsliding in Singapore after 2015', *Democratization*, Vol. 27, No. 7 (2020): 1123–41.
Curato, Nicole, 'Flirting with Authoritarian Fantasies? Rodrigo Duterte and the New Terms of Philippine Populism', *Journal of Contemporary Asia*, Vol. 47, No. 1 (2017): 142–53.
Diamond, Larry, 'Democratic Regression in Comparative Perspective: Scope, Methods, and Causes', *Democratization*, Vol. 28, No. 1 (2021): 22–42.
Dressel, Bjorn, and Cristina Regina Bonoan, 'Southeast Asia's Troubling Elections: Duterte versus the Rule of Law', *Journal of Democracy*, Vol. 30, No. 4 (2019): 134–48.
Hafner-Burton, Emilie M., Susan D. Hyde and Ryan S. Jablonski, 'When Do Governments Resort to Election Violence?' *British Journal of Political Science*, Vol. 44, No. 1 (2013): 149–79.
Levitsky, Steven, and Lucan Way, *Competitive Authoritarianism: Hybrid Regimes after the Cold War* (Cambridge: Cambridge University Press, 2010).

Levitsky, Steven, and Daniel Ziblatt, *How Democracies Die* (New York: Crown, 2018).

Linantud, John L., 'The 2004 Philippine Elections: Political Change in an Illiberal Democracy', *Contemporary Southeast Asia*, Vol. 27, No. 1 (2005): 80–101.

Ortmann, Stephan, 'Singapore: Authoritarian but Newly Competitive', *Journal of Democracy*, Vol. 22, No. 4 (2011): 153–64.

Smith, Peter H., and Melissa R. Ziegler, 'Liberal and Illiberal Democracy in Latin America', *Latin American Politics and Society*, Vol. 50, No. 1 (2008): 31–57.

Zakaria, Fareed, 'The Rise of Illiberal Democracy', *Foreign Affairs*, Vol. 76 (1997): 22–43.

Part II

Democratization from without: Considerations of the global age

6

Threats to democracy: Backsliding, coups and populism

In contrast to past periods of waves of democratization, the most recent decade has been one of democratic retraction. By most indicators – the number of democracies worldwide, the number of people living under a democratic system and the democratic quality of regimes – democracy has been in retreat. Several liberal democracies have transitioned to illiberal or even authoritarian regimes, demonstrating that political movement can occur in both directions. Other liberal democracies remain intact, but have recently been severely wounded and teeter on the brink of illiberalism or one-party rule.

This chapter discusses the extent of democratic backsliding around the world over the past decade, as well as the forms which this recession has taken. The discussion demonstrates that while in the past coups by military personnel were the main route to the end of democratic systems, in the contemporary global era, democracies are far more likely to be eroded by democratically elected civilian leaders. Rather than felling democracy in a dramatic action overnight, these would-be authoritarians undermine democratic institutions and norms over the course of several years. Many of these demagogues are populists, using anti-establishment sentiments and (in many cases) the fear of outsiders to win power. The chapter discusses the causes of the rise of populism and democratic backsliding. It examines two very different liberal democracies, India and the United States, where democracy has recently been under challenge.

Backsliding and the degradation of democracy

For the past fifteen years, the world has seen a dramatic period of democratic retreat (Diamond 2021: 25). Many electoral and liberal democracies have seen a decline in accountability, transparency and the protection of rights. This has been the case in middle-income countries such as Hungary and Poland and higher-income countries such as the United States. The International Institute for Democracy and Electoral Assistance (IDEA) finds that one in four people live in a 'backsliding' democracy. At the same time, authoritarian regimes, such as China under Xi Jinping, have become more autocratic. Adding to this trend, fewer democratizations are occurring now than in the past. For the first time since the start of the Third Wave of democratization, the past five years have seen more democratic breakdowns than democratizations (ibid.: 29).

The year 2006 was the high point for global democracy: this has been in retreat ever since. In 2006, 61 per cent of all states and 57 per cent of states with a population of more than 1 million were democratic (ibid.). Those figures are now 55 and 48 per cent respectively. Between 2006 and 2021, the number of people in the world living in a democracy also declined, from 55 to 47 per cent. By one measure, twelve countries have experienced democratic breakdown in the past five years, including several large and important states such as Bangladesh, Thailand, Turkey and a member of the European Union, Hungary (ibid.: 26). Freedom House also measured a decline in freedom for most regions and calculated that more countries have seen reduced freedom than improvements. In 2020, more people lived in a country in which democracy declined, 'shifting the international balance in favour of tyranny' (Repucci and Slipowitz 2021: 1). This is the case even for many of the world's largest states which remained democracies, including the United States, India, Indonesia and Brazil.

Using the main coding systems for quality of democracy (V-Dem, Freedom House, Polity and the Economist Intelligence Unit), Stephan Haggard and Robert Kaufman identified sixteen cases of democratic backsliding between 1974 and 2019. They define democratic backsliding as 'the incremental erosion of institutions, rules, and norms that results from the actions of duly elected governments' (Haggard and Kaufman 2021: 28).

The main challenge to democracy is now different to that of past decades. Rather than coups (see below), which were more frequent in the past, the most common threat to democracy now comes from elected civilians with authoritarian goals who seek to undermine democracy and accountability from within. In a process sometimes referred to as executive aggrandizement, these elected leaders, often riding to power on a populist election platform (see below), have little commitment to the democratic norms and institutions which limit the power of the executive and protect liberties and rights (Merkel and Lührmann 2021: 870). They often undermine democracy gradually and incrementally, often raising little alarm or opposition. Administrations make changes which undermine accountability, transparency and media freedom and avoid any potential for criticism of the government. At the same time, they often make it more difficult for political opponents to win power. These changes are often enacted through legal channels, using greater influence over the judicial system, by passing laws or through binding referenda. Each successful change makes the next step easier, and the weakening of one democratic institution has a negative effect on others (Haggard and Kaufman 2021: 38). Elected leaders have recently undermined democracy in this way in Venezuela, Sri Lanka, Hungary, the Philippines, Russia and other countries.

Diamond identifies an 'autocrats' twelve step program' for undermining democracy (Diamond, 34). Although the following steps can occur in any order or even simultaneously, their combination is often present in many cases of democratic regression. Authoritarian leaders weaken the institutions and actors which might constrain them (such as the opposition, media and courts) by portraying them as part of the corrupt and unpatriotic elite which stands in the way of the will of the people. Others identify control of legislatures, often through winning elections, as a key path to reducing oversight and restraint on the power of executives (Haggard and Kaufman 2021: 34). Compliant legislatures then help to co-opt or weaken other democratic institutions such as judiciaries. Administrations stack institutions with loyalists, starve them of funding and intimidate them into working with the administration rather than against it.

The leader creates a new crony capitalist class of loyal businesspeople who financially and publicly support the administration and in turn receive lucrative government contracts and deals. Authoritarian leaders also attack the groups within civil society which often criticize or hold leaders to account: intellectuals, academics and universities, artists, non-governmental organizations (NGOs), human rights organizations and similar. Leaders and their allies portray these actors as the epitome of the 'out of touch elite', who often look at the common people with scorn. Attacks on media are central to all cases of backsliding. Just as importantly, autocrats restructure the electoral system to ensure that one-party rule is no longer challenged. They do so in many ways, including redrawing electoral boundaries and changing voting rights as well as the process and personnel involved in approving results.

The incremental nature of these changes is crucial. While groups and individuals directly affected or tasked with protecting rights and democracy may notice and oppose the changes, for most citizens, the gradual nature raises little concern and each quickly becomes normality (ibid.: 38). Administrations driving a breakdown in democracy maintain the façade of elections and political freedom; indeed, many budding populist autocrats tell their people they are in fact strengthening democracy.

Coups

While backsliding driven by elected leaders is now the most common threat to democracy, in previous eras, democratic breakdown was most often driven by the forceful ousting of an elected government by members of the state's security forces. While there has been a steady decline in the frequency of military coups in recent decades, 2021 saw four successful coups (Myanmar, Mali, Guinea and Sudan). The year also saw several other attempted coups and the January 2021 attempt to overturn the results of the 2020 United States election (discussed further below).

The generals or other military officers who perpetrate coups often present their actions as necessary measures in order to save democracy from corrupt or incompetent civilian leaders, and often promise to hold elections in the near future. These promises are often not met. When elections are held in the years after a coup, the perpetrators often win, suggesting less than free and fair polls (Bermeo 2016: 9). Few countries which experience coups move to a freer political system after the ousting of a democratically elected administration, even when the opponents of coups win subsequent elections.

Control over the use of force has long been considered to be a central feature of the modern state. Max Weber famously defined the state as that entity which had a monopoly over the legitimate use of force. Control over the use of force differentiates the modern state from states in previous eras.

The control of militaries by democratically elected civilian governments is a crucial part of the balance of power and the checks and balances of a democratic system to ensure that the military is not used in a monopolistic fashion by the executive. And because militaries have the means to impose their will on society and are not democratically elected, they must themselves remain uninvolved in politics: any exercising of power by them undermines democracy. Constitutions, laws and popular mandates are worth little if the institution that holds the arms can overthrow the system. Gaining civilian control over militaries involves empowering civilian institutions, professionalizing and installing democratic norms in the military and ensuring its members concentrate on external military matters rather than domestic affairs, among other approaches. In reality, there are few if any situations where the military plays no role in politics. A central paradox in state building is how to build a military that is strong enough to protect the state and deter potential enemies, but that will not try to use the force at its disposal to take over the state.

The question of civil military relations is therefore central to understanding the durability of democracy. There are several main explanations for when and why militaries will intervene in domestic politics or even seek to dominate it. These revolve around the professionalism of the military, the need for coercion in government, the level of economic development, the efficacy of civilian government and the level of international and domestic military threat. Samuel Huntington argued that a professional military focused on its institutional responsibilities is very unlikely to try and dominate politics (1985). Yet militaries can be very professional and take a great interest in improving their skills and technologies but also seek to be involved in politics. The Pakistani military is given as a case of such a military.

Another common argument is that the level of coercion that is required in state building and in politics in general determines the role that the military plays in politics. The more coercion by the state, against political opponents or against ethnic militias, for example, is seen as necessary, and the more the state expands, the more important the military is thought to become, the more advantaged the military institution is and the more disadvantaged this makes other institutions. In turn, the level of coercion that is used or seen as necessary depends on the domestic and international legitimacy of the state.

The level of economic development is also seen as important. Economic development creates new forces within society, such as a middle class which demands a say in politics and a judicial system which is stable and functions as expected; these new groups also have more communication with the outside world, and begin to replace old actors such as the military. But in some cases, such as Indonesia in the 1970s and 1980s, for example, decades of economic growth may actually give legitimacy to military rule.

The military's role in politics, and the extent of it, often has its source as much in rivalries, competition, and efficiency within the civilian elite as it does in the interests of the military itself. The more effective civilian institutions are, the less likely it is the military will interfere. If civilian leaders are fragmented, corrupt or indifferent to economic development or they meddle in internal military affairs or try to manipulate the military as a political tool, the military is more likely to become involved in politics. Civilian control over the military therefore depends a great deal on the skills within the civilian elite.

Some countries develop what is sometimes referred to as a 'coup culture', whereby particular characteristics of the local political economy lead to a recurrence of coups over several decades. Thailand has experienced nineteen coups or coup attempts since the revolution that ended absolute monarchy in 1932. Most recently, coups ended the democratic governments of Thaksin Shinawatra in 2006 and that of a caretaker government during a six-month political crisis in 2014. Another case is Fiji, which has seen coups in 1987, 2000 and 2006. At the time of writing, in February 2022, despite holding two elections since 2006, Fiji remains only partly free, and the political process subject to substantial influence by the military.

Populism

One of the key trends of the current era is the rise of populism and the ascension to power of populist leaders and parties. As we will see in the discussion below, populist movements emerge from both the left and right of politics, and have assumed political prominence in advanced industrialized democracies and in developing states. We will also see that populism has a chameleon-like character, able to alter its appearance to best win votes and power depending on local circumstances. Populism's relationship to democracy is ambiguous and complex: on one hand, it demands a greater voice and representation for the 'people', on the other, it often both excludes those it considers to be outsiders and resists any opposition to its chosen 'will of the people'.

Populists are at heart anti-establishment; they create a binary opposition between 'the people' and 'the elite'. Ernesto Laclau saw populism as a political logic which involved an appeal to the community against a particular enemy, often unresponsive elites (2005). Similarly, Mudde and Kaltwasser defined populism as a 'thin-centred ideology that considers society to be ultimately separated into two homogeneous and antagonistic camps, "the pure people" versus "the corrupt elite," and which argues that politics should be an expression of the volonté générale (general will) of the people' (2017: 6). Populism therefore contains several elements: a focus on the people; the notion that the people have a 'general will'; and anti-elitism.

Populism is not a fully formed ideology with a cohesive worldview. As a consequence, it is often found attached to other more complete ideologies such as nationalism, socialism, fascism or neoliberalism. Populist ideologues and leaders take many of their ideas from these more cohesive ideologies. Populist movements can therefore be either right-wing, which are often more exclusive of minorities and nationalistic, and left-wing, which are generally more inclusive. This characteristic of populism also makes it more malleable: populists can adjust their demands to win as many votes as possible depending on the local political context. Populism sometimes emerges in a nationalistic and nativist form (such as in the United States) and sometimes in a radical left form (such as in Venezuela). Populists are also often flexible and hypocritical in which 'elites' they depict as enemies of the people, often befriending some oligarchs and media moguls while attacking others.

A notion central to populism is that of 'the people', which in turn is perceived in opposition to the elite. For Mudde and Kaltwasser, the people are those groups excluded from power 'due to their sociocultural and socioeconomic status' (ibid.: 10). Populists seek to bypass elite institutions and media and establish a direct relationship with the people. They portray opponents or the media as 'enemies of the people'. Populists often openly abhor and distrust not just politicians but all forms of elites: political, health, academic, cultural, media and economic (apart, of course, from members of those groups, particular media commentators, academics or politicians, for example, that take the same positions as they do). This distrust goes beyond the elite to include many key democratic institutions. Populists sometimes blame the political elite, or murky international forces which cannot be clearly defined, for the ills of society. Often key targets are supra-national organizations such as the United Nations or European Union, which populists claim are taking away the rights of the people and sovereign states.

Yet who is a member of the people and who is excluded can change almost overnight. This ambiguity of 'the people' means populists can define the boundaries of the group in different ways to further particular political interests at different moments. As discussed, populism exists in both civic and ethnic forms; the former is more pluralist and inclusive in its understanding of the people, while the latter defines the people in ethnonationalist terms. It is this ethnic (or nativist) populism which is a key defining feature of contemporary far-right populism in the West and elsewhere.

Populists often mobilize resentments within the populace, whether against the system, the main political parties, the political, economic and cultural elite, or immigrants. Populist appeals are therefore based on emotion rather than a rational approach to society's problems. Populists seek to re-politicize certain issues such as immigration, corruption and other issues, which they believe the elite is ignoring or intentionally hiding from public consultation. They often co-opt particular issues, such as anti-corruption, as a way of manipulating popular sentiment. Populists often take pleasure in violating the norms of good behaviour and language (even body language) observed by the elite, often revelling in contravening 'political correctness'. This helps construct a sense of the populist leader as 'one of us', and crude language creates a visceral rejection of the status quo and gives voice to the 'people's' frustration (Curato 2017: 149).

Populism's relationship to democracy

Populists often present themselves as the true defenders of democracy: only they defend the rights of the common people. They do so by taking on the powerful political, economic and cultural elites who have for too long ignored the ordinary members of society. A case can be made that populism is a reaction to long-standing restrictions on the will and interests of the people. In this view, populist movements emerge because the existing system, political parties and institutions are failing to respond to the needs and demands of the masses. Populism also often mobilizes groups which have been depoliticized for long periods. Scholars explain the rise and appeal of minor populist parties such as the Freedom Party of Austria (FPO) and Italy's Lega Nord (LN) as deriving from their opposition to the major established parties' long-standing dominance during which they simply shared power between them. Parties such as the FPO portray this monopolization of power as the key cause of the political apathy and disillusionment of the population.

In reality, however, the relationship of populism to democracy, particularly liberal democracy, is often negative. Populism almost naturally leads to rule by the majority. Populism contends that nothing should restrain the will of the *pure* people and therefore rejects the notion of minority rights (Mudde and Kaltwasser 2017: 81). In prioritizing particular ethnic communities and excluding minorities and less represented groups, populism directly challenges the foundations of liberal democracy. It is important to recognize, however, that this applies most strongly to right-wing, national populists, and far less to left-wing populists, who often take a more inclusive view of the people. National (or nationalist) populists sometimes use vigilante groups and the intimidation or repression of minorities to increase their power, thereby also damaging democracy. While they may not call for violence themselves, populist leaders often do not condemn it, thereby contributing to its prevalence.

Once in power, populists often claim that any opposition is illegitimate (because by definition it opposes the people). This applies to both left- and right-wing populists. They often claim that institutions are undemocratic and opposed to the will of the people and seek to undermine them. 'As it tends to distrust any unelected institution that limits the power of the demos, populism can develop into a form of democratic extremism or, better said, of illiberal democracy' (ibid.: 82). Many also change laws in ways which undermine pluralism and democracy, using disinformation and control or pressure media. Some also override or change limits on terms in office so that they can stay in power, claiming that only they can represent the people.

According to Mudde and Kaltwasser, the effect of populism on democracy will to some extent depend on the political system of the time. If acting in the context of an authoritarian regime, populist movements can be profoundly democratic, giving voice and cohesion to the demands of the people (ibid.: 88). They give the example of the Solidarity movement during Poland's communist era.

Populists can also play a key role in eroding democracy. They often gradually erode the legitimacy or undermine the independence of democratic institutions by depicting them as controlled by the elite and opposed to the will of the people. In reality, of course, they often oppose these institutions because they present an obstacle to the augmentation of their own power. Viktor Orbán's undermining of democratic institutions in

Hungary since the election of his political party Fidesz in 2010 is a dramatic recent example. His administration has introduced a range of new laws which have weakened legal checks on his authority, undermined judicial independence and freedom of the press and severely damaged minority rights. Orbán has gone so far as to implement a new national constitution to ensure his ongoing dominance.

Causes

Explaining why democracy is retracting is of crucial importance. Yet any complete explanation is likely to be complex, identifying a large number of connected causal phenomena. It is first helpful to consider which phenomena keep democracy strong. The key barriers to democratic breakdown include acceptance of democratic norms and of political opponents being legitimate and the rejection of political violence, and strong state institutions which balance and counter the centralization of power (Diamond 2021: 33). If strong norms of commitment to democracy are prevalent across society, this makes it more difficult for authoritarian leaders to come to power and to undermine democratic practices and institutions. The strength of democratic institutions is also crucial to holding in check the ambitions of authoritarian leaders. Courts, parliaments/legislatures, anti-corruption watchdogs and other bodies which can provide a balance to leaders are crucial in preventing backsliding. Strong and independent legislatures which have oversight powers are important in restraining the executive. Most democracies which have broken down over the past five years have been illiberal democracies already strongly affected by corruption and weak rule of law.

Many budding authoritarians are unsuccessful. Those who might seek to undermine democracy must have the political skills and ambition to do so and adeptly take advantage of the surrounding political and economic context. As discussed above, populist authoritarian politicians must not only successfully appeal to the resentments and emotions of large sections of society but also have sufficient charisma to manipulate, exacerbate or even create those fears. To undermine long-standing institutions and norms of democracy, budding authoritarians must not only develop a loyal and dedicated mass following but also overcome the 'free rider' (or collective action) problem, to mobilize large numbers to collective action. They must mobilize an army of dedicated supporters and activists. This mass following and movement in turn can deter other elites from opposing them as they break down the components of democracy. Yet those intent on undermining democracy do not need a majority of the population to support them. What is most important in resisting or facilitating democratic decline is political parties and institutions.

Budding authoritarians must weaken the democratic institutions which, among other roles, balance the power of the executive. The most important among these are legislatures, judiciaries, media, security agencies and electoral commissions. They must provide incentives or coercion to ensure that these institutions assist or at least do not oppose their autocratic mission. Leaders can stack these institutions with loyal supporters, particularly if they have a majority in the legislature, can restrict funding if certain conditions are not met or can threaten and intimidate officials into acquiescence. They must also undermine or even dismantle those civil society bodies which oppose them, including NGOs, universities and human rights organizations.

Social and political polarization is an important factor in the deterioration of democracy. Most if not all cases of democratic backsliding have been preceded by periods of polarization. When political parties and their supporters are deeply polarized, they find it difficult to cooperate on the important issues of the day. The resulting ineffectiveness in turn drives further dissatisfaction with the democratic system. Haggard and Kaufman point out that in polarized polities, each main political party, and therefore sometimes overall power itself, is more likely to be won by populists or would-be authoritarians (Haggard and Kaufman 2021: 31). One sign of increased polarization is what is known as negative partisanship, a situation in which people focus on the party which they hate and would never want in power, more than they do on the party they support. Importantly, too, when electorates are deeply polarized, supporters are more inclined to ignore and support their leader ignoring democratic norms and doing whatever it takes to win because they so deeply hate their opponents.

The advent of social media has also been important in both the rise of populism and the recent democratic recession. Compared to traditional forms of media such as newspapers, television and radio, social media is a powerful tool with which demagogues can quickly generate a mass following if they are sufficiently 'social media savvy'. These platforms allow them to speak directly to the people and bypass the elite. Just as importantly, however, social media is designed with a 'self-publishing' model which gives ordinary citizens a voice for the first time. Online platforms allow disgruntled citizens to express their dissatisfaction with the government, or the elite or other topic, in a way never possible in the past (Gerbaudo 2018: 746).

Social media can also play a key role in driving polarization, which, as discussed, is often an important precursor to democratic backsliding. The algorithms of mainstream online sites such as Facebook and Twitter encourage users to congregate with those of like mind, where a process of 'groupthink' (the process of dissenting voices gradually disappearing and all participants agreeing on a particular position) takes hold. Online users engage with others who disagree with their positions far less regularly, and users within a 'bubble', whether left or right, can be incentivized to take increasingly extreme variants of the group position. This polarization makes ready-made and suggestible audiences for populist politicians while pushing the political elite and political parties further apart.

International and domestic social and economic forces have played an important role in placing pressures on democracy. Many democracies have seen striking and rapid change in the nature of their economies, in levels of inequality, in social norms and laws and in the demographic makeup of their societies. Over the past two or three decades, many Western democracies have seen progressive advances in protections of the rights of women and minorities, and legal restrictions on discrimination. Much of the backlash against the 'liberal establishment' has been in response to these changes. High levels of immigration over the past two decades, along with rising levels of ethnic diversity, have had a particular impact on increased nativist populism among sections of the white community in the West. Many have turned to authoritarian populists who promise a return to an idealized past, and a reinstatement of lost privileges.

As discussed above, many individuals and groups in society, particularly in the West, have seen these changes as a direct threat to their interests, culture, worldviews and status. For some people, these changes lead to a sense that they are on the verge of losing their country, a claim often made by populist authoritarians. When political opponents are viewed as such an existential threat, the focus becomes winning power no matter the pathway to doing so, rather than following the rules of democracy (Haggard and Kaufman 2021: 31).

Technological advancements, particularly related to the internet and digital communications, have also played a key role in destabilizing democracies. The effect of social media in creating siloed online communities trapped in separate echo chambers has driven political polarization and allowed the spread of misinformation and provocation. This in turn has led to the rise of authoritarian populists who can play on fears of ethnic others or political opponents. Demagogues have been able to exploit these echo chambers to undermine objective truth, cultivating suspicion of the elites or minorities and ultimately damaging faith in democracy.

The ascendancy of neoliberalism and deregulation in most Western states, including the United States, and their role in creating the Global Financial Crisis, undermined the reputation of democracies for economic management, and increased inequality, poverty and resentment. The international context is also crucial in influencing, or even determining, the strength of democracy worldwide. The Third Wave of democratization was to a large extent driven and supported by the foreign policy of the United States and its allies. At that time, and particularly from the end of the Cold War, the United States enjoyed global hegemony and supported democracy movements in many communist and authoritarian states. With the failure of the invasion of Iraq, partly for reasons of regime change and democracy promotion, the leadership and legitimacy of United States foreign policy was severely undermined. The United States itself also focused far more on security and the so-called War on Terror in the years after September 2001 instead of human rights and democracy. Whether or not a regime was democratic or democratizing was far less important to the White House than whether that state assisted it in its fight against Islamist terrorism.

In the past decade, in contrast, authoritarian regimes have increased in confidence and influence, and even in their willingness to interfere in established democracies. Diamond writes that Russia and China have together eroded the post-Cold War hegemony of liberal values and institutions (Diamond, 37). Both have befriended and supported authoritarian leaders and regimes in smaller states. Russia has played a key role in fomenting division within Western societies and using propaganda and other techniques to politicians who undermine Western policies and alliances antagonistic towards Russia. China's vast and increasing financial influence in much of the developing world through the provision of aid, infrastructure and development, has undermined the influence of the Western democracies. The Chinese model of authoritarian government increasingly gains legitimacy in many developing nations at the expense of liberal democracy. Simultaneously, the election of Donald Trump to the United States presidency was a boon for authoritarian regimes, seemingly providing proof of the corrupt, nepotistic, unpredictable and chaotic nature of liberal democracy. Backsliding also has demonstration (or copycat) effects. As one state becomes more authoritarian it can influence others (particularly in the region) to do the same. Viktor Orbán's undermining of democracy in Hungary influenced Poland, while the rise of Chávez in Venezuela had an impact on Bolivia, Ecuador and Nicaragua.

Outcomes

When democracies retract, the outcome can be a form of illiberal democracy or competitive authoritarianism or even outright autocracy with few vestiges of public participation. Even where democracies remain liberal, democratic decline can have other impacts. Reduction in the transparency and accountability of government can push larger numbers of people towards populist leaders. Declining faith in the legitimacy of major parties can also lead to greater political fragmentation. Richard Pildes points out that declining faith in major parties to deliver on important policy promises has led to the proliferation of smaller parties (30 new political parties entered European parliaments between 2015 and 2017 for example) or serious divisions within the main parties themselves (Pildes 2021). These divisions and the splintering of large parties into many smaller ones, ironically has the effect of making effective policy-making, even the formation of governments after elections, more difficult. If democracies do not fight wars with each other, it also follows that the retreat of democracy will be accompanied by a greater number of conflicts.

Nativism and the vilification of minorities

As regimes degrade their democracies, attacks by increasingly illiberal governments are often targeted at minority groups within society. Populism in particular is inherently at odds with liberal democracy because it holds that nothing should restrain the will of the pure people and therefore rejects the notion of minority rights and government protections of them. These minorities can be LGBTQIA, ethnic, religious, immigrant or other groups. Authoritarians portray these groups as illegitimate members of the nation undermining the real culture of the nation, as groups which pose a threat to the majority. They claim too that the elite is protecting these groups at the expense of the majority.

In many cases, populism and democratic backsliding are closely aligned with nativism – the notion that the interests and identities of the native community must be prioritized over those of immigrants. Mudde has written that 'The key feature of the populist radical right ideology is *nativism* ...' (Mudde 2010: 1173). Many populist movements are nativist in character, with anger over immigration driving frustration with mainstream political parties and the elite. Mudde and Kaltwasser point out, however, that it is nativism, not populism per se, which drives exclusion. One potential reason for the connection between nativism and populism (and democracy) is that a key goal of populism is to bring to the fore issues such as immigration, which they claim have long been ignored by the elite.

In one of the earliest definitions of nativism, John Higham wrote that 'Nativism, therefore, should be defined as intense opposition to an internal minority on the ground of its foreign (i.e. "un-American") connections' (Higham 1988: 4). More modern definitions are often broader. Myron Weiner defined nativism as 'that form of ethnic identity that seeks to exclude those who are not members of the local or indigenous ethnic groups from residing and/or working in a territory ... Nativism is anti-migrant' (Weiner 1978: 747). Guia writes that nativism is 'a philosophical outlook and an eclectic collection of policies that redefines who the "real" people of a political unit are and who ... should have more rights and decision-making power to determine the characteristics of that society vis-à-vis a group considered exogenous and incapable of assimilating' (Guia 2016).

Nativists see immigrants, or a particular immigrant community, as a threat to the culture, jobs, land or security of the native population. In many post-colonial societies, the descendants of European settlers have assumed a self-appointed role as the true owners and 'natives' of the land, often comprising the main constituents for far-right parties. Nativism tends to be nostalgic, positing an idealized past before society was altered by new arrivals. At the very least, nativists demand that immigrants assimilate into the host culture. At its most extreme, nativism demands the expulsion (or even elimination) of immigrant groups.

Nativist populism has been present in most regions of the world, including both the West (Europe, the United States, and Australia for example) and the non-West (including India and Indonesia). It has been the core principle of both national parties and movements and those with more local goals. Far-right groups have targeted immigrants in several recent cases of backsliding including the United States, Hungary, Poland and Greece. The direct effect is often politics restricting immigration or the rights of immigrants. More indirectly, this trend often leads to extremist violence by non-state actors such as the El Paso attack against Mexicans in the United States.

In the next section, we examine two cases of democracy which have undergone backsliding in recent years. The two cases, India and the United States have two of the world's three largest state populations, confirming the importance and reach of this trend of democratic recession.

Case study 6.1: India

India has long been a democratic success story. Since the end of British India and the onset of independence, India has maintained 'unity in diversity' through a federal democracy, becoming the largest democracy in the world. Yet over the past decade, India has seen a rapid democratic decline. In 2018, Varieties of Democracy Institute categorized India as an 'electoral democracy' rather than a liberal democracy because of a closing of political space and a decline in transparency. In 2020, Freedom House stated that India had shown the largest democratic decline of any country, and in 2021 moved India from free to partly free status.

This change has been driven to a large extent by the rise of Narendra Modi, first to the position of Chief Minister in the state of Gujarat, and then to Prime Minister in 2014. Modi, along with the Bharatiya Janata Party (BJP) have overseen the rise of a combination of Hindu nationalism and national populism. Jaffrelot writes that India is now an 'ethnic democracy'. In an ethnic democracy, the state is much less democratic towards minorities, and certain minority groups in particular, than it is to the majority group. He claims that India has transitioned to an authoritarian Hindu raj (a Hindu nation-state).

Populism
Narendra Modi and the BJP won the 2014 national election with a programme of national populism. In the campaign he used a range of national populist appeals including development 'a la the Gujarat model', hostility to the establishment, particularly the Congress Party, subordination of institutions to the people's will, and an ethno-religious definition of the people. Modi effectively used his

lower social background, comparing himself to the elite, along with promises of development, to appeal to lower caste voters. He presented his campaign and administration as in opposition to elites in Delhi.

Both in power as Chief Minister in Gujarat and when campaigning for national office, Modi used a highly personalized style, developing a cult of personality which focused almost exclusively on him as leader rather than the party. Like most populists, Modi chose to communicate directly with his voters, often via Twitter or rallies, circumventing and weakening mass media. He developed a heroic image of himself (having swum with crocodiles for example), as a common man who had renounced the luxuries of life to serve the people.

While Modi's populism was based on appeals to lower socio-economic groups, this has not translated to advances for the poor. Jaffrelot writes that the ultimate goal of both him and his party was to regain power for the upper classes after years of positive discrimination for the lower castes. 'The subtext of national populism, indeed, is elite revenge, and upper-caste politicians have continued to stage a political comeback since 2014' (Jaffrelot 2021: 153). Upper-caste Hindus have reclaimed power in national and state assemblies over the BJP's two terms in national office. At the same time the government has diluted positive discrimination for scheduled and lower castes and weakened anti-poverty programmes.

Nationalism

Also central to Modi's populism has been nationalism and the strategy of using communal issues and the targeting of minorities as a way of polarizing the electorate. Ever since the large Gujarat riots of 2002 in which two thousand people (mostly Muslims) died, Modi has portrayed himself as the protector or *Chowkidar* (sentinel) of the Hindu nation. He emphasized his status as a 'son of the soil' (in opposition to supposed immigrant groups, particularly Muslims). Hindu nationalist groups position Hindus as victims, claiming that despite being the vast majority of India's population, Hindus faced the threat of a higher birth-rate on the part of Muslims and from claimed proselytizing and conversion by Christians.

The government has allowed and encouraged vigilante groups to harass and attack minorities, secularists and political opponents. These groups have attacked churches and mosques, beaten and murdered (referred to as lynchings in India) individuals involved in the cow trade, and assaulted interreligious couples. This latter campaign, targeting what nationalist groups call 'love jihad', has seen numerous assaults and arrest of Muslim men accused of engaging in intimate relationships with Hindu women. Using groups not directly connected to the government allows it to deny complicity and continue to refer to harmony and unity. Yet the BJP has not completely disassociated itself from these actions, in some cases listing leading perpetrators as party candidates.

One particularly extensive initiative against Muslims was the update to the National Register of Citizens conducted in the state of Assam. This state-wide register of names effectively identified who was recognized as a citizen, and the update was intended to identify illegal immigrants from Bangladesh. The anti-Muslim nature of the campaign was shown by the subsequent addition of the Citizenship Amendment Act (CAA) by which all those without citizenship documents from neighbouring countries would be given refugee status, yet this would only apply to those from all religious communities apart for Muslims. The BJP argued this was because Muslims were the majority religion in neighbouring states (Bangladesh and Pakistan), and that it was alleviating the suffering of religious minorities from those countries. In 2019, the government stated that they would implement a nationwide National Register of Citizens (NRC), with the leader of the BJP, Amit Shah, stating that all illegal immigrants would be cast into the Bay of Bengal. He also stated that this national version of the NRC would be preceded by the CAA meaning that only Muslims would be captured and affected by the NRC. In other words, religion has increasingly become the key criterion for determining who is an Indian citizen. As Indian citizens have protested against these changes, the state has resorted to repression. In January 2020, Jawaharlal Nehru University was raided by a mob connected to the government. Students protesting the Citizenship Law were assaulted.

Rather than moderating over time in office, the government has become more polarizing and extreme in its approach to diversity and minority groups. The government has made legislative changes such as the CAA facilitated by its increased mandate afforded by the 2019 election. India has also faced little concrete resistance from international actors which might restrain its path to national populism. This is partly due to the rise of populism in the United States and elsewhere.

Attack on pluralism and democracy

Since coming to power, Modi and the BJP have eroded the strength and quality of democracy in India on a number of fronts. Jaffrelot argues that the government has successfully weakened all state institutions which might be in a position to balance the administration's power (ibid.). The government have frequently bypassed Parliament, with the Prime Minister addressing it only infrequently, meaning it is now the site of little debate or able to hold the government to account. Under pressure from the government, the Supreme Court has relinquished much of its independence and balancing role. The BJP attempted to prevent the formation of an anti-corruption watchdog, the Lokpal and weakened the institution once it was created. Groups connected to the government have harassed journalists, and the government has banned television channels critical of it or for their reporting of events, such as the 2020 Delhi riots, which portrayed the government in a poor light.

The former chief justice of the Delhi High Court wrote that the way the government has undermined institutions has 'rendered the Indian democratic state practically comatose, and given the executive the upper hand in most matters' (As quoted in Jaffrelot, 309). As a result of this pressure on state institutions, elections have become far less equitable than in the past. The government has also sought to make elections more difficult for the opposition, by providing fewer resources for those outside government, and undermining the impartiality of the Electoral Commission. According to Jaffrelot, the 2019 elections were a turning point for India's democracy. These elections much more than those in 2014, exhibited an uneven playing field. Some of the factors which demonstrated this included: biased media, unequal access to financial resources for the opposition, a lack of impartiality by the Electoral Commission tasked with managing the election.

Case study 6.2: United States

Indicators of backsliding

In 2016, Donald Trump, a real estate tycoon and reality TV star with no experience in politics, was elected President of the United States. Trump's period in office was relatively brief and so much of the path towards democratic decline or even authoritarianism was cut short. However, many of the trends which drove his election – polarization, declining faith in institutions for example – predate his presidency.

In 2021, IDEA classified the United States as a backsliding democracy for the first time. Polls show that most (two-thirds) of Americans fear that democracy is under threat in the country. One 2021 poll showed that 83 per cent of Republicans believe that democracy is under threat, likely driven by claims that the 2020 election was stolen and by the fact that a Democrat President was in the White House. State governments have recently introduced numerous bills designed to restrict voting rights. By May 2021, 389 such bills in 48 states had been introduced. Republicans in the Senate have also blocked bills introduced by Democrats designed to ensure voting rights are upheld. In December 2021, three retired United States Army generals wrote in the Washington Post of their fears of a military breakdown, increasing fears that the security services may choose to become more involved in the political process in the future.

Although Trump further radicalized the Republican Party (and his presidency is the focus of this case study), many Republicans had already started to subvert democracy by referring to President Obama's Administration as an existential threat and alluding to the use of violence. And the party's retreat from democracy has also been driven from below by predominantly white Christian voters feeling threatened by economic, cultural and demographic change. The drivers of America's vulnerability to populism and vulnerability include the economic precarity generated by the 2008 Global Financial Crisis, and the drastic reduction in manufacturing and job losses that went with it. This left large swathes of the population facing unemployment and uncertainty, and easily convinced to blame minorities and other scapegoats for their difficulties. High rates of immigration and rising diversity have made most Republicans feel a sense of existential threat.

The United States has in recent decades seen increasing polarization, a key driver of democratic backsliding. As discussed above, polarization prevents opposing parties and communities from cooperating in the national interest, meaning government is less likely to be effective. The inability of the Trump Administration to contain the Covid outbreak is a case in point. The United States has seen increasing polarization at both the elite and public level.

Elite polarization has led to an inability to make effective policy, in turn contributing to a decline in confidence in Congress and even in democracy itself (Haggard and Kaufman 2021: 36). Yet importantly polarization extends beyond policy to cultural and even existential concerns and conflicts.

Populism

Donald Trump used an almost archetypal populist approach to winning power, exploiting these fears and speaking directly to the people through Twitter and at rallies and calling media 'fake news'. He used classical populist terminology such as Make America Great Again. He presented himself as a man of the people despite his great wealth and elite background, using crude language and publicizing his affection for fast food. Trump referred to the 'swamp' of corrupt elites in Washington which were betraying the American people.

Nationalism

Key to both Donald Trump's populism and his attack on democracy has been the manipulation and amplification of racial and religious tensions and the vilification of minorities. Throughout his campaign and then his one term in office, Trump directly appealed to white identity politics and nationalism. He referred to 'fine people on both sides' after the deadly Charlottesville far-right rally and requested violent white nationalist group Proud Boys to 'stand back and stand by'. Immigration was perhaps the most important issue in the 2016 election. During his term too, Trump regularly referred to immigrants as rapists, criminals, and spoke of a wave of illegal immigrants entering the country, sometimes saying this was facilitated by the Democrats.

Attack on pluralism and democracy

While democratic institutions and actors continued to exert accountability upon and otherwise balance Trump's antidemocratic, the erosion of the norms and practices of democracy during his term is clear. Trump announced and then sometimes pursued a range of policies which stretched the boundaries of illegality, including jailing his opponent Hilary Clinton, using collective punishment against the families of terrorists, banning immigrants from Muslim-majority countries, and other policies. He frequently and publicly criticized the judiciary when legal decisions went against him. The President attacked and undermined media in the United States in a way never seen before. He referred to media in general and particular publications or television channels as 'enemies of the people', which in turn sometimes led to threats and even violence against journalists.

President Trump's capacity to undermine democracy was enhanced by the acquiescence of Republicans in both houses of Congress, demonstrated most clearly by the failure of sufficient Republicans to vote to impeach him for the January 6 attack on Capitol Hill (discussed below). The response to the assault has further polarized supporters of the two parties. This willingness to accept backsliding and centralization of executive power was in turn driven by high levels of polarization and partisanship. The ability and willingness of Congress to balance the President's authoritarian tendencies has varied depending on the relative strength of Democrats and Republicans in the Senate and House.

Particularly damaging, Trump and his allies publicly cast doubt on and undermined the fairness of the electoral system both during the 2020 election and then publicly failed to accept his defeat to Joe Biden. In the election, more than 80 million Americans voted for Biden, compared to more than 74 million for Trump. Biden also won the electoral college vote. Yet Trump publicly claimed the result was fraudulent, pressured election officials to overturn the result, and in January 2021 exhorted his followers to march on Capitol Hill to prevent the certification of Biden's victory. This resulted in an unprecedented attack on the American democratic process. A majority of Republicans now say they do not accept the so-called 'Big Lie', that Joe Biden won the 2020 election. During the election campaign the President sought the assistance of outside actors to undermine his rival Joe Biden, claimed without evidence that there was widespread voting fraud, and Republicans also sought to restrict the voting rights of some Americans. Ongoing attacks against the result of that election have continued to undermine American democracy.

Conclusion

Democracy is facing challenges perhaps unprecedented in the post-Second World War era. In previous eras, the main threat to democracy came from the armed forces, disgruntled with the trajectory of the nation or their treatment by civilian leaders. Military coups against democratically elected governments were common, and few countries return to a stable democracy in the decades following. However, today popularly elected demagogues pose the greatest threat. These civilian politicians often take their democratic mandate and seek to dismantle democracy as a way of centralizing power around themselves and weakening constraints and balances on the executive. They do so incrementally, with each step only a gradual and further erosion of political freedom, that very few notice the gravity of the process or mobilize in opposition.

Many do so using populist rhetoric, in which they position themselves as the true representative of the people, who is seeking to fight back against the national and global elites who have stolen the ordinary citizen's democracy. In many if not most cases, they do so by targeting scapegoats, in particular minority groups, who are deemed to be illegitimate and exploitative members of the nation. As demonstrated, the consequences for liberal democracy can be severe and lead to extensive political violence.

Questions for discussion

1   What explains the rise of populism in the past five to ten years?
2   What are the key differences and similarities between left and right-wing populism?
3   What is driving the democratic recession of the past decade to fifteen years?
4   What is nativism and what causes it?
5   Why do militaries overthrow democratically elected governments through coups?

Further reading

Bermeo, Nancy, 'On Democratic Backsliding', *Journal of Democracy*, Vol. 27, No. 1 (2016): 5–19.

Curato, Nicole, 'Flirting with Authoritarian Fantasies? Rodrigo Duterte and the New Terms of Philippine Populism', *Journal of Contemporary Asia*, Vol. 47, No. 1 (2017): 142–53.

Diamond, Larry, 'Democratic Regression in Comparative Perspective: Scope, Methods, and Causes', *Democratization*, Vol. 28, No. 1 (2021): 22–42.

Gerbaudo, Paolo, 'Social Media and Populism: An Elective Affinity?' *Media, Culture & Society*, Vol. 40, No. 5 (2018): 745–53.

Guia, Aitana, 'The Concept of Nativism and Anti-Immigrant Sentiments in Europe', European University Working Paper 20 (2016): 1–16.

Haggard, Stephan, and Robert Kaufman, 'The Anatomy of Democratic Backsliding', *Journal of Democracy*, Vol. 32, No. 4 (2021): 27–41.

Higham, John, *Strangers in the Land: Patterns of American Nativism, 1860–1925* (New Brunswick, NJ: Rutgers University Press, 1988).

Laclau, Ernesto, *On Populist Reason* (London: Verso, 2005).

Mudde, Cas, and Cristobal Rovira Kaltwasser, *Populism: A Very Short Introduction* (New York: Oxford University Press, 2017).

Weiner, Myron, *Sons of the Soil: Migration and Ethnic Conflict in India* (Princeton, NJ: Princeton University Press, 1978).

7

Globalization and democracy

For most of its history, the study of democratization has focused predominantly on domestic-level processes. As we saw in chapters 1 to 5, this is still true today. Economic development, education levels, elite interests, political cultures, demographic composition and even national or local geographies all shape the prospects for initial democratic opening and the long-term durability of democratic institutions.

Yet democracy's fortunes are, now more than ever, contingent upon factors beyond the scope – and sometimes the control – of domestic political leaders. This chapter is about some of these external pressures for democratic reform but pays particular attention to the diffusion of democratic values via global actors and technologies. Over the last three decades, such diffusion processes have shown a disregard for national boundaries and met with considerable pushback from autocrats seeking to resist them.

'Globalization' is a ubiquitous but notoriously slippery term to define, and one that subsumes the transborder diffusion processes we explore here. Scholars have defined globalization in different ways, often focusing on particular forms of the phenomenon. Key emphases have been economic internationalization, liberalization and interdependence, cultural universalization and 'Westernization' and globalization of communication and connections between people. Many understandings incorporate most or all of these processes. Jeffrey Haynes, however, writes that 'to have analytic utility, the concept of globalization must involve more than the geographical extension of a range of phenomena and issues for which a pre-existing term – "worldwide" – would suffice' (Haynes 2005: 8). In this chapter, we focus on political globalization and the connection between global civil society and democratization.

To speak of 'the globalization of democratic values', then, is to speak not merely of their spread across regions and continents, but of the mechanisms and processes that make that spread possible. We use 'globalization' to refer to interconnectedness – the networks of actors, ideas and institutions that operate across or beyond conventional borders to affect domestic political change, and which are facilitated by rapid technological advancement (Keohane 2002: 31). Some scholars (particularly political scientists) refer to this concept as 'linkage', viewing the prospects for democratization to be far greater where linkages – geographic, cultural, social, diplomatic or economic – to the established, consolidated democracies of the Western world are densest (Levitsky and Way 2005). However, as we saw in chapter six with the worldwide trend of democratic backsliding and decay, values and ideas such as populism are also gaining traction worldwide, suggesting a parallel and troubling 'globalization of undemocratic values'.

In an effort to uncover the machinery of global pressures for democratization, we open the chapter with a brief overview of the changing position of the state in a global age, and of the 'global civil society' which has arisen principally since the end of the Cold War. Instead of replacing states entirely, as some theorists suggested it might, we contend that global civil society co-exists with states, and is at once shaped by and capable of shaping state behaviours. This means that while some states may be vulnerable to external pressure for change, global civil society tends to reflect the views and interests of the strongest within it, namely actors from the wealthy, democratic Global North. This, we contend, is partly what explains the global transmission and wide acceptance of liberal democracy in the early twenty-first century, but also the pushback against it from some quarters. We then engage these rival perspectives to revisit the age-old debate concerning the universality or cultural particularity of democracy.

The latter portion of the chapter then examines the 'neighbourhood' or 'snowball' effect, in which democracy emerges within groups of countries sharing contiguous borders (and, conversely, fails to emerge in some others). Specifically, we note the role of the technologically induced information flows at work in multiple 'clusters' of transitional states over the last thirty years, including the 'Colour Revolutions' of 2006 in Eastern Europe, and the 'Arab Spring' cases of the early 2010s.

Globalization and the state

Throughout this book, we have taken the state to be our primary unit of analysis. Most of the time, studies of democratization are focused on understanding processes of political reform in particular countries. 'Countries' is often taken to mean 'states', defined by sociologist Max Weber as entities having a monopoly on the legitimate use of force within a defined territory. This is the most common definition of 'stateness' and carries an implicature of 'capacity'. As explained in chapter three, states not only require the moral authority to exercise force in pursuit of their goals but must also possess a structural ability to do so. Those successfully able to enact their will are called 'strong states', while those unable to marshal the necessary resources to get what they want done are typically termed 'weak states'. Some states lack any ability to enact their preferences. These are often called 'collapsed' or 'failed' states, and are typified by extreme poverty, an absence of law and order, rampant social factionalism, terrorist activity or some combination of these factors.

However, much early scholarship on globalization spoke of states as though they were outmoded, or even on the verge of extinction (Strange 1996; Evans 1997). Scholars envisioned an increasingly borderless world in which states – the very entities that had waged two world wars, engaged in a nuclear arms race, put people on the moon and engineered their economies to achieve levels of wealth and development previously unknown in human history, and in doing so had defined the twentieth century – appeared to matter less and less. At the very least, there was growing consensus that states now shared the stage with many different kinds of actors, such as multinational corporations, non-governmental think-tanks, charities, foundations, churches, scholars, scientists and practitioner communities, all of which had a growing global reach and an ability to transmit information and effect outcomes on a global scale as never before (Haas 1992). During the 1990s and early 2000s, the growth of international bodies such as the European Union (EU) and World Trade Organization, and an increasingly dense web of United Nations (UN) agencies, also suggested that many states would willingly exchange an element of their sovereignty for membership privileges in a kind of supra-national club. Such institutions, the transborder partnerships they form and their influence on domestic politics the world over have collectively come to be known as 'global governance' (Barnett and Duvall 2005; Finkelstein 1995).

But what does global governance imply for democratization? If states do the democratizing, and states are declining or disappearing, does this mean democratization will also be a thing of the past? Or is there an alternative to state-focused democratization in a global age? Is there such a thing as 'global democracy'?

Global civil society, political participation and democratization

Global governance does not imply the existence of a 'global government' in a formal legal sense. The UN is global in its membership, but it is not a democratic body. No members are elected to the General Assembly, and the Security Council grants veto power to its five permanent members, while others take part on a rotational basis and many more have no voice at all. The European Parliament is the only EU institution to which representatives are democratically elected, and many have written of the EU's 'democratic deficit' (Bowman 2006; Featherstone 1994).

However, the concept of global governance does invite us to think about the actors and organizations beyond the state which may serve as agents of democratization, or the diffusion of democratic values. Scholars now write of a 'global civil society', sometimes called a 'transnational public sphere', ostensibly modelled on the domestic version of civil society, which incorporates a variety of non-state actors that operate across traditional borders (Castells 2008; Kumar 2007; Anheier, Glasius and Kaldor 2001). Some of these play a role in democratization by performing the functions of a conventional civil society, but from a global position. Some act as watchdogs and call out abuses of power. Others serve as clearinghouses for information and report on the quality of democratic governance. Still others directly intercede in the political affairs of states by providing funding to domestic political organizations or monitoring elections, while some of the largest global non-governmental organizations (NGOs) fill several of these roles at once. Amnesty International, for example, is among the most trusted sources of on-the-ground information on human rights abuses, publishing regular reports and attempting to impose pressure on the perpetrators by upping the weight of global public opinion. While direct advocacy of democratization falls outside the organization's mandate, it does anchor its stance on human rights in liberal values (Hopgood 2006: 105). The Ford

Foundation takes a similar approach, framing its mission as a commitment 'to the inherent dignity of all people' without explicitly mentioning the democratic institutions it promotes to achieve this end.

While constituent parts of global civil society may be forces for democratization, there is no stipulation that groups in global civil society must stand for liberal democracy. Moreover, nothing precludes members of global civil society from working with states and interstate organizations. Many do so, just as their counterparts in domestic civil society work with state actors at many levels. Such cooperation is especially common in the field of international democracy promotion, a subject to which we will turn in the next chapter.

Within global civil society, many kinds of non-state actors express their interests and vie for influence. Many seek to influence domestic state policies, but there is no single goal that unites the transitional public sphere. The diversity of viewpoints, cultures and nationalities present might lead one to think that global civil society itself is a highly participatory, broadly representative construct. Many times, marginalized individuals and groups living in remote parts of the world have been able to use technology to transmit ideas and objectives to audiences a world away, far further than would ever have been possible for previous generations.

Case study 7.1: The Zapatista movement

Among the first to capitalize on global communications technology in this manner were the Zapatista rebels (Ejército Zapatista de Liberación Nacional (EZLN)) of Chiapas, Mexico. Chiapas is among Mexico's poorest states. Mexico's economic liberalization was connected to the process of globalization and neoliberalist approaches to economic management, and the removal of subsidies and price controls which led to rising local prices but reduced income from crops, as well as the termination of land reform benefiting peasants, pushed many *indigenas* in Chiapas towards supporting the EZLN against the state. On 1 January 1994, EZLN guerrillas took control of the municipal buildings of seven towns in the southern state of Chiapas. They declared a range of revolutionary goals focused on Indigenous rights, better health, education and infrastructure in the region, true democracy, socio-economic reforms and the abrogation of the North American Free Trade Agreement (NAFTA). The group argued that ongoing neoliberal reforms would further impoverish agricultural workers in Chiapas and throughout Mexico.

As the world watched on, the group made effective use of communication to the outside world, declaring it was not associated with the (by this time unpopular) Marxist ideology and was instead an Indigenous movement against globalization. The group took an inclusive approach to resisting globalization, involving a blend of Mexican, Indian and Mestizo identities. The Zapatistas were closely connected to and influenced by local Indigenous communities and activists. This was in part a driver of the group's focus on democratic processes and outcomes. Indigenous communities were opposed to the centralization of power and hierarchical structures, relying instead on consensus and deliberation (Ronfeldt 1998: 32). 'All activists were in basic agreement that they were not interested in seeking political power or in helping other actors seek power. Rather, they wanted to foster a form of democracy in which civil-society actors would be strong enough to counterbalance state and market actors and could play central roles in making public policy decisions that affect civil society' (Collier and Collier 2005: 450). The group called for international support and solidarity for its goals.

In response to the movement, the Mexican government mobilized a military force and began attacking EZLN positions. The campaign was accompanied by reports of human rights abuses, evoking widespread international sympathy, particularly among NGOs and activists. Within nine days of fighting between the Zapatistas and the Mexican government, the country's President accepted a ceasefire, despite his army having an overwhelming advantage over the insurgents. He did so because the rebels were waging an information war from inside their cordoned off territory, publicizing the conflict and their goals to the world, and this sparked widespread global sympathy and threats of economic repercussions for, and withdrawal of investment from, Mexico (Martinez-Torres 2001: 347). The Zapatistas had such an impact because they were connected to a global network of NGOs and activists, a global civil society. Two transnational networks were crucial in this regard: the human rights and Indigenous movements.

In the years since, the group has occupied a substantial portion of Chiapas' territory, and become synonymous with opposition to economic globalization, all the while embracing technological globalization to remain visible and relevant internationally. The movement had an influence well beyond its very local origins and small size. One study referred to the Zapatistas as 'the most powerful force for democratization in Mexico'.

The Zapatistas' story implies that technological change affords marginalized groups new opportunities or abilities to participate in political action, and that emergence of global civil society is therefore desirable. How else could a collection of poor farmers from the remote Mexican jungle have captured the global imagination? Isn't it a good thing that they, and many others like them, have found a voice and built coalitions with like-minded others around the world? As we saw in chapter four, the aggregation of interests that takes place at the domestic level is indicative of a liberal civil society that strengthens and supports democracy. Could the same thing be happening on a global scale?

In reality, the extent to which global civil society is itself democratic or democratizing is dubious, for several reasons (Kaldor 2003). Traditionally, democracy-enhancing civil societies are understood as separate from, yet bound by, processes at work within states – that is, within territorially defined legal and institutional contexts. But global civil society removes states from the equation altogether, operating in a conceptual space that is paradoxically a) beyond the reach of any one state's legal and institutional framework, and b) therefore not formally subject to any of these. In other words, global civil society is still the Wild West, an essentially lawless place where no sheriff is recognized, and the weak and marginalized are vulnerable to predation by the relatively strong. It is, to borrow a phrase from international relations theory, 'anarchic'. The absence of any overarching or broadly subscribed authority to govern the way global civil society operates or to ensure that rules of democratic representation or fair play are adhered to in turn has two major consequences.

The first is that there is little to prevent some members of 'global uncivil society' from asserting themselves or wielding a tremendous amount of influence. Just as domestic societies sometimes face challenges to participation from white supremacist groups or other ethnic chauvinists, so global civil society faces threats from transnational terrorist organizations. Often these are domestic entities that use the internet as a kind of megaphone, broadcasting their messages and carrying out recruiting and fundraising activities across national boundaries. And, just as with domestic civil society, such organizations stifle the democratic potential of global civil society when those messages are violent or aimed at limiting the participation and representation of others. Examples are legion, but could include Hamas' advocacy of Israel's destruction, East Africa's Al Shabaab, Japan's Aum Shinrikyo or Sri Lanka's Liberation Tigers of Tamil Elam.

A second, more general problem is that there are major inequities in whose concerns are given voice within global civil society, since there is nothing to formally oversee or police the distribution of resources and ensure basic representation, as might happen at the domestic level (Clark 2014; Edwards and Gaventa 2001). As the above example of the Zapatista rebels suggests, one could argue that globalization levels the playing field, creating openings for those located in the most far-flung reaches of the planet to broadcast themselves to new audiences – audiences they never would have had were it not for the shrinking of space and time by digital technology, and which in many cases have produced new transnational allies, amplifying the political impacts of such groups on the ground. In this sense, global civil society is seen as becoming more pluralistic – that is, open to participation by many kinds of entities representing many kinds of claims and viewpoints.

However, groups or individuals located physically in the relatively well-developed, northerly parts of the planet are more easily able to assert themselves in global space. As one study put it, 'the communication networks that compose the transnational public sphere are uneven in terms of authorship and consumption and thus move ever further away from the egalitarian presumption of democratic public spheres' (Guidry, Kennedy and Zald 2000: 7). In part, this occurs because of a 'digital divide' problem – internet access (and access to technology in general) is near-total in places like Canada, the UK, Australia, the Netherlands and Japan. This means that organizations in these places face fewer problems in placing their claims before the global public. But those based in places like Guinea-Bissau, Haiti, Tuvalu or Timor-Leste will have diminished capability to reach a wider audience (Landers 2017; Ragnetta and Muschert 2013; Norris 2001). There, low levels of internet penetration reduce opportunities for participation in global civil society and affect the agenda-setting power of local organizations.

Moreover, even if digital divides and material inequalities were less significant than they are, it must be remembered that the internet itself has a major democratic deficit. 'We risk irreversible losses of human freedom and privacy if we do not impose democratic controls on digital technologies', as Larry Diamond has written (2021: 183). To date, however, few such controls are in evidence, though a few practical recommendations have been made (Deibert 2020).

The upshot is that organizations in more materially prosperous parts of the world can project their ideologies, values and frames of experience onto global civil society. Indeed, one common critique of globalization is that far from creating a more pluralistic world, it has a homogenizing effect on global culture, crowding out local or Indigenous cultures while promoting the views of the powerful. Those whose values are elevated the most sometimes meet with accusations of 'cultural imperialism', deliberately erasing or side-lining marginal interests and perspectives.

It is probably not an accident that groups originating in the Global North (i.e. North America and Western Europe, and perhaps a scattering of allies in the most developed parts of Oceania and East Asia), are the most numerous and prominent actors in global civil society. These places also happen to be where the world's oldest and best-consolidated democracies can be found. US culture is the most frequent target for these kinds of charges. Transnational NGOs hailing from the United States are frequently thought to be carriers of US political culture, and the 'tip of the spear' in terms of democratic value diffusion, just as Hollywood actors and movie studios are global purveyors of US popular culture. This can have the effect of conflating US values with 'global culture' and give the sense that these values have broader appeal than is in fact the case. To put it in the terms of sociological International Relations theory, the United States and its allies from the developed, wealthy 'West' are taken to be 'norm makers', since it is they who are most able to project their values and have these take root as rules of conduct or standards to be observed by everyone else. Hence, it is of little surprise that in an era in which the United States was the leading, and, for a time, the only, superpower, liberal values and democratic institutions would achieve global recognition and widespread adoption. However, the dominance of US culture under conditions of globalization could also lead to false impressions about its popularity and, indeed, considerable pushback from alternative value systems in global space. The supreme irony of global civil society is that its agency of democratization derives from its own undemocratic structures.

The universalism/particularism debate

At the outset of this book, we discussed a so-called 'democratic consensus' that predominated during the latter portion of the twentieth century. Particularly after the Cold War and the demise of Soviet-style communism, it appeared that there remained no meaningful, practicable alternative to liberal democracy. Thus, it gained broad acceptance as the best form of government, and one to which states either aspired, or ought to aspire. As the Churchillian adage went, democracies were the worst form of government, except for all the others, most of which had been tried and failed; this left democracy as the last ideology standing. So strong was the global consensus for democracy that even states which were plainly not democratic and had no democratic aspirations still used 'democracy' in their official names – the Democratic Republic of the Congo and the Democratic People's Republic of Korea being two key examples. This trend was at least in part a legacy of the socialist camp during the Cold War.

Famed political theorist Amartya Sen wrote of this phenomenon in terms of 'democracy as a universal value'. For Sen, universalism does not imply total agreement on what constitutes democracy, and it certainly does not mean democracy is perfect. Far from it. Rather, Sen refers to the general recognition that democracy has value for virtually any society, to the degree that it became the default setting within and among most countries of the world (1999: 5). Sen saw the shift to democracy as a universal value as a very recent occurrence. During the earlier parts of the twentieth century, he notes, it was common to ask whether certain societies were 'fit for democracy' – that is, whether democracy could or would take root, given pre-existing values and social structures. We now think of many places, he argues, as becoming 'fit through democracy' – that is, of states and their citizens reaching their maximum potential through the use of representative, participatory and competitive institutional practices typical of democracy (ibid.: 4). By extension, this shift to fitness through democracy in a huge assortment of places, each with their own histories, cultures and needs, must mean that democratic institutions are capable of being adapted to unique circumstances while retaining core principled commonalities. In other words, to be recognized as having universal value, democracy must also be diverse (Beetham 2009).

Critics of this universalist position have been quick to point out that the institutions associated with democracy arose in a particular time and place. For these critics, liberal democracy is a specific variant or subtype that premises itself on values not found everywhere, and is therefore culturally bound and cannot claim universal validity (Parekh 1992). Hence, what was presumed to be a global ascendance and triumph of democratic principles may be a widespread adoption of the stylings of democracy but not its substance. If the institutional trappings of democracy – recall Schumpeter's 'procedural minimums' – can be built without a foundation in liberalism, the result is likely to be a blossoming of 'pretender' democracies around the world, or illiberal or hybrid regimes, as we saw in chapter five. We have already named numerous examples throughout this book, most of which are characterized by weak attachments to liberal values hidden behind a veneer of electoral competition.

Of course, one must be careful not to adopt an approach to culture that is insufficiently dynamic to allow for rapid changes in political values (Inglehart and Welzel 2005). No culture stands still. Yet there may also be limits to the likelihood, pace and direction of values-based change, and particularists would claim these must be taken seriously. Many of the authoritarian populists noted in chapter six would be particularists, arguing that certain elements of forms of democracy were unfit for their country and that they alone understood their people's needs (perhaps even some democratic populists would fit this bill, were they to argue that a given aspect of democracy or democratic result contravened 'the will of the people'). Further, as suggested in the previous section, values gaps between 'the West and the rest' animate much of the early scholarship on globalization and may only be deepened by perceptions of a Western values hegemony (Huntington 1993; Friedman 2000; Barber 1995).

Value diffusion in action: Neighbourhood (snowball) effects

One curious feature of democratization over the past several decades is the tendency for certain countries that are geographically close to one another to embrace or resist change together. Casual observation confirms that democracies tend to cluster or bunch regionally, resulting in democratic 'neighbourhoods' – that is, identifiable parts of the world where democracy is the norm rather than the exception among adjacent or proximate states. In some places, adoption of democracy may even be required for membership in multilateral bodies, creating a kind of 'neighbourhood association' that enforces democratic standards for the wider region and all but ensures democracy remains the exclusive form of government, as is the case with the EU (that is, the states that comprise the EU, not the EU itself, as noted above). Of course, the same phenomenon has also been observed in non-democracies. In the 1950s, communism engulfed nearly half the world. In 2020, just five nominally communist states remain. Four of these share contiguous borders – North Korea, China, Vietnam and Laos – with Cuba being the lone exemplar in the western hemisphere. Today, institutional legacies, communist, colonial and otherwise, all play a role in preserving pockets of authoritarianism in different regions of the world.

In this section, we hypothesize that this clustering phenomenon – variously called the 'snowball', 'demonstration', 'contagion' or 'domino' effect – may be not only correlation but causation. This allowance enables us to explore a range of explanations as to when and why clustering occurs.

The first and most important plausibility is that democratic change in one country creates grounds for comparison with another, leading to an idea that what was possible in one place might be an option somewhere else (Huntington 1991: 101). Such demonstrations of democracy's viability rest upon reliable information about the exemplar-in-transition travelling to the follow-on country, followed by an assessment of the conditions within the exemplar to determine whether the same might eventuate in the follow-on. However, several important caveats must be borne in mind.

First, the information about the exemplar must be accessible and trustworthy in the follow-on society. The medium by which information is carried may matter a great deal. Timeliness might also be a factor. In some past instances, information might have been carried from person to person across borders in real time, by way of personal contacts and clandestine resistance movements, especially where restrictions on freedom of the press, speech or assembly were in effect. At times, the transmission of information was aided by underground printing and copying enterprises, which disseminated books, leaflets and other dissident literature in secret, as with the *samizdat* of the former Soviet Union. As mass communication modes became more broadly available in the latter half of the twentieth century, pirate radio, television, satellite signals and, finally, the internet could be used to reach more people quickly. Thus, the role of technology in causing demonstration effects has broadened – and its importance increased – over the same period.

Second, the rapid transmission of information electronically means that demonstrations need no longer occur between close neighbours only. Because details about a given country's democratization process can now be sent around the world instantaneously, the comparative assessments noted above may happen between two or more geographically distant places, at least in principle. We might therefore expect to see 'temporal clustering' (i.e. democratizations happening in geographically disparate places at the same time), as well as neighbourhood effects (i.e. democratization processes that spill over international borders).

Third, while technology sees to it that demonstration effects need not take place between societies sharing a contiguous border, contagion effects are still likeliest in countries geographically and culturally close to each other. This could happen because of parallel conditions occurring in neighbouring states, such as wars or natural disasters, a major recession in which several national economies within a region are particularly hard-hit, similarities in ethnic, religious or linguistic makeup and any history of conflict or instability arising from these factors. Regional snowballing becomes especially likely if democratization already showed itself to be an effective antidote to these or other social and political ailments. Alternatively, democracy might appear to be a feasible option if one society judges its values to be sufficiently close to those of its democratizing neighbour. Gazing across the border, reformers in the follow-on country may observe foreign demonstrators and think 'we are not so different … what works for them may work for us'.

Beyond the recognition of similar problems and solutions in neighbouring states, demonstration effects are typically stronger where the demonstrator is taken to be a politically or culturally significant model. Adding to their theory of international linkage and democratization, noted at the start of this chapter, Levitsky and Way use the term 'leverage' to refer to 'the degree to which governments are vulnerable to external democratising pressure', while hastening to add that 'leverage without linkage has rarely been sufficient to induce democratization since the end of the Cold War' (2002: 379). One further way of thinking about this kind of peer influence might be to use the term 'bandwagoning'. In this version of the concept, borrowed from international relations, relatively small and less influential states play follow-the-leader with preponderantly powerful regional hegemons (Mearsheimer 2001: 162–3).

Fourth, and perhaps most importantly, we note that 'comparison' does not mean 'sameness'. Transitions to democracy are more likely to eventuate where reformers in one country observe similarities in another, but comparison also has a way of highlighting differences. Instead of thinking 'we are not so different …', the kind of cross-border gazing mentioned above may be just as likely to highlight the obstacles and challenges to democratization, conditions which may not have been present (at least to the same degree) for the demonstrator as they are for the follow-on society. Making a clear-eyed assessment of the risks involved in pushing for reform may be extremely important in shaping the timing and tactics used in the follow-on country, and thus could be an explanation as to why democratization occurs in some societies and not in others.

Case study 7.2: Post-communist Europe

Many of the foregoing propositions about demonstrated democratization took shape in the context of clustered transitions across Eastern Europe in the wake of the Soviet Union's collapse. Indeed, because it coincided with significant technological innovations – not least the advent of the personal computer – the collapse of communism in former Soviet client states which brought on democracy's 'Third Wave' is a paragon illustration of the snowball effect at work. In this example, democratization on a regional scale was driven primarily by a growing awareness within communist states of conditions within nearby democracies, which in turn fuelled popular dissatisfaction with the political status quo and a belief in the greater efficacy of democratic institutions.

Some of the first rumblings of this democratic turn are thought to have been heard in Poland in 1988, when the Solidarity trade union won a partly free election. The following year, amid growing calls from their citizens for political liberalization, and emboldened by Mikhail Gorbachev's new policies of *perestroika* (restructuring) and *glasnost* (openness) within the Soviet Union, reform-minded communist leaders began to hold meetings to discuss the necessity of change, the potential for a democratic alternative and, crucially, an end to the Soviet military presence in their countries. It was a risky proposition. The Iron Curtain was both a symbol of Soviet dominance in Eastern Europe and a physical barrier that separated the communist satellites from neighbouring democracies. Movement from east to west and vice versa had been restricted since the Berlin Wall went up in 1961. By holding discussions about democratization, reformist leaders were testing Gorbachev's resolve, as well as Soviet military supremacy and security in the region. Indeed, they were also pushing the stability of European communism to the breaking point.

It was the 'Pan-European Picnic' of 1989 that touched off a chain reaction of events that concluded with the total collapse of the Soviet bloc. On 19 August, an outdoor gathering was held at Sopron, Hungary, a town near the Austrian border. The event had been widely promoted to the public in Hungary, mostly with paper leaflets, and with the knowledge and approval of Hungarian Minister of State Imre Pozsgay and Prime Minister Miklós Németh, who had become convinced of the need to open borders and allow Hungarians to travel more freely. Németh's main motivations stemmed from the struggling Hungarian economy, though the 'picnic' itself had been suggested to him by Ferenc Mészáros of the Hungarian Democratic Forum (MDF) and Otto von Habsburg, heir of the Imperial House of Habsburg and President of the Austrian chapter of the Pan-European Union.

Many of those in attendance were Hungarian, though a sizeable contingent had come from the German Democratic Republic (GDR) as well, meeting no resistance to their travel from either the Ministry of State Security of the GDR or the Hungarian state security service, both of which had information about the event but apparently chose not to act upon it. Many reached Sopron on foot, having hiked from the Hungarian capital – today, the routes they took serve as walking and cycling trails on the outskirts of Budapest. As had been arranged in advance by the Hungarian and Austrian governments, a border crossing was to be opened for a period of three hours so that Europeans could experience international travel, at least symbolically. However, picnickers arriving at the side found the crossing was still guarded and tore down the wooden gate, with dozens of mostly young people rushing to the Austrian side. Ultimately, about 600 East Germans are thought to have fled to the West that day. News of the exodus spread quickly, as did reports that armed border guards did not intervene to stop it and may have been ordered to stand down. Nor was there any reported retribution from Moscow against those who had known about and planned the gathering.

The combination of encouragement from influential actors, wilful negligence on the part of border patrols, endorsement from reform-minded governments and the absence of repercussions from authoritarian holdouts meant that there were no meaningful disincentives for the exercise to be repeated. Subsequent picnics were planned and carried out throughout 1989, resulting in the Austria–Hungary border being formally opened in September. Then, on a fateful day in November, the nerve demonstrated by the East German refugees at Sopron was put to the test on a much larger scale in central Berlin. At 6:00 pm on 9 November, a televised press conference was held at which Günter Schabowski, top spokesperson for the ruling Socialist Unity Party, announced that East Germans would be able to cross to West Berlin immediately, and without the paperwork normally required. Crowds began amassing shortly after 7:00 pm, demanding that all six checkpoints be opened in accordance with Schabowski's announcement. At around 10:45 pm, unwilling to use force against peaceful protesters, guard commanders relented, and East Berliners poured through. Around the world, televisions sets were alight with the sights and sounds of the reunification, complete with champagne, street parties and swarms of East Germans scaling, dancing on and then tearing down the Iron Curtain. The GDR was dissolved, and Germany's reunification formalized in October 1990. Facing political challenges of its own, the Soviet Union was dissolved on 26 December the following year. Communism was at its end in Europe, and with the notable exception of Romania, it had fallen without violence. Rather, the demonstration of democratic possibilities within politically liberal neighbouring countries, and the rapid transmission of information about the security implications of border crossing fed the boldness of reformers. It's also worth noting that this may have been the first time demonstration effects transcended regional boundaries at speed, again because of the technology involved.

Communist regimes in Asia faced similar insurrections to those in Europe. Wary that their own regimes may befall a similar fate as the Soviet Union, communist leaders in Asia were inspired to devise a range of strategies in response. For China's leadership, especially state security czar Li Peng and other close advisers of Deng Xiaoping, this meant a military crackdown to crush calls for political freedom, a strategy that ultimately succeeded. Elsewhere, such as in Vietnam and Cambodia, leaders spent the early 1990s in a guided process of reform from within that worked to preserve authoritarianism through a kind of halting liberalization process.

Case study 7.3: The 2003–6 Colour Revolutions

A second example of clustered regional change occurred in the mid-2000s, with the 'Colour Revolutions', including in some long-time authoritarian holdouts that had persisted since the end of the Cold War. Interestingly, most did not share contiguous borders, but were scattered across Central and Southern Europe, the Middle East and central Asia. These include the 2003 Rose Revolution in the Republic of Georgia, the Ukrainian Orange Revolution of 2004–5 and Kyrgyzstan's 2005 Tulip Revolution, with some observers also including Kuwait's Blue Revolution of 2005, Lebanon's Cedar Revolution that same year and the Denim or 'Jeans' Revolution of 2006 in Belarus. In most cases, these were non-violent movements consisting primarily of strikes and large street demonstrations in response to democracy denied, usually in the form of disputed election results, or to call for open, free, fair electoral processes.

While most of the Colour Revolutions of this period earned their names from colours or symbols associated with national identities – for example, the cedar tree is the national symbol of Lebanon – these were not the first cases where patriotic images had been invoked to lend credence to a democratic movement. Indeed, the Colour Revolutions of 2003–6 have any number of historic antecedents in popular movements against authoritarianism. The first was probably the 1986 'Yellow Revolution' in the Philippines that toppled Ferdinand Marcos' regime. Czechoslovakia held its 'Velvet Revolution' in 1989 in defiance of Soviet occupation. Yugoslavia's 'Bulldozer Revolution' of 2000, which led to the overthrow of Serbian leader Slobodan Milošević, was based almost entirely on demonstrations held elsewhere in Southern and Eastern Europe, including in Slovakia in 1998, Bulgaria in 1999 and Croatia early in 2000. In each of these instances, the downfall of dictatorship was wrought by massive civic participation in a get-out-the-vote campaign resulting in coalescence of opposition forces. Frequently, the impetus for mass protests came from student activism. In the former Yugoslav capital of Belgrade, it was a student movement called Optor! (lit. 'Resistance!') that began the demonstrations against Milosevic in the fading stages of the Kosovo War. Optor! is thought to have provided direct inspiration for similar student movements in Georgia (Kmara), Belarus (Zubr), Ukraine (Pora) and Albania (MJAFT!).

One further distinguishing feature of the Colour Revolutions is that they were subject to allegations of foreign sabotage from two strong authoritarian regimes – Russia and China. Unlike the clustered collapse of communist regimes in 1989–90 noted above, the Colour Revolutions are viewed by Moscow and Beijing as the imperial machinations of the United States (Bolt and Cross 2018: 216–89). According to a report by the Washington-based Center for Strategic and International Studies, Russia's view is that the Colour Revolutions reflect a 'new US and European approach to warfare that focuses on creating destabilizing revolutions in other states as a means of serving their security interests' (Cordesman 2014). Similar claims have been made in Beijing, where reference has been made to the attempts to destabilize China by fomenting a Colour Revolution there as a new form of containment. A 2015 White Paper produced by China's state council alleges that 'anti-China forces have never given up their attempt to instigate a "colour revolution" in this country' (People's Republic of China 2015).

Case study 7.4: The Arab Spring

A third and more recent set of uprisings swept across the Middle East and North Africa in the early 2010s. Some of these bore names like those of the Colour Revolutions from the previous decade, such as Tunisia's Jasmine Revolution of 2010, Egypt's Lotus Revolution the following year and Bahrain's Pearl Revolution, which ran from 2011 to 2014. Also, like earlier clusters, the diffusion of the Arab Spring protests is commonly thought to have spread through demonstration effects – what was possible in one context appeared plausible in a neighbouring one. The potential for parallel revolutionary change was strong enough that a common slogan emerged among protest movements and transcended international boundaries. Chants of 'Ash-shaʻb yurīd isqāṭ an-niẓām' ('the people want to bring down the regime') were heard in Tunis, Cairo, Bahrain, Tripoli and Damascus, though this was softened in some other places to the less antagonistic 'Ash-shaʻb yurīd islah an-niẓām' ('the people want to reform the system').

As with the Colour Revolutions, there were some notable instances of dictators deposed. Beginning on 25 January 2010, a date selected by protesters to coincide with the annual 'police holiday' in a symbolic gesture against abuses by state security forces, demonstrators began to assemble in Tahrir Square in central Cairo. They brought with them a grab bag of grievances against the government of President Hosni Mubarak, including allegations of systemic police brutality and abuses of Egypt's emergency powers legislation, as well as more general complaints about the denial of civil liberties, official corruption and economic matters such as inflation, wage stagnation and unemployment. Peaceful at the outset and centred mainly around the occupation of public spaces, strikes and marches, tensions between protesters and security personnel escalated over a period of two-and-a-half weeks, with the Central Security Forces being joined by the Egyptian Army to restore order. The result was violent clashes that left 846 protesters dead and more than 6,000 injured. By 11 February, realizing he no longer had the moral authority to govern, Mubarak handed power over to a military junta which suspended the Egyptian constitution and dissolved Parliament until fresh elections could be held. Ultimately, the Muslim Brotherhood would form Egypt's next government under Islamist leader Mohamed Morsi, who was himself deposed in a coup after ruling for just a year. The coup was led by then-Minister of Defence, General Abdel Fattah Saeed Hussein Khalil el-Sisi, who in 2014 was selected as President when millions of Egyptians again took to the streets to demand early elections be held. Similar fates befell incumbent authoritarian governments in Tunisia, Libya and Yemen, with significant protests happening in Saudi Arabia, Algeria, Morocco, Oman and Mauritania as well.

However, the Arab Spring is distinct from the earlier instances of the snowball effect in several ways. First, while the movements of the 2010s had enhanced ability to organize and direct protests with cell phones and social media in ways that were simply not possible in Europe in the late 1980s, they also encountered significant resistance within the authoritarian governments they opposed. In many cases, government security forces were not only capable of counter-intelligence and surveillance activities to keep pace with protesters' technological sophistication, but were also willing to use violence, including military force, to suppress riots and restore order when they had to. This stands in clear contrast to the unwillingness of East German guards to fire on crowds at Checkpoint Charlie in 1989.

Second, changes within some Arab Spring countries occurred alongside significant foreign military intervention, clouding the issue and making it more difficult to attribute the spread of protests to demonstration effects alone (Brancati and Lucardi 2019). Libya is one such notable case. In 2011, armed rebel factions overthrew the Libyan Arab Jamahiriya of Colonel Muammar Gaddafi which had ruled in Libya since 1977. An interim government known as the National Transitional Council (NTC) was established as Gaddafi fled the capital in a convoy to the city of Sirte, a last stronghold of support for his government. With Sirte itself about to fall, Gaddafi again fled and was fired upon by NATO forces ostensibly present to protect civilians in compliance with UN Security Council Resolution 1973. Following the strike and destruction of his convoy, Gaddafi took shelter nearby and ultimately was killed by pursuing NTC forces. Video of his capture and death then circulated on the internet. One of these showed NTC fighters holding up Gaddafi's head by the hair, with gunshot wounds visible on the head and torso. Another reportedly showed his lifeless body being sodomized with a bayonet. Afterwards, the NTC government displayed the corpse publicly as proof that Gaddafi was dead. While it is unclear whether NATO forces realized they were firing on Gaddafi specifically, its role in the demise of a larger-than-life dictator and long-time US enemy adds a dimension of complexity and intrigue to the Libyan case not found in some of the other examples of regional clusters noted here.

Third, while in some places, such as Egypt, lagging civil liberties or delayed elections were a key rallying point for demonstrators, many Arab Spring protests were expressions of dissatisfaction with incumbent dictatorships rather than calls for democracy per se. Consequently, coherent, well-organized opposition forces sometimes failed to crystallize. This allowed for militias, insurgencies or other extremist organizations to fill the power vacuums left behind by authoritarian strongmen (and they were, without exception, men). In some cases, the result was a near-total breakdown of law and order, and the collapse of the state itself. Bashar al-Assad's Syria is probably the best-known example, though violent insurrections, separatist movements and pan-National Islamist organizations also gained prominence in places like Morocco, Sudan, Iraq and Algeria. The first rumblings of the Syrian Arab Spring were felt on 26 January 2011, when protesters gathered in old Damascus to demand the release of a man arrested after his assault by a police officer. In March, 15 children were arrested in the city of Daraa, which thereafter became the site of the first open protests against the Ba' athist government. By mid-month these had spread to Damascus, Aleppo and beyond, and called for Al-Assad's resignation. The state responded with heavy-handed crackdowns, including one in late July in which tanks were dispatched and some 130 protesters killed. While both the protests and government crackdowns drew the attention of the world, neither eventuated in collapse of the Al-Assad government. Instead, Syrian security forces entered into a now-decade-old civil conflict against a cohort of rebel and jihadist organizations, including most notably Islamic State of Iraq and the Levant (ISIL). Syria's descent into chaos and the rise of terrorist groups where a functional state once stood in turn drew interventionist forces from around the globe, whose presence has been criticized many times by Al-Assad, who still clings to power. Thus, the Arab Spring stands alone among the examples here as a cautionary tale of democratizations that never materialized.

Conclusion

In the above sections, we have provided a brief overview of globalization's effect on recent democratizations. Because this effect revolves mainly around the diffusion of values and ideas via technological exchanges, it has been by necessity an examination of recent history. Advances in telecommunications in particular have shrunk the globe, and news of political events in far-flung places now spread with much more speed and reliability than was possible just two or three generations ago.

This change has brought a number of consequences. One of these is that many different kinds of actors now consume information and exercise influence or pressure for democratization. Non-state organizations active in a global civil society exercise many of the functions of domestic civil society, acting as watchdogs against government abuses, spreading information that may help to set the tone of international debate on key issues and providing many who may otherwise be disenfranchised with an outlet that allows them to reach a global audience and participate in transnational political debates. Their influence became so strong that some scholars even began to question the relevance of traditional states. However, as we argue above, neither global civil society nor the broader institutions of global governance are democratic structures. Rather, they tend to reflect the values and preferences of the most dominant actors within them. It was in this context that we raised the universalism/particularism debate – an ongoing dialogue about democracy's origins, adaptability and well-suitedness to diverse situations, cultures and contexts around the world. We submit that this debate is only likely to retain its relevance in an age when knowledge about foreign political systems can be so easily accessed and transmitted by so many people across the globe.

In the latter half of this chapter, we explored three examples of the 'domino' or 'snowball' effect in order to illustrate how information about regime change crosses international boundaries to produce regional clusters. While democracy did not eventuate in all countries or clusters examined, these examples do point to the continuing role of pressures from beyond state boundaries. These sorts of pressures, too, are only likely to continue in the future, as more and more people acquire access to mobile phones, laptops and tablets, as well as social media platforms. From here on out, all democratizations – even the ultimately unsuccessful ones – are affected by globalization. While the role of technology and cross-border demonstrations is likely to proceed apace, it is important to remember that the ideas being transmitted and demonstrated may be as destructive of democracy as conducive to its thriving. The rise of populism worldwide noted in chapter six is just one example, though scholarship in that area remains too recent to be able to say with certainty whether that rise is underpinned by global demonstration effects, or region-specific populist clusters are emerging.

We hasten to add that this is not, and cannot be, an exhaustive consideration of all international issues at play in democratization. In our next chapter, we explore the role of aid programmes specifically designed to foster political opening.

Questions for discussion

1 What are the key processes involved in globalization?
2 What is the relationship between globalization and inequality?
3 How important are 'demonstration effects' in democratization (and its reversal)?

4 Is global civil society a force for democracy or autocracy?
5 Is democratization now fundamentally driven by international phenomena?

Further reading

Bhagwati, Jagdish, 'Globalization, Sovereignty and Democracy', Columbia University, Revised March 1995 (August 1994), Discussion Paper Series No. 723, pp. 1–29.
Bottici, Chiara, and Benoît Challand, *The Myth of the Clash of Civilisations* (London and New York: Routledge, 2010).
Gleditsch, Kristian Skrede, *All International Politics is Local: The Diffusion of Conflict, Integration and Democratization* (Ann Arbor, MI: The University of Michigan Press, 2002).
Hawkins, Darren G., 'Domestic Responses to International Pressure: Human Rights in Authoritarian Chile', *European Journal of International Relations*, Vol. 3, No. 4 (December 1997): 403–34.
Houle, Christian, and Mark A. Kayser, 'The Two-step Model of Clustered Democratization', *Journal of Conflict Resolution*, Vol. 63, No. 10 (2019): 2421–37.
Inglehart, Ronald, and Pippa Norris, 'The True Clash of Civilisations', *Foreign Policy*, Vol. 135 (2003): 62–70.
Laxer, Gordon, and Sandra Halperin, eds, *Global Civil Society and Its Limits* (Houndmills: Palgrave, 2003).
Ronfeldt, David F., *The Zapatista Social Netwar in Mexico* (Santa Monica, CA: Rand 1998).
Tolstrup, Jakob, 'External Influence and Democratization: Gatekeepers and Linkages', *Journal of Democracy*, Vol. 25, No. 4 (October 2014): 126–38.
Whitehead, Laurence ed., *The International Dimensions of Democratization: Europe and the Americas*, Expanded Edition (Oxford: Oxford University Press, 2001).

8

Funding change: International democracy assistance

The early chapters of this book examined democratization as an *endogenous* process – that is, one driven mainly by factors found within a country. Economic conditions, education levels, class coalitions, the role of the military, demographic disposition, political history, and so on, all exercise an influence on democratic prospects. Such conditions therefore have the longest tradition of scholarly research behind them, and remain the dominant approach to studies of political change. By contrast, chapters in Part II survey a range of *exogenous* factors that have underpinned democratization processes over the past twenty-five to thirty years, many of which are themselves driven by processes of technological advancement and information diffusion around the globe.

With this chapter, we explore yet another external source of pressure for democratization – democracy assistance programming. Also referred to as 'democracy promotion' or 'political aid', the term refers to a specific category of development assistance designed to either foster democratic opening in an authoritarian country, or strengthen and consolidate democratic rule in countries undergoing transition (Carothers 1999: 6). Defined in this way, democracy assistance can be understood as a vehicle for the advancement of providers' foreign policy interests. These interests may stem from a belief in democracy as an inherent good, but also from a sense that it is associated with other desirable outcomes, like economic development, the rule of law, enhanced transparency and international peace. Whether or not these premises are accurate or true is a matter of debate, but the latter idea in particular nevertheless holds a great deal of currency among aid providers –

if democracies do not go to war with one another, then the global spread of democratic institutions is a path to a more prosperous, peaceful world.

Unsurprisingly, most donors of democracy assistance are governments of the world's wealthiest and most-established democratic states. In contrast to other areas of the democratization field, which are almost exclusively the remit of scholars and theorists, the study of democracy assistance also includes a strong element of 'applied' research driven by the desires of donor governments to understand whether or to what extent their efforts are effective and their money well used (Perlin et al. 2008: 3).

Nearly all programmes and expenditures now classified as democracy assistance have occurred since the end of the Cold War. One report commissioned by the United States Agency for International Development (USAID) found that between 1990 and 2004, the agency spent an average of more than US$1 billion per year on some 40,000 different projects (Finkel et al. 2008). A 2019 report estimates that expenditures across all US government bodies have topped US$2 billion annually over the last decade (Lawson and Epstein 2019).

During this period, democracy assistance has been distributed mainly on a bilateral basis, though some multilateral organizations – such as the UN Development Programme, UN Democracy Fund and International Institute for Democracy and Electoral Assistance – and some regional bodies like the Organization for Security and Co-operation in Europe and the Organization of American States have now entered the field. Most democracy aid flows from government to government, sometimes with the help of semi-governmental foundations or arms-length agencies, think-tanks, NGOs or charitable foundations. By extension, this means that 'it takes two' for democracy promotion to happen. One government must provide it, and another must be open to receiving it. Recipients may be unlikely to request support for democratic institutions when the political costs are perceived as being too high (i.e. could it risk the collapse of an autocratic regime?) or the benefits too low (i.e. will it actually help to strengthen elections?). From a donor perspective, donors may be less likely to provide democracy assistance when they judge its likelihood of impact to be minimal (Borzyskowski 2016).

A key issue in understanding who provides or rejects democracy assistance is the measurement of its results. Even defining what is or ought to be a good goal for democracy aid has proven fraught. If 'success' were judged solely in terms of whether new democratic regimes arose where authoritarian ones fell, the record of democracy promotion initiatives would appear to be very poor indeed. While some research emphasizes the need to rethink our definitions of success and what can reasonably be accomplished through such programmes, the question of whether or not democracy promotion is something that ought to be provided or is worth the investment remains a feature of international debate. Consequently, the future of democracy aid is uncertain.

The first section below takes up definitional matters, outlining in detail what does and does not qualify as democracy promotion. A second section then develops an explanation for its provision based on conceptual understandings of donor interests. However, the bulk of the chapter is given over to exploring some of the more commonly funded and studied elements of democracy promotion, such as funding for the conduct and monitoring of elections, building democracy-enhancing political parties, funding the rule of law in a manner that prevents over-concentrations of power or arbitrariness in its application, and the construction of an active liberal civil society that broadens avenues for citizens to participate in politics.

What democracy promotion is (and is not)

Democracy promotion is a particular category of foreign development assistance. Instead of improving access to education, building public health systems, providing sanitation infrastructure or sealing roadways, this kind of assistance aims to develop political institutions, both formal and informal, in the interest of effective, efficient, socially responsive and transparent governance.

UK-based Emeritus Professor Peter Burnell developed a set of three basic criteria to help us distinguish democracy promotion from other types of aid (Burnell 2000). First, it must target the reform or improvement of a political system as its primary goal. This qualifier is an important one, because some economic and social development programmes may have a positive effect on democratization even when this was not their express purpose, and donors sometimes combine the aims of such projects with the more general task of tackling 'governance challenges'. Some democracy promoters also regard certain levels of social or economic development as necessary preconditions for sustainable democratization, and thus tend to view programming in these areas as part of the larger democracy promotion rubric.

Second, democracy assistance activities must be not-for-profit undertakings, operating as traditional development assistance does. In many donor countries, provision of official development assistance is driven in part by a domestic aid industry composed of international non-governmental organizations (INGOs), think-tanks and private enterprises to whom contracts are awarded in exchange for expertise in a given development sector (Van Rooy 1998). Their inclusion may be required to cement domestic support for large and expensive overseas programmes, but commercial gain by any of these actors has the potential to undermine the integrity of donor commitments to democracy.

Third, democracy assistance must be peaceful. Some donor countries conflate democracy promotion with security provision, (correctly) deeming security to be the cornerstone of meaningful, lasting peacebuilding efforts, which in turn are necessary for a functional democratic state. This logic was used during the presidency of George W. Bush as a partial justification for US incursions in both Iraq and Afghanistan, though tied inextricably to rhetoric on the need to eradicate global terrorism. Indeed, spreading democracy was an essential pillar of what became known as the 'Bush Doctrine', with the President himself declaring in 2005 that 'freedom can be the future of every nation', and that bringing about a 'global democratic revolution' that included the Middle East 'must be a focus of American foreign policy for decades to come' (Reynolds 2003). The difficulty comes when democracy-building outcomes arising from military operations are measured indirectly through evaluation of military operations, or are incorporated into military budget appropriations. The challenge is similar to the one noted above with respect to conventional aid – sometimes benefits to democratization occur as a result of programmes designed for other purposes, making it difficult to distinguish genuine effort to promote democracy from incidental benefits arising from military actions. Stipulating that democracy promotion must be peaceful helps to offset this confusion.

Moreover, many have noted the historically poor record of democracy promotion by military means. Japan, whose constitution was enacted in 1947 by a US occupation force, is touted as a notable example of success, significantly downgrading the role of the emperor, limiting the power of Japan's military, establishing a parliamentary regime and guaranteeing universal basic rights. However, Japan is an exception that proves the general rule. In fact, most theorists advise against the imposition of democracy by a foreign military power due to the difficulty of achieving success (or at least the high human and monetary costs of achieving success). They note that where foreign military intervention is involved in democratization, greater success has been achieved through UN peacekeeping operations or those of regional international organizations involved in activities such as ensuring elections are held safely or that incumbent dictatorships are not allowed to interfere in the results (Russett 2005).

Explaining democracy aid: Unpacking national interests

Why would the United States, or any entity, provide aid to foster foreign democracies? What business is it of theirs? Isn't this colonialism by another name? International Relations theories offer some plausible answers. One possibility, based on liberal theories of complex interdependence, suggests there may be economic benefits to creating new democracies. According to this rationale, democratic institutions, being more open and transparent than those of non-democracies, reduce the transaction costs associated with doing business in partner countries. Countries with more accountable forms of governance may provide more compelling assurances against the prospect of corruption, something of immense value to foreign investors. Ergo, democracy promotion efforts aimed at building the rule of law – for example by strengthening a foreign court system – are in fact laying a framework for future economic engagement.

For many donors of democracy aid, particularly the United States, the promotion of free markets has gone hand in hand with that of free people – though an emphasis on opening international markets has historically been a focus of democracy promotion projects by the EU, Japan, Canada and others. As one observer has put it, 'Free markets and democracy formed a symbiotic and reciprocal relationship that produced free, stable, prosperous societies [and] both produced benefits for the United States' (Travis 1998: 253). The importance of this objective in US foreign policy was a particular feature of democracy promotion under the Clinton administration, with Clinton's deputy secretary of state declaring forthrightly that 'Countries whose citizens choose their leaders … are more likely than those with other forms of government to be reliable partners in trade' (Talbott 1996). The same sentiment was later echoed by President Barack Obama, who in 2009 told the Ghanaian Parliament: 'Governments that respect the will of their own people, that govern by consent and not coercion, are more prosperous, they are more stable, and more successful than governments that do not' (White House 2009).

A second line of logic is based on national security considerations. Democratic peace theory centres on the hypothesis that democracies do not go to war with one another. If this proposition is true, and not everyone agrees that it is (Layne 1994; Layne 2001), then expanding the number of democracies should bring about a more peaceful world. As with the economic interdependence argument, democracy is viewed here not merely as a good in its own right, but as a means to another worthy end.

Historical examples of this thinking abound, but the US government has led the way. Indeed, the messaging from recent presidential administrations (barring that of Donald Trump) has been remarkably consistent. Bill Clinton's 1993 policy of 'democratic enlargement', which included a focus on overseas democracy promotion efforts, was framed explicitly in terms of the security needs of the United States. 'Ultimately, the best strategy to ensure our security and to build a durable peace is to support the advance of democracy elsewhere. Democracies don't attack each other,' said Clinton in his 1994 State of the Union Address. Clinton's security-orientated take on democracy promotion provided direct inspiration for the strategies of George W. Bush's administration, which tailored its messaging to the contemporaneous 'war on terror'. According to at least one critical commentator, the difference between the democracy promotion policies of the two presidencies is 'merely one of degree' (Søndergaard 2015: 547).

A related yet clearly distinct version of this rationale applies to peacebuilding at the domestic level. Termed 'liberal peacebuilding', these interventions serve donor interests by using the machinery of democratic governance to foster secure conditions within a recipient country, instead of addressing propensities for interstate conflicts. In part, this focus on establishing domestic peace and stability is justified by a belief that civil wars are now more common around the world than are conventional interstate conflicts, but it is also grounded in a 'means-to-an-end' type of thinking by donors. As former US Secretary of State Madeleine Albright put it,

> [T]here is nothing foreign about foreign policy anymore. When we make innovative investments in peace, prosperity, and democracy overseas, as we now propose, we help to secure those blessings for our own citizens here at home. And when we fail to make the needed investments, we place our own future in jeopardy.
>
> (1999)

Conflating democracy promotion with statecraft, liberal peacebuilding efforts are grounded in an instrumental logic, one designed to serve the interests of those funding post-conflict reconstruction by transforming formerly divided or unstable societies into more functional contributing members of the international community.

Of course, liberal peacebuilding has its detractors, too. A quarter of a century on from its post-Cold War heyday, critics have pointed out the disappointing results of liberal peacebuilding, and the folly of believing that elections, the very heart of liberal democracy, signal sustainable democratic institutions in the long run, much less guarantee long-term democratic outlooks or the healing of divided polities (Paris 2010).

A third possible explanation for providing democracy aid is premised on a non-instrumental view: that democracy carries intrinsic value. Such a view might best be described as 'constructivist', in that it reflects the shared beliefs of actors within the international community and provides a basis for their individual and shared behaviours. According to this view, democracy aid provision follows a logic of appropriateness, rather than a logic of consequences (Finnemore and Sikkink 2001). Donors need not be self-interested. They need only to have pro-democracy convictions, and to be sufficiently motivated by these to make aid available. The adage that democracy is the worst form of government except for all the others carries more than an implicature that democracy is not perfect. Indeed, it may frequently disappoint (Shapiro and Hacker-Cordón 1999: 1–4). Yet true believers in democracy can still be found and tend to regard attempts to spread democratic values as benevolent and virtuous, rather than imperialistic. For them, democracy promotion is not just smart politics, but 'the right thing to do'. This line of thinking is perhaps most evident in the justification for democracy promotion offered by the European Parliament: 'Democracy remains the only system of governance in which people can fully realise their human rights, and is a determining factor for development and long-term stability' (European Union 2019).

What democracy promotion does

So, what do democracy promoters do? Most political aid concentrates on four programmatic areas: electoral assistance, especially international monitoring and technical support; fostering competition through party-building; fighting corruption, strengthening accountability and promoting due process in political institutions; and the encouragement of civic participation and grassroots advocacy in civil society.

Electoral assistance

As we've noted elsewhere, elections are an essential, inescapable aspect of democracy. For this reason, it should come as no surprise that electoral assistance features prominently among international democracy aid programming types. Of course, many non-democracies hold elections too. To provide support for genuine and sustainable democracies, such contests must be open, free and fair. International electoral assistance is therefore designed with these ideals uppermost in the mind.

Aid to support elections usually fits into one of the following categories:

- institutional design (i.e. provision of legal and technical assistance to support creation of policy and implementation frameworks that govern electoral processes);
- Establishment and training of oversight bodies and their professional staff;
- get-out-the-vote activities, including assistance to create and maintain a register of voters, as well as voter education initiatives and the raising of popular consciousness of the importance and role of elections;
- cash and supplies to facilitate the physical conduct of elections (i.e. printing ballots, providing boxes and screens to protect voter privacy, paying election workers);
- provision of international observers to monitor and assess the veracity of electoral activities and their outcomes.

Additionally, some donors classify financial and technical support to social actors such as political parties, civil society organizations and journalists as electoral support, since these actors may all participate in and uphold the integrity of the voting process.

The relatively wealthy governments of developed countries in the Global North provide the overwhelming bulk of electoral aid in the world, either through state development agencies, diplomatic ministries or, occasionally, the outreach efforts of their own electoral commissions. For example, Elections Canada, the federal government body that oversees national elections in Canada, regularly cooperates with its counterparts in other countries, a role which is enshrined in law through the Canada Elections Act of 2000. Its mission 'is to strengthen the independence, impartiality, integrity, transparency and professionalism of electoral management both abroad and in Canada to ensure the conduct of free, fair and inclusive election processes' (Elections Canada 2020). This goal is met through a variety of efforts to share and exchange knowledge of effective electoral management practices by: responding to enquiries from foreign electoral authorities; hosting international delegations participating in multilateral and regional fora, such as the Commonwealth Electoral Network (CEN), the Réseau des compétences électorales francophones (RECEF), the Four Countries Partnership (which includes Australia, Canada, Great Britain and New Zealand) and networks of election authorities in the Americas and Europe; and participating in the ACE Electoral Knowledge Network, the world's largest online repository of electoral knowledge.

Among bilateral donors, USAID is by far the largest. However, multilateral agencies play a critical role in the support of elections too, with the UN Development Programme

(UNDP) and EU providing the most. One study conducted in 2008 found that these three donors were consistently the largest overall (Perlin et al. 2008: 44). More recently, the UN has established the Electoral Assistance Division (EAD) of its Department of Political and Peacebuilding Affairs, which supported over seventy electoral missions in some fifty UN member states in 2019, its first year of operation. Among the activities funded by the UN body are professional training programmes for staff in regional and subregional bodies, strengthening the role of the media in reporting elections and monitoring to ensure orderly voting procedures and the prevention of 'electoral violence'. In collaboration with the UNDP, UN Country Teams and UN Women, these efforts have also sought greater inclusion of women in electoral administration and oversight roles, particularly in El Salvador and Guinea-Bissau and throughout the Arab world. With planned expenditure of US$135 million to support electoral projects over the 2020–2 period, the EAD identifies the deployment of up to eighty missions in fifty member states as a key priority, along with the establishment of new peacebuilding partnerships, convening a forum for officials with the Organisation of Islamic Cooperation on good electoral practices, and training for member states of the Association of Southeast Asian Nations (ASEAN) and the Pacific Islands Forum (United Nations 2017).

For the EU, support for elections internationally goes hand in hand with its commitment to human rights. It boasts both an elaborate policy framework derived from the Universal Declaration of Human Rights and, since 2015, a 2030 Agenda for Sustainable Development, goal 16 of which outlines the importance of accountable institutions and participatory decision-making. Incentives – also termed 'conditionalities' by the international development community – have historically been a key part of the EU's toolkit, and observation missions a mechanism of enforcement. As the only democratically elected body within the EU, the European Parliament takes an active role in monitoring activities (European Union 2019).

As this discussion suggests, international observation and monitoring is probably the most thoroughly studied of all aspects of electoral assistance. Not only has the topic received much attention from the scholarly and policy communities, but consultants who work on behalf of donor governments and multilateral organizations submit post-election reports on their in-country experiences. These are then published, making information concerning successes, failures or irregularities broadly available. As a result, a great deal of information is available concerning the strengths and vulnerabilities of electoral aid programming.

One upshot of the international donor community's focus on monitoring has been a concerted effort to develop a set of common standards and codes of conduct for election observers. Both have achieved broad support within international agencies and practitioner communities, with a view to building consensus around precisely what 'free and fair' means. Adopted in 2005, the Declaration of Principles for International Election Observation and the Code of Conduct for International Election Observers have been ratified by interstate bodies including the UN, the African Union, the European Commission, the Organization of American States (OAS), the Commonwealth Secretariat and the Pacific Islands Forum, as well as a range of non-profit, NGO and quasi-governmental entities engaged in monitoring, such as the Carter Center, Inter-Parliamentary Union, International Republican Institute, National Democratic Institute, Electoral Institute of Southern Africa, International IDEA and Center for Electoral Promotion and Assistance.[1] While the Principles are too many and too long to be quoted verbatim, they stress that voting is a human right, elections are an expression of national sovereignty and that observer missions must be impartial.

---

[1]The full text of the Principles can be found at https://www.osce.org/files/f/documents/4/1/16935.pdf, 27 October, 2005. Accessed 16 June 2020.

However, the extensive literature on electoral assistance outlines a range of challenges and critiques as well. Here, we describe three of the most common. First, democracy is more than elections. One cannot have democracy without elections, but one can have elections without democracy. Elections support transitions to democracy, and its consolidation, only when and where they reflect stewardship for the values of accountability, transparency, participation and competition. Thus, to rush into elections in places where democratic values are weak or poorly recognized, or on the assumption that democracy-supporting values will necessarily follow the act of voting, may be folly. For this reason, many donors have chosen to diversify modes of democracy promotion, so as to balance electoral support in the short-to-medium term with longer-term initiatives to create a 'democratic culture'.

A related problem concerns bureaucratic inertia in the process of monitoring electoral integrity. Carothers, for example, describes the tendency for observing elections to get put on 'autopilot' when monitors rely too heavily on a menu of prescriptive options or checklists of evaluation criteria (Carothers 2015: 64). Others have likewise noted that too often such interventions 'become tame through an emphasis on routine technical exercises' (Bush 2015, as cited in Uberti and Jackson 2018). The risk is that when electoral support becomes too standardized and familiar, it creates opportunities for corrupt practices to creep in, perhaps even undetected.

An excessively formulaic approach to electoral aid can introduce other hazards as well, namely an inappropriate application of idealistic 'principles' to situations or contexts where they do not fit well, leading to inaccurate reporting of electoral processes and the pre- and post-electoral dynamics at work in a recipient country. In turn, incomplete or misreported in-country experiences may lead to a sense within donor countries that electoral aid chases unrealistic aims. While professionalization and training activities for observers are ongoing and are increasingly sophisticated, a lack of familiarity with local contexts – and local languages – remains a particular pitfall for electoral aid practice.

Finally, international observer missions tend to be expensive for donors, who must pay for observer salaries, travel costs and accommodation, security measures and sundry other overheads. These costs get even steeper when one considers that often they must be spent anew for each mission in each place – that is, unless multiple elections are held in quick succession. Politicians, diplomats and other policy professionals must consider these costs alongside what can be achieved through observer missions and may come away sceptical of the value of their programmes.

Political party development

Political parties serve the goal of democratic development in a variety of ways. As the prime vehicle by which social interests seek and attain public office, they form a crucial link between citizens and government. As one classical political science text put it, 'political parties created democracy, and modern democracy without parties is inconceivable' (Schattschneider 1942: 1).

However, as with elections, political parties are a common feature of non-democracies. Many countries, particularly those whose political systems developed from the Marxist-Leninist tradition, have *ruling* or *hegemonic* parties. The Communist Party of China (CCP) is one such example, but ruling parties have existed in non-communist states as well. Still other states have had *ruling coalitions* or parties that have dominated politics at the exclusion of opposition forces for very long periods. Examples include Malaysia's Barisan Nasional, which formed the country's government from independence in 1973 until 2018. The People's Action Party (PAP) has ruled Singapore without interruption since 1959. South Africa's National Party remained in power from 1948 until the collapse of the apartheid regime in 1994. Even Japan's Liberal Democratic Party (LDP) has governed almost continuously since 1955, with only brief interruptions occurring from 1993 to 1994, and again from 2009 to 2012.

How, then, is one to tell political parties that enhance democracy from those designed to forestall it? Are the above examples of sustained popularity, or exceptional electoral luck? Or is there something about the institutional environments in which these parties operate that accounts for their good fortune? Because non-democracies have parties too, international efforts at political party development include the creation of parties themselves but extend beyond this to address party systems – that is, the laws and policies that provide a framework for contesting public office.

From the standpoint of liberal theory, parties and party systems support democracy when:

- They ensure broad social representation, such that no element of society is consistently denied an opportunity to express political viewpoints. Representation may be upheld through the act of voting for a political party or by seeking office under party affiliation.
- They serve to aggregate interests among diverse groups within society. This forging of alliances among societal interest groups in turn works to deepen representation and tolerance and provide for more stable and

efficient governance. Accordingly, interest aggregation via omnibus parties is an especially important step in post-conflict situations or where societies show deep division along ethnic, religious, linguistic or cultural lines.

- They perform the function of educating the public. This may take the form of disbursing information over the importance of certain issues, laws or policies, but can also mean teaching liberal values such as tolerance, compromise and accommodation.
- They uphold the principle of accountability by fulfilling the role of opposition inside and outside legislatures, for instance by forming shadow governments or offering public critique of political elites. Accountability of elites may also occur at the intra-party level, such as when leadership conventions, primaries or votes of no confidence in party leaders are held.
- Through processes of outreach and engagement, they encourage citizen participation in public affairs.
- They operate in a manner that strengthens public confidence in political leaders and systems. In this sense, the building of citizens' faith in democratic institutions is the cumulative effect of all the other functions of parties. As noted in chapter four, public trust is critical to the longer-term survival of democratic systems and can be a serious impediment to their emergence in places where public trust in leaders and institutions is very low.

Though obviously important for democratic transition, research on support to political parties is sparser than that for electoral aid, and the volume of international support for this crucial area of work is also smaller. One estimate pegged party development at around 7 per cent of all democracy aid from major players (Carothers 2006: 86).

As with other areas of democracy assistance, governments of developed nations provide the bulk of party support, though interstate organizations like the UNDP and the OAS, and International IDEA, have increasingly done work in this area (Catón 2007; IDEA 2020). Key areas of focus for organizations engaged in party-building include:

1 Organizational aid to parties, to assist in professionalizing internal management structures and staff so that they can work more effectively (including and especially matters of internal party governance and finance). Initiatives in this area might also include a range of public

outreach activities designed to foster more inclusive representation. International IDEA, for instance, operates gender equity initiatives to get more women engaged in party politics (IDEA 2018).

2 Electoral aid (i.e. providing money or technical resources to help parties to contest elections). This can be especially important where multiparty elections have never been conducted, and thus the funding structures for opposition parties are limited or non-existent.

3 Governance aid – resources to help a party's capacity to legislate and work with other parties, agencies or branches of government. For example, the UNDP incorporates party-building into its Parliamentary Development Program, which focuses on strengthening and coordinating relations between parties, legislatures, executives and judiciaries.

4 Aid to party systems – 'modifications of the underlying legal and financial framework in which parties are anchored' intended to 'foster changes in all of the parties in a country at once' (Carothers 2006: 190).

Up-to-date estimates of the relative amounts spent on each of these activities are not readily available. However, it is generally expected that of these four areas, organizational aid to parties makes up the lion's share. One 2005 study pegged the figure at roughly 70 per cent of all funding for party development (Wersch and de Zeeuw 2005). As in other areas of democracy promotion, however, some of the above (such as governance aid) may be subsumed into other funding categories depending on the donor.

There is consensus that party and party system aid could benefit from greater awareness among donors of the local and national contexts in which these activities are carried out, as well as more refined tools for measuring their effectiveness (or the lack of it). Indeed, very few organizations publish systematic information on the nature and scale of party aid cross-nationally. This lack of information carries several consequences. One of these is that 'the recommendations they [donors and reporting bodies] offer draw heavily on those found throughout the broader democracy assistance literature, and are almost wholly tied to delivery approach, as opposed to issues of programming content, timing, sequencing, or sustainability' (Perlin et al. 2008: 39). This means that there is very little reliable information on whether party-building meets its objectives or not, and only a vague sense of how it factors into the overall results of democracy assistance programmes. Absent reliable information to the contrary, party-building is thus perceived as riskier by many donors, since aiding particular parties may be viewed as 'political' or even as 'tampering' in the elections of other states, which may carry serious diplomatic consequences.

Promoting the rule of law

The rule of law is more than existence of a formal legal code, known by and applied to all citizens. Were the existence of such a code the only standard, Germany under the Third Reich, China under the Han and Qin dynasties and present-day Philippines under Rodrigo Duterte would all qualify as having rule of law. Instead, each of these provides an example of *rule by law* – a classic instrument of dictatorial power, insidious not only for the harsh punishments imposed for rule-breaking, but for the air of legitimacy such actions acquire when done 'according to law'.

Where it supports democracy, the rule of law refers to placing restrictions on the arbitrary exercise of power by subjecting it to legally defined limits. Because authoritarian rulers may resist legal efforts to rein them in, rule of law development and in particular 'horizontal accountability' (i.e. checks and balances among branches of government to ensure none is disproportionately powerful), are likely to emerge at the post-transition phase of democratization and are necessary for democracy's long-term consolidation and proper function (O'Donnell 1996). To be sure, there are varying degrees and forms of self-restraint present in a wide assortment of states which have not reached consolidation, but these tend to be either exceptional instances that prove the rule, or designed specifically to create a veneer of accountability and thus head off pressure for more aggressive democratic reforms (Schedler, Diamond and Plattner 1999; Gilley 2010).

Deepening a democratic rule of law can entail international support for a dizzying assortment of institutions and tools. Here, we focus on three of the most common. First, rule of law support can help to establish neutral watchdog institutions such as ombudspeople or anti-corruption bureaus. By adhering to the principle of neutrality, such offices operate above the level of opposition political parties, whose critiques of power are more likely to be viewed as politically motivated (because ombudspeople's offices do not contest elections for state power, they are much less vulnerable to this sort of charge). The role of these bodies may be investigatory, aimed at bringing certain facts to light, a function which, though sensitive, may be especially important for countries transitioning from dictatorships with a history of human rights abuses or strict controls on access to information. By establishing politically neutral facts and correcting a national narrative about a dark past, 'truth commissions' (like those that have been held in places like Argentina, Sierra Leone and Cambodia) can provide a basis for a country to move on to a more stable democratic future. In situations where the facts of historic atrocity are interwoven with cultural, linguistic, religious or ethnic division, commissions may also be charged with the social reconciliation so vital to that same future. These were key objectives of the truth and reconciliation commissions in Rwanda and former Yugoslavia after the civil wars of the 1990s.

In other countries, including those with longer histories of social stability and democracy, politically neutral ombudspeople are important for safeguarding the effective functioning of government, establishing facts and holding elites to account, and therefore for maintaining the credibility and legitimacy of democratic institutions. In Westminster-style parliamentary democracies (like New Zealand or Canada) the role is sometimes fulfilled by a 'Royal Commission' or other type of public inquiry, whose neutrality is all the more important given that executive and legislative powers are fused in these systems rather than separated, as in presidential ones.

A second area of international support involves ensuring judicial autonomy and sufficient training for jurists to be able to apply the law evenly and impartially. The challenge is a complex one because, as Thorbjørn Jagland, secretary general of the Council of Europe writes,

> the judiciary is not immune to the environment in which it operates. In recent years, creeping populism and attempts to limit political freedoms among some member states have resulted in challenges to the judiciary's independence at home – and at the international level too. For example, we have seen draft legislation which allows political influence over appointments or disciplinary procedures, politically motivated changes to the composition of judicial self-governing bodies, and proposals to weaken the security of judges' tenure or empowering the executive to discretionally replace court presidents. We have also witnessed attempts to challenge the primacy of the Convention and to give national courts the power to over-rule judgments from the Court. We have also seen examples of member states refusing to implement Court judgments for political reasons.

(Council of Europe 2018)

If left unchecked, these kinds of practices threaten to undermine the rule of law and, therefore, the outlook for democracy too. There is, however, a pronounced lack of systematic research comparing efforts to improve judicial autonomy, and (ironically), collection and reporting of primary data from experience in the field is thin. Thus, there are few workable benchmarks for the performance of this aid type beyond broad agreement among donors that it matters.

A third type of aid focuses on support for press freedom, on the understanding that independent media are similarly important for holding powerful elites in check. From the standpoint of democratic theory, what distinguishes the media from the judiciaries and commissions of inquiry discussed above is that while the former two are state-based entities, the press is not, at least not in the same sense. This means that there is no specific requirement for the media outlets to be apolitical. Indeed, a central function of the media is providing a forum for free expression, which in turn means that neutrality need not be upheld so long as standards of journalistic ethics are followed. The difficulty arises when the state itself is a large (or perhaps the largest) player in the media field. What are we to make, for example, of the democracy-serving role of the British Broadcasting Corporation (BBC), or other widely trusted and respected forms of state media? How is its role different from that of China Central Television (CCTV), or similar state-owned media in non-democracies? The idea is that aid in this sector supports the prevention of information monopolies that could seriously undermine the tone or quality of public debate. This includes not only encouraging pluralism within the journalism sector but ensuring the independence of voices within that sector from unreasonably narrow political interests. For example, it would be highly problematic for UK democracy if the BBC were not independent from say, the Labour or Conservative Party. On the other hand, there is no problem with state-owned media in democratic regimes, provided control of the state itself is regularly up for grabs in an open, free and fair electoral competition.

Civil society-building

Most civil society-building projects focus on cultivation of the awareness, skills and values necessary for democracy's deepening and survival. Usually, these programmes justify themselves as an 'attempt to influence the cultural norms and expectations of public servants and citizens, thus encouraging bottom-up change within society through an emphasis on power and culture instead of laws and institutions' (Dahinden 2013). However, civil society-building can also involve development of the necessary legal and institutional framework within which groups of political actors can freely and successfully mobilize.

In practice, this means that most civil society programmes engage in the broadening of citizen engagement in public affairs through involvement in grassroots NGOs, the development of consultative fora that facilitate closer interaction between citizens and political leaders, the dissemination of information and knowledge development around particular policy matters and the practical know-how required for voting and the execution of other key aspects of democratic citizenship.

In chapter four, we explored the various ways in which civil society serves democracy at both the transition and consolidation phases of a regime change, and the ways in which it helps to protect the ongoing vitality of democracy in the years that follow. These do not need to be rehashed here. However, as with other areas of democracy promotion activity, it is very difficult to tell whether support for civil society accomplishes what it sets out to do, and how we would know if that were the case. Suppose that a donor government established funding to create a range of new NGOs intended to facilitate the broader participation of women in Zambian public life. Suppose that a target of twenty such NGOs was set, but that ultimately double that figure were established. Would we take the proliferation of NGOs as a reliable indicator that Zambian women were more able to participate in politics than before, or that this sector of civil society was twice as vibrant and democratic as it was projected to be?

Obviously not. The mere existence of new NGOs – a measurable *output* of democracy promotion programmes – is very different from an *outcome* (i.e. the issue of whether Zambian democracy is any healthier for it). One of the reasons may be a lack of self-sufficiency. What would happen to these new NGOs if foreign support dried up? Another problem may be one of credibility in the new foreign-funded organizations. Do they have sufficient buy-in from local political actors to operate within the targeted political system, or are they seen merely as puppets for foreign interests (McIntosh-Sundstrom 2006; Mendelson and Glenn 2002)? Crucially, is the operating environment conducive to the deepening of democracy-enhancing values this type of programming requires? Because growing numbers of NGOs does not mean a civil society or a democracy is emerging, donors face a need to recalibrate their expectations, and to take a relatively long-term view of values diffusion (Ottaway and Carothers 2000). Part of this effort may also involve a need to more effectively target democracy promotion activities at those actors and groups for whom the programmes will do the most good.

Conclusion: Does democracy promotion work (and how would we know)?

A central and long-standing debate in the field of democracy promotion is whether any of these initiatives, either individually or together, accomplish what they set out to do. It is very difficult to say whether any positive change in the number of worldwide democracies was attributable to the resources expended by democracy promoters. This problem has bred a certain malaise about democracy assistance, which after all, premised itself on encouraging democratic opening in authoritarian regimes. This was a core part of the working definition of democracy aid tabled at the outset of this chapter, yet it may never have been a reasonable goal for such programmes. Is it possible that democracy promotion may be a victim of its own lofty ambitions? If so, what, if anything, can be done about it?

As we've seen in this chapter, there are numerous challenges in measuring the success of democracy promotion. Part of the issue derives from contested definitions. For the sake of analytic clarity, we have provided some criteria for identifying democracy promotion when we see it. Yet there are many understandings of what democracy entails, and hence what the outcome of democracy promotion ought to look like and how particular funding schemes may serve that end (or not).

There is also a tendency on the part of some donors to conflate democracy and 'good governance', an equation that is ultimately unhelpful because it implies the democracies are, *ipso facto*, more effective, efficient, transparent and socially responsive than non-democracies. Many – perhaps most – do perform better on these measures than do authoritarian governments. Democracies are certainly more law-bound and more competitive, by and large. But it is not true of all democracies all of the time, and it is a mistake to presume that democracies inherently govern better simply *because* they are democratic. Some semi-authoritarian governments, such as Singapore's, are highly efficient and responsive, while some weak democracies, such as Zambia, fare relatively poorly. Again, this problem arises because measures of state capacity (i.e. how well a state governs) overlap with indicators of democratic progress, creating a kind of social scientific 'distortion' that clouds our ability to track genuine democratic progress.

These measurement difficulties are further compounded by the lack of any central or overarching clearinghouse for measuring democratic outcomes in a clear and consistent way. As mentioned previously, many tens of thousands of organizations and states engage in democracy promotion, and they do not necessarily use or publicly explicate the indicators of their success (or lack of it). This means that ultimately, success can mean whatever provider governments say it means, since they are the ones that must justify their budgets and are accountable to their own electorates.

Finally, democracy promotion may bear the reputational costs of a perceived decline in the quality of democracy within and among donor states. One might think that whatever their motivations, or whatever the difficulties of measuring democratic progress, states seeking to advance democracy abroad could and should lead by example. Yet as Thomas Carothers has noted, US democracy promotion receded considerably during the tenure of the forty-fifth President, Donald Trump. More than that, 'Trump repeatedly signalled a lack of interest in or concern about violations of democratic norms and rights in other countries, a strong disinclination to prioritize democracy support in U.S. foreign policy, and an admiration for repressive strongmen, from Russia's Vladimir Putin to Iraq's Saddam Hussein' (Carothers 2017), in addition to causing widely condemned damage to democratic processes in the United States. This kind of poor example-setting creates what Carothers calls 'top-down trouble' in democracy promotion and may only fuel views abroad that democracy is not worth adopting, since it is apparently valued so little by democratic leaders.

Questions for discussion

1 If foreign assistance were promoting democracy successfully, how would we know?
2 Is it hypocritical for countries to fund democracy promotion amid a perceived slip in the quality of their own democracies?
3 Can democracy be promoted using military means? Ought it be?
4 What are the differences between standard forms of development assistance and democracy promotion?
5 Are there important differences between promoting democracy and promoting 'good governance'?

Further reading

Anderson, Elizabeth S., 'Democracy: Instrumental vs. Non-Instrumental Value', in T. Christiano and J. P. Christman, eds, *Contemporary Debates in Political Philosophy*, 212–27 (Malden, MA: Wiley-Blackwell, 2009).

Bouchet, Nicolas, *Democracy Promotion as US Foreign Policy: Bill Clinton and Democratic Enlargement* (London and New York: Routledge, 2015).

Cox, Michael, G. John Ikenberry and Takashi Inoguchi, eds, *American Democracy Promotion: Impulses, Strategies, and Impacts* (Oxford: Oxford University Press, 2000).

Cox, Michael, Timothy J. Lynch and Nicolas Bouchet, eds, *US Foreign Policy and Democracy Promotion: From Theodore Roosevelt to Barack Obama* (London and New York: Routledge, 2013).

Graham, Gordon, 'Liberalism and Democracy', *Journal of Applied Philosophy*, Vol. 9, No. 2 (1992): 149–60.

Norris, Pippa, *Strengthening Electoral Integrity* (Cambridge: Cambridge University Press, 2017).

Peou, Sorpong, *International Democracy Assistance for Peacebuilding: Cambodia and Beyond* (New York: Palgrave Macmillan, 2007).

Wetzel, Ann, Jan Orbie and Fabienne Bossuyt, eds, *Comparative Perspectives on the Substance of EU Democracy Promotion* (London and New York: Routledge, 2017).

Youngs, Richard, ed., *The European Union and the Promotion of Democracy: Europe's Mediterranean and Asian Policies* (Oxford: Oxford University Press, 2003).

Youngs, Richard, ed., *The European Union and Democracy Promotion: A Critical Global Assessment* (Baltimore, MD: Johns Hopkins University Press, 2010).

9

After the 'end of history'?

The introductory chapter to this book commenced with an overview of a global trend towards democratization in the decades after the Second World War. During this period, processes of decolonization in Africa and Asia, the crumbling of military dictatorships in Latin America and the demise of communism in Europe all contributed to a worldwide increase in the number of countries that could be considered 'democracies'. Acceptance of democratic principles became a norm that nearly all states adopted, at least rhetorically. So great was the consensus for democracy that many plainly undemocratic countries attempted to pass themselves off as democratic or as having the basic institutional features of a democracy, in accordance with global standards and expectations. We discussed this phenomenon of 'democracy as a universal norm' in detail in chapter seven, noting that in some respects, it appears to have expanded beyond the state to encompass the international sphere. Many international bodies not originally designed with democratic principles in mind, but which are thought to be lacking in some aspect of participation, representation and inclusion, are sometimes said to have a 'democratic deficit' (Follesdal and Hix 2006; Moravcsik 2004; Crombez 2003). To what could this thinking be attributed if not to the widespread belief that democratic ideals are not just applicable but worth striving for in many different areas of human social organization?

However, much of the content of this book – and certainly many of the examples we provide from the early twenty-first century – call the democratic consensus into question, or at least suggest its superficiality. Whereas prominent authors of the 1990s hailed the global victory of democracy as the 'end of history' (i.e. the final phase of political development in which viable alternatives to democracy no longer existed), this book has detailed a number of challenges confronting democratic transitions and even the nature of consolidation in well-established places where democracy is usually thought be 'safe'. These include the proliferation of illiberal democracies, guerrilla movements, insurgencies, terrorist threats and, in some cases, a conscious effort by populist politicians to undermine the integrity of long-established democratic processes, among other factors. Thirty years removed from the triumphalism of the immediate post-communist 'Third Wave', modern democracy appears to have arrived at a time of pessimism, doubt and, indeed, peril.

With this final chapter, we ask whether there may be some workable alternatives, perhaps too far off on the horizon to be clearly envisioned or anticipated by previous generations of scholars. In doing so we call attention to two distinct categories of phenomena: alternatives *to* democracy – non-democratic types of political organization which at the time of this writing appear strong and stable, with a high degree of efficacy and popular approval – and alternatives *within* democracy, which highlight the dynamic nature of democratic institutions across time and space. Both categories suggest that debates about democracy's utility and superiority are far from over.

One of the key issues dealt with in this concluding chapter concerns just how far the pursuit of institutional alternatives can go before the line demarcating democracy from non-democracy is crossed. Often, alternatives are envisioned as a way to improve a democracy's functionality and efficiency, or to remedy some inequity or gap in representation. As we saw in chapter three, careful constitutional engineering can serve as an important means of mitigating violence, protecting group rights or ensuring communal autonomy, for example (Gagnon and Keating 2012). If democracies can be more fairly and effectively governed by granting regional autonomy, or by creating specialized electoral rules, there is nothing at all wrong with exploring these options, since, as we have seen, democracies already vary greatly in their forms and function.

But what if more radical changes were to be considered, such as doing away with popular elections altogether? Proponents might reasonably consider this proposal as a concession to practicality. After all, elections are expensive and time-consuming. Many citizens are either poorly informed about policy issues or candidates, or opt out of voting altogether. 'Surely there must be a better way?' supporters of innovation might say. If there were some other methods of enabling people to choose their leaders, what would be the harm in giving it a try? Could we remain true to the principles that sustain a democracy while exploring ways to make it better, on the understanding that even consolidated democracies have room to improve?

On the other hand, those who view voting as their birthright and a personal contribution to communal wellbeing may chafe against the change, viewing efforts to explore or adopt alternative mechanisms as a regression away from purer, more open and participatory forms of democracy. Democracy may be more than elections, but electoralism is still a defining characteristic of democracies. If one did away with popular elections, costly and inefficient as they may be, what sort of democracy would one be left with? Could it be called a democracy at all? UK sociologist and political scientist Colin Crouch has written of 'post-democracy', in which a desire to experiment is encouraged by the many seemingly preferable non-democratic options and widespread disaffection with the way democracies work. The risk, he argues, is the further hollowing out of democracies. In his words,

> A post-democratic society ... is one that continues to have and to use all the institutions of democracy, but in which they increasingly become a formal shell. The energy and innovative drive pass away from the democratic arena and into small circles of a politico-economic elite.
>
> (Crouch 2013; see also Crouch 2004)

In other words, a state of post-democracy may risk strengthening or multiplying the number of illiberal democracies worldwide.

Our purpose here is not to assess the sincerity or intentions underpinning attempts at systematic improvement, or to brand any particular proposal for doing so as decadence or progress. Rather, our purpose is simply to highlight how debates about democracy's efficacy are unsettled, as are questions about the extent of its malleability. Thus, the core conundrum with which we must grapple is just how far interpretations of democracy can stretch and how much innovation can be realized while still usefully differentiating democracies from non-democracies. If the concept of democracy is too elastic, it loses all meaning – anything and everything could qualify as democratic. To avoid watering down democracy beyond recognition, its defining benchmarks need to be applied consistently, even as the tools and methods for achieving those standards are prone to shift.

We begin below with the premise that envisioning new forms of democracy is nothing new at all. Indeed, many of the traits now commonly associated with democracy are relatively recent innovations, perhaps stemming from changing social conditions over just the last few decades. The remainder of the chapter is then split into two parts, one for democratic alternatives (which are designed to improve upon existing models of democracy in some way) and one for alternatives to democracy (which deny liberal democratic supremacy and pose themselves as better options). Our focus in the first of these sections is on two mechanisms: digital democracy and sortition. While these are hardly the only ongoing efforts to alter the democratic character, they are two of the most commonly debated. We examine their meaning, strengths and drawbacks in turn.

The last portion of the chapter is not a rehashing of all the various forms of non-democracy in existence today. This book has given many detailed examples of these already, including absolutist monarchies (Eswatini, Saudi Arabia), still-surviving Lenin-inspired party states (Cuba, Vietnam) and military dictatorships (Mali, Myanmar). Instead, the space is devoted to exploring the so-called 'China Challenge'. Unlike the late twentieth century, when liberal democracy appeared to be the last ideology standing and the United States the only remaining superpower, the world today is once again characterized by bipolarity. This time, it is China that is the chief rival to the United States, and which presents the most striking alternative to the democratic consensus. The twist, as we note, is that China nevertheless characterizes its political model as a 'democratic' one, different from the version practised in the United States and, to some, superior to it as well. Because the Chinese system operates with a seemingly high level of popular approval, and because China is rising while US-style democracy appears to be on the decline, the Chinese way of politics is sometimes interpreted as a threat to the liberal democratic order, not just an alternative to it.

Finally, because the implications of China's rise, post-democracy and the frontiers of institutional experimentation are all relatively new and ongoing areas of research, our word on them cannot and will not be the final one. Conclusions are meant to say something conclusive, but ours provides a round-up of challenges and changes which suggest that the future of democratization is open-ended.

The concept of democracy: A moving target

One of the consistent and recurring messages of this book has been that democracy is not static but varies widely. It is fairly common for democracy to be characterized as emerging from a specific cultural context, or to hear the modern liberal variant referred to as 'Western' democracy, even though it has been widely adopted in places that unquestionably fall outside what could be called 'Western'. The modular nature of democracy applies not just in a geo-spatial sense, but over time too.

Forms of government called 'democracy' may have originated in Greece some 2,600 years ago, but the ancient Athenians might have trouble recognizing the versions of democracy practised today. To be sure, the Athenian system exhibited aspects of what we now call 'procedural minimums' – laws were debated and decided upon by an assembly of citizens, with membership in the assembly being chosen by a vote, and staff of some key government positions were chosen at random from a pool of qualified citizens. However, that pool was quite shallow, because Athens adhered to a very different understanding of citizenship from today and did not enumerate the individual rights now associated with democratic citizenship. Instead, citizenship was conferred by the ability to take part in military campaigns, and thus was restricted to adult men who had completed the requisite training, perhaps just 10 per cent of the total population of Athens at the time (Lape 2009). Completion of this training in adolescence both required and reinforced a strong social standing, such that citizenship became hereditary and restricted to those of (preferably legitimate) Athenian parentage. Slaves (including those previously freed), women, foreigners and those below the age of military service were not considered citizens and were therefore not permitted to take part (Rhodes 2017).

As the first of its kind, Athenian democracy was not designed to contend with the challenges faced by later democratic models. For one thing, it pre-dated the nation-state by nearly two millennia. The ancient world was also far less integrated than today's. Athenians were certainly aware of their neighbours, trading and occasionally warring with them, but Greek city-states did not face the same questions of sovereignty that internationally connected modern states do, and, being less geographically diffuse, did not have to govern over populations of the same social complexity across the vast swathes of territory that most nation-states now occupy. Additionally, markets did not exist for the Athenians in the sense that we now know them – compatibility with capitalism was a question that would not be countenanced anywhere for many more centuries. In order for later democracies to survive and thrive in the conditions of their day, the received understanding of democracy itself had to adapt.

Democracies of the industrial age developed and practised different understandings of the concept, related to but obviously distinct from those of prior eras, and better suited to meeting their needs. It may be tempting to view these changes as progressive by the standards of their time, but the democratic concept employed in nineteenth century US or the UK, like wise proved dynamic and seems very crude indeed by any contemporary measure.

In Victorian Britain, the scope of eligibility to cast votes or run for office was heavily proscribed, and electoral integrity was highly suspect. Before the 1830s, the British electorate was tiny. In the 1780s, the total number of legal voters was thought to be about 214,000, just 3 per cent of the total population (UK National Archives n.d.). The system for allocating seats to population centres was also lopsided. The UK National Archives recount that large industrial centres like Birmingham, Leeds and Manchester had no members of Parliament between them, while the 'rotten boroughs' (those with few or no eligible voters), mostly in London, had more than their share. Reforms began in 1832, with passage of new measures approved by then-Prime Minister, Lord Grey, to 'prevent the necessity of revolution' (ibid.). These extended voting rights to men who owned property with a value of not less than £10 per year, which effectively meant that most were still precluded from participating. By 1885, the total number of voters had risen to just below 8 million. However, it would be another thirty-three years before any women got the right to vote. Legislation adopted in 1872 also sought to crack down on corruption, but it remained commonplace in the voting process. According to the UK Parliament,

> Treating, bribery, influencing and intimidating were commonplace practices well into the late 19th century, with candidates often attempting to influence voters through alcohol, food, indirect payments and employment arrangements. Due to the lack of a secret ballot, voters could be dismissed from employment or evicted from housing if they were known to have voted the wrong way.
>
> (UK Parliament n.d.)

This example illustrates that the definition of democracy and of democratic citizenship now practised in the UK are fairly recent developments, and hard-won and contentious ones at that. Indeed, the process of extending the franchise in Britain – that is, rethinking the nature and scope of political representation – was halting, with many of its more notable supporters espousing reforms that appear repugnant by modern standards. John Stuart Mill, who is best known for his philosophical writings and served as a Member of Parliament for the City of Westminster from 1865 to 1868, was a staunch advocate for extending the franchise but wrote of practical limits on both rights and the suitability of expanded participation under democracy, notably favouring weighted voting (i.e. assigning greater value to the votes of some than others), perhaps as a means to introduce votes for women without appearing too radical. While he supported the extension of working-class suffrage, he also felt that there were those too lacking in education, drive or discipline to be given responsibility in collective decision-making. Until the skills needed for the effective representation of interests could be developed, technocracy (i.e. rule by a skilled elite for the common good) was preferable to democracy, for Mill (1861: 479–81, 415–18).

If those who stood against changing the nineteenth-century status quo had difficulty envisioning voting rights for women or unpropertied men, and even strong supporters favoured extending democratic rights only in increments, how might they conceive of modern Britain, where elections are open to all adults over eighteen years of age regardless of wealth, status or education? Would they recognize contemporary democratic institutions as descended from those they knew?

One further example might be US politics in the era of the Jim Crow laws. These were state and local ordinances that perpetuated the historical disenfranchisement of Blacks across the former Confederacy through a system of institutionalized racial separation. What is especially interesting about this system, which first came into being shortly after the American Civil War, is that it remained in place for a century without the implications for democratic participation, which seem obvious in hindsight, being officially examined or altered at a national level. Indeed, the Jim Crow laws acquired a stamp of legitimacy in 1896, when the Supreme Court upheld as constitutional the position of 'separate but equal' that in principle made Black citizens equal with whites before the law but precluded their mixing when accessing public services such as schools, mass transit, restrooms or drinking fountains. In some places, mixing in spaces such as restaurants or cafes was illegal as well. Because dedicated services for Blacks in the United States were either non-existent or under-resourced and therefore not of the same standard as those for whites, the Jim Crow laws effectively institutionalized racial inequality in the southern United States. Because polling stations were subject to segregation laws too, this meant that the laws were also directly responsible for the suppression of Black voters. Black citizens often had little recourse, since segregation was supported by large segments of white America, in some cases enforced by white supremacist politicians and organizations like the Ku Klux Klan.

By the mid-twentieth century, the growing power of the civil rights movement began to bear fruit. The landmark Brown v. Board of Education of Topeka, 347 U.S. 48, case of 1954 meant Blacks and whites could be educated in the same classrooms, though in practice it would be many years before most schools desegregated. The Twenty-fourth Amendment, ratified in 1964, ostensibly outlawed the poll taxes that had long excluded Black voters. Substantial disenfranchisement remained, however, and prompted the famous march led by Martin Luther King Jr, Rosa Parks and John Lewis from Selma to Montgomery the following year, an event that was televised and shared with the wider world together with footage of Alabama state troopers beating peaceful demonstrators. A key turning point for civil rights in the United States, President Lyndon B. Johnson signed the Voting Rights Act into law soon after.

How is this relevant to our concern for innovation in democratic models? All of what has just been described took place long after Abraham Lincoln waged a bloody civil war to ensure, as he told those assembled at Gettysburg in 1863, 'that government of the people, by the people and for the people should not perish from the earth'. The struggle for the franchise was still being waged decades after the United States fought the First World War to 'make the world safe for democracy', and later defended democracy against fascism in Europe. Not only that, but there is much evidence to suggest that ideas about democratic citizenship in the United States continue to evolve and experience major challenges. In June 2013, the Supreme Court repealed Section IV of the 1965 Voting Rights Act. According to the Library of Congress, the Section 'provided special protections for voters in states in the South with a history of violations' (Library of Congress n.d.). The National Low Income Housing Coalition, a non-profit based in Washington DC, argues that 'voter suppression is an unfortunate but consistent feature of the US political system', adding that since the 2013 Supreme Court ruling, '25 states have created new obstacles to vote', such as restricted registration, unequitable voter identification laws and cutting voting times (National Low Income Housing Coalition 2020).

This excursus on Athenian, British and American politics shows that conceptions of democracy are not very stable. Not only have democratic practices changed over time, but so have the values that underpin democracy and the rights and meanings associated with democratic citizenship. Historically, democracy has captured the prevailing social mood and mores of given times and places, while shifting as necessary in response to changing structural conditions and outside pressures. Even in the countries that have been consolidated the longest, democracy only recently came to mean what it means.

Perhaps this is as it should be. What if no one had ever taken it on themselves to alter the meaning of democratic citizenship as practised in Athens? What if no one had innovated British democracy, albeit incrementally, to enable women to participate in public life? What if the civil rights movement had not pushed forward the frontiers of the franchise in the United States? And what if no one took it upon themselves to address continuing gaps in rights, citizenship and participation?

Given what we know about the modularity of the democratic concept over time, would it be a mistake to think that democracy was done evolving? Why would we expect that democracy as known and practised today was done evolving new forms, and that the conceptions of democracy prominent worldwide in the late twentieth century were the final stage of human political development?

What happens after 'the end of history'?

Alternative institutions: Democracy reimagined

For our purposes, perspectives on democratic futures are sorted into two parts. In this first part, we examine some methods of expanding and thus preserving democracy. In the next, we consider efforts to displace it. We emphasize two main institutional alternatives to the way in which most democracies currently operate: sortition and e-democracy.

Sortition

Sortition is a mechanism by which public officials are chosen through random selection, rather than the standard democratic method of filling posts using elections. A variety of historical examples exist, with the most notable being Athenian democracy, where public positions were granted partly by lottery. Even though eligibility was limited to men of a certain age and social standing, equality among those qualified to serve was considered sacrosanct in ancient Greece, and sortition a fairer and more equal way to make appointments than voting. As Aristotle wrote, '... Democrats, on the

grounds that they are all equal, claim equal participation in everything …
it is accepted as democratic when public offices are allocated by lot; and as
oligarchic when they are filled by election' (*Politics*, 4, pp. 1294, 1301).

Probably the most common use of sortition mechanisms today takes place
in countries having common law traditions, where trial by jury is a standard
tool used in criminal or civil proceedings. Usually, a panel is selected from
a pool of qualified citizens identified at random and sent a summons
or notification stating a place and time where they are to report for jury
service. Qualifications typically centre on eligibility to vote and whether or
not one has a criminal record, or is a police officer, judge, member of prison
management or security staff, employee of a government agency involved
in law enforcement or other occupation that may raise conflict-of-interest
concerns. It is important to remember that sortition describes only the
initial phase of identifying and contacting qualified persons to *potentially*
serve on a jury through random selection. The process of setting the panel
itself is separate, presided over by a judge, with assistance from legal counsel
as required, to provide an extra layer of screening to ensure the legal process
is as fair as possible, though in practice most of the eligible population of
potential jurors are not actually chosen to serve.

Besides juries, sortition-like systems have sometimes been used to fill
other public roles too. For example, while technology has made the draft a
thing of the past in many countries, military conscription was historically
used to fill ranks in times of need. As with jury service, serving one's country
in the military has often been considered an obligation of eligible citizens,
and dereliction of duty an offence. In the 1960s and early 1970s, many young
American men burned their draft cards or fled to avoid being sent to fight in
Vietnam and were pursued by US authorities abroad as 'draft dodgers'.

What if other public service roles were chosen by lottery? Would such a
thing be practical? How, or under what conditions? What kinds of roles, and
in what kinds of political environments might sortition be best used?

Because the Athenians practised a type of direct democracy, one
might think that modern-day sortition is most readily suited to direct
governance situations in municipalities rather than whole nation-states.
Such local applications might include, for example, citizen's committees
or advisory bodies where members are chosen randomly and may serve
as a complement to elected bodies. In October 2021, a permanent citizens'
assembly was created for the city of Paris to consult on and challenge public
policy decisions. The 100-member body, drawn by lot, was created using
two selection rounds. The first, held in August 2021, preselected a pool of

5,000 citizens, of which about 700 responded positively. A second round then winnowed the pool to 100 members based on four criteria – geography, socio-economic bracket, age and gender – to ensure representativeness. The initiative was billed as a 'world first on the scale of a city of 2 million inhabitants' (Greco 2021). A variation on this process was used previously in the 2014 selection of the Grandview-Woodlands Citizens' Assembly in Vancouver, Canada. In that case, notification letters were distributed to approximately 19,000 area residents to fill the 48-seat Assembly, though the pool was subsequently narrowed to only those who responded to the initial invitation. The city of Gdansk, Poland, has chosen three citizens' assemblies by random selection since 2016.

All of these cases contain elements of what is known as 'deliberative democracy', which entails close consultation and consideration of public affairs matters by qualified, committed and informed lay citizens (Fishkin 2009; Fishkin and Luskin 2005). The chief advantage of this type of participation is that it lends greater legitimacy to political decisions by enabling citizens themselves to gather for informed debate, instead of merely voting on the platforms of others. Sometimes, public consultation takes place by means of a questionnaire distributed to prospective respondents. These 'deliberative polls' replicate the logic of standard surveys but differ in that they give participants a chance to reflect on their position by polling them before and after they have had a chance to deliberate. Though these are not usually given as examples of sortition, they are an example of citizen participation taking place through random but representative sampling (Fishkin 2003). They also illustrate that there are many distinct participatory models and formulas to be found under the wider category of democratic innovation, some of which may overlap or borrow from each other in various ways, to greater and lesser degrees (Chwalisz 2020).

There are also examples of assemblies composed by sortition being used at higher levels of government. In 2019, the Parliament in Ostbelgian (a collection of German-speaking municipalities in Wallonia, Belgium) voted to establish a new citizens' council to serve alongside Parliament itself. The council's 24-member roster is to be chosen using a civic lottery and will be replaced in its entirety at intervals of six months. Within just a few years, it is anticipated all qualified residents will have received an invitation to participate, providing the kind of close consultation envisaged by deliberative democracy, broadly representative of the Ostbelgian population but chosen at random (Chwalisz 2019). Though the council has an agenda-setting role, it works with the Parliament and is not intended a replacement for it. Since

2020, the Local Government Act of the Australian state of Victoria has mandated that local councils use 'deliberative engagement practices' when developing council and financial plans, with many of the deliberative panels having been chosen by random selection (Sortition Foundation 2021).

It is notable that the uses of sortition described so far are all recent examples, and that further-reaching applications have been suggested but remain at the proposal stage as of this book's writing. One of the more interesting proposals has been to use random selection to fill positions in the upper chambers of bicameral legislatures (Abizadeh 2021; Gastil and Wright 2019). In Canada, appointments to the Senate are made by the Prime Minister and are lifetime positions. They are not elected, as in the United States. The public has no direct input in the selection of senators, nor any electoral means of removing them. Choosing senators from among a pool of eligible Canadian citizens, and rotating the entire roster at regular intervals might go a long way to legitimizing a body which is often argued to be in need of reform by making it more participatory and representative. Similar ideas have also been tabled for reform in the UK. One proposal suggesting members of the House of Lords be chosen by sortition was put to a Royal Commission on the matter in 1999. Other advocates for sortition are more radical still. Australian philosopher John Burnheim argues that a statistically representative sample of citizens could consider and decide on public policies, leading to the restructuring or obsolescence of the state (2006).

Those in favour of sortition make a number of claims for its efficacy. First, as is implied by the discussion above, sortition may be more representative and egalitarian than electoral methods. Random selection sees to it that no particular gender, age, income level, ethnicity, religion or language group is disproportionately powerful or unpowerful. Because all qualified persons are given an equal chance to participate, sortition can help to overcome the demographic imbalances common to many elected bodies. Second, it has been argued that sortition lends itself to greater 'cognitive diversity' in governing bodies, producing a healthy amalgam or cross-section of interests capable of governing more effectively than an elite cohort (Landemore 2013). A third argument is that sortition processes may be less vulnerable to corruption than voting. In particular, sortition has the potential to dramatically reduce the influence of money in shaping electoral outcomes, and overcome the problems created by campaign finance regulations (or a lack of them). Fourth, the egalitarian nature of sortition is thought to be able to reduce factionalism in politics. Giving all qualified people an equal chance to participate could reduce excessive partisanship, a key political problem in the United States and many other democracies (Graham and Svolik 2020; Abramowitz and McCoy 2018). Indeed, a sortition-based system could ultimately negate the need for political parties altogether, allowing those selected to make legislation according to their conscience rather than their affiliation. Free from the electoral incentives of career politicians, ordinary citizens replaced at regular intervals may be empowered to provide input in the public interest. In smaller-scale settings especially, where assemblies comprise those who live and work locally, that empowerment may be enhanced by a sense of greater personal investment in making policies with direct impact.

Sortition has its detractors as well. One line of critique is that random selection opens the door to incompetence and mismanagement because there is no means of screening those who would serve for any special qualifications or skills that might make them effective policy-makers. 'Having good ideas' is not among the qualification criteria used to select citizens – the point of sortition is that everyone gets a fair chance at having their ideas heard. Electoral systems produce incompetence too, of course, but voting enables the public to judge a candidate's fitness for office, to reject those it deems unsuitable, or at least to express a preference for others.

A second problem concerns accountability. If all citizens were given an equal chance for public service, and participation by anyone was not permanent but subject to rotation, then one could simply 'put in one's time' before the position shifted to the next randomly chosen citizen, without much performance pressure. Elections, held at regular and predictable intervals, repeatedly subject the job performance of officials to voters' will, and provide an opportunity for their removal. In many places, elected officials may be subject to recall if the public is unhappy with their job performance. Not only are there no such mechanisms in sortition systems, but these would make little sense, since returning to affirm the public's desire for someone to continue in office could interfere with others' equal opportunity to serve.

Finally, sortition is controversial because it fundamentally changes the nature of contestation, representation and participation. In this book, we have flagged these as core characteristics of democracies and marks that distinguish authentically democratic regimes from mere pretenders (Coppedge, Alvarez and Maldonado 2008). Throughout democracy's relatively recent history, wider representation and higher levels of participation are imagined to be good things – that is, the quality of democracy is thought to be better where levels of representation and participation are higher. In the examples of the

United States and the UK raised in the last section, activists fought long and hard to see participation and representation expanded because they saw both as worthy democratic goals worth striving and sacrificing for. No one could claim the quality of British or American democracy was higher when such large portions of the public were unable to make their voices heard, or when one segment of the population was legally considered to have the value of 'three fifths of all other persons', as was agreed at the US Constitutional Convention in 1787. Known as the 'three-fifths compromise', this was the formula agreed by representatives of the northern and southern states when determining the relative weight of slave populations for purposes of direct taxation and apportioning seats in the US House of Representatives.

Sortition may level the political playing field by giving all those qualified a chance to have input in policy-making, but, were it to replace elections, would also end a key means of obtaining the public's consent. Lacking a popular mandate, policies made by those chosen at random may be seen as less legitimate or authoritative. Replacing elections with sortition could choke off a key avenue for representation and thus restrict opposition viewpoints. Citizens would effectively be swapping out their ability to register opinions regularly at the ballot box with the prospect that someday they too may have their turn at making public policy. Limiting the role and impact of citizen voices, including healthy and valuable opposition voices, could seem a risky proposition even if it did produce more efficient and deliberative governance, given the protracted struggle to expand the franchise over time. What appears to be more inclusive from one standpoint seems exclusive, even regressive, from another. Thus, a hybrid model that combines electoral competition with citizen assemblies chosen by lot achieves a reasonable balance of democratic goals.

E-democracy

This discussion of institutional innovation implies a strong role for technology. E-democracy, or 'digital democracy', is the application of digital communication technologies – especially the internet – to democratic practice in order to expand participation and improve policy-making (Boehlen et al. 2005; Schapals, Bruns and McNair 2018; Hacker and van Dijk 2000). Such applications may take a variety of forms. For example, allowing voters to cast ballots online, in addition to the conventional 'pen and paper' option, might lower the costs of voting for some and therefore provide added incentive for participation in the electoral process. Yet e-democracy can influence participation in other ways too, and is about more than the availability of technology itself. The dissemination of information by candidates, the receipt and interpretation of that information by likely voters and the ensuing free and open discussion on social media platforms are also examples of digital democracy. In other words, e-democracy can be procedural, but has a discursive, deliberative character as well.

E-democracy supporters make a range of arguments in its favour. One of these is that it is efficient. Digital technologies allow for information to be transmitted to large numbers of citizens more quickly and cheaply than in the past. Consider the example of citizens' assemblies or deliberative polls as described in the last section. In these cases, organizers could notify thousands of potential participants of their eligibility within seconds using email, and without the cost of postage. The interactive nature of the internet also makes it possible to network in ways not possible in the pre-internet days of television and radio, meaning it's easier to coordinate replies and allocate resources. Likewise, candidates for office can now 'tweet' their positions to millions of followers instantaneously, instead of addressing crowds from atop a tree stump in their town square like the office seekers of yesteryear. Because democracy requires an informed citizenry, the efficiency of digital democracy is a blessing to both state actors and citizens alike. The former are concerned with the best way to put their message before the voting public, while the latter seek the quickest and most reliable means to gain information to evaluate the policy proposals on offer.

By lowering the costs of political participation, digital democracy may encourage more citizens to engage in democratic behaviours (Nabatchi and Leighninger 2015). Whereas serving on a citizens' assembly, joining a neighbourhood association or even voting may require substantial time commitments not everyone is able to make, internet access makes it easier for almost everyone in developed countries to participate in less formal ways from cafes, libraries or the comfort of their own homes. It also allows for ongoing citizen engagement in politics on a day-to-day basis, rather than just at election times, making digital democracy an effective tool for consistent monitoring of politicians and governments, thus strengthening accountability (Keane 2011).

There are also claims that digital democracy holds the promise of being more inclusive. One stream of argument is that the internet itself is democratic in the sense that virtually anyone with access can use it as a platform to promote their views. Indeed, the lack of central control or oversight of online communities means that almost anyone can share almost anything. In principle, this means that the internet is a vehicle for free speech and can be a source of alternative viewpoints and healthy debate. Relatedly, the concept of digital inclusion holds the promise of creating equitable chances for political participation for citizens regardless of ethnicity, linguistic or religious background, gender, age, sexual orientation, income or disability. Indeed, where access is even, the ability of the internet to facilitate social networking has the potential to create the kinds of 'cross-cutting ties' that bridges social divisions and build tolerance, enhancing social capital and the outlook for democracy more broadly.

However, in the twenty years since research on digital democracy began to appear in earnest, a number of criticisms have emerged. Some have begun to write of a 'dystopian' image of e-democracy, posing it in contrast to the overly optimistic 'utopian' picture of democratic experimentation of the early 2000s (van Dijk 2012; Dahlberg 2011). One problem is that a high volume of information transfer does not necessarily translate to a deeper, better quality of political engagement. The internet may lower the costs of participation for some, but this same characteristic may lead to relatively shallow exchanges that do not require or incentivize investment in one's community as, for example, in-person involvement in local civic groups might (i.e. do Facebook groups facilitate the same kind of democracy-enhancing community spirit that joining organizations in face-to-face meetings does?).

The sheer amount of information now available also exceeds what most people can consume or have time to think critically and form opinions about. Amid the online cacophony, consumers tend to seek out and stick to those sources of information that affirm views they already hold. The result is the fragmentation of media markets along political lines, and the polarization of public opinion. Without sufficient oversight, antipathy over opposing views is sometimes taken to extremes, with opportunities for genuine exchange becoming mired in personal or partisan attacks in anonymous message rooms, chat broads and social media threads. Anonymity and open access are also a breeding ground for 'fake news', extremist rhetoric and conspiracy theories, which can circulate unchecked and undermine the values of tolerance or compromise that sustain democracies. Too much information, it seems, can be as damaging as too little. Additionally, there is some research suggesting control of the agenda remains highly concentrated in a relatively small proportion of sources. One study showed that most web traffic was concentrated in the top twenty news outlets and skewed towards a readership of socially elite groups (Hindman 2009). Finally, there are the technical challenges (Ebert 2020; Schill and Hendricks 2017). Online interactions are vulnerable to security breaches and cyber-attacks that raise privacy concerns and may undermine confidence in the tools of digital democracy. Is e-voting ultimately any less susceptible to tampering or outside interference than elections by conventional means (Hanson et al. 2019)?

'Whole-process people's democracy': The rise of China and the challenge to liberal democracy

Noting that the concept of democracy has not stood still over time, this chapter has primarily examined proposals to alter the nature and scope of political participation, and to make the role of citizens in decision-making more equitable and accessible, and more responsive to popular voices. Such experiments remain mostly in their infancy. Some of these may be improvements. Others may not. Regardless of feasibility or results, these reflect an attempt to make liberal democracy better, and are undertaken 'by democracies for democracy'. We might even think of them as efforts to 'democratize democracy'. Each of the proposals examined here reflect a view of liberal democracy as something that can and should be improved upon, not as a system fundamentally flawed and in need of replacement.

At the close of the twentieth century, it appeared to learned observers of world politics that there was no longer any alternative to liberal democracy. We have returned to this premise many times throughout this book – the collapse of communism in the wake of the Cold War effectively left liberal democracy as the last ideology standing, and the United States as the world's only superpower. In the 2020s, this no longer seems an accurate description of global politics. Neither the United States nor liberal democracy stands unopposed.

The rise of China and its political model is the most prominent alternative to liberal democracy in the world today. Curiously, however, it has co-opted democratic terminology to do so, presenting itself as having a more evolved and functional type of democracy than its rivals.

Talk of democracy in China, even within elite political circles, is a regular occurrence. Indeed, it is common enough to be unremarkable. However, something drastically different is implied by the official usage of the word by China's government.

Unless one is a specialist in Chinese politics, this probably sounds strange. After all, China is one of the last surviving Marxist-Leninist states, and famously suppressed a millions-strong democratic movement with military force in full view of the world at the Tiananmen Square uprising of 1989. For many scholars of Chinese politics, it was a watershed event that led directly to policies designed to forestall regime collapse and keep democracy at bay ever since. Yet use of the term 'democracy' has long been a feature of political rhetoric in the People's Republic of China (PRC) and features prominently in guiding documents (Yu 2009). As in other communist states, the Chinese Communist Party is organized according to a principle called 'democratic centralism', something designed to uphold party supremacy rather than keep it in check. Initially adopted in the early years of the regime under Mao Zedong, Article 1 of the PRC constitution still refers to the country as the 'People's Democratic Dictatorship'.

What exactly is the Chinese model of democracy? How does it work? A government White Paper published in 2019 refers to a 'whole-process people's democracy', and positions it as the natural evolution and next phase of an ever-changing concept, 'embodying the Party's innovation in advancing China's democratic theories, systems, and practices' (Information Office of the State Council of the People's Republic of China 2019). The document states:

> Whole-process people's democracy integrates process-oriented democracy with results-oriented democracy, procedural democracy with substantive democracy, direct democracy with indirect democracy, and people's democracy with the will of the state. It is a model of socialist democracy that covers all aspects of the democratic process and all sectors of society.

Supporters of this model contend that compared to liberal democracies, where politics is increasingly exclusive and dominated by a wealthy elite, Chinese whole-process democracy allows more opportunities for participation, and in a variety of different ways, making it more accessible and attuned to the wishes of ordinary citizens (Zhang 2021). Because it combines electoral and consultative methods, some regard it as more active or 'open' in the sense of providing multiple continuous channels for participation. As Vice Foreign Minister Le Yucheng remarked, 'China's whole-process people's democracy is not the kind that wakes up at the time of voting and goes back to dormant afterwards' (Yew 2021).

Calling it 'a true democracy that works', the White Paper also argues for the superiority of people's democracy to other extant models:

> Whole-process people's democracy, giving full expression to the socialist nature of the state and the people's principal position, serves to better represent the people's will, protect their rights and fully unleash their potential to create.
> (Information Office of the State Council of the People's Republic of China 2019)

Others have suggested that the meritocratic nature of China's political system makes it superior to democracy as practised elsewhere (Bell 2015).

Finally, the White Paper asserts its own criteria for the classification of democracies and defends the Chinese interpretation of the concept as both justified by and an expression of national sovereignty.

> Democracy is the right of the people in every country, rather than the prerogative of a few nations. Whether a country is democratic should be judged by its people, not dictated by a handful of outsiders. Whether a country is democratic should be acknowledged by the international community, not arbitrarily decided by a few self-appointed judges. There is no fixed model of democracy; it manifests itself in many forms. Assessing the myriad political systems in the world against a single yardstick and examining diverse political structures in monochrome are in themselves undemocratic.
> (Information Office of the State Council of the People's Republic of China 2019)

Here, the authors of China's White Paper are making a defiant stance against universalist interpretations of democracy and asserting their right to remodel the central meaning of the concept so as to best fit China's needs. As the passage above indicates, this position is justified by the high level of popular support for China's system of government (Perry 2019; Dickson, Shen and Chan 2016; Zeng 2014). Yet this is also why the rise of China is such a meaningful challenge to liberal democracy. Just as belief in the quality of democracy seems to be declining in many consolidated countries, including the United States, China's geopolitical ascendance, rapid development and seeming orderliness and stability have emerged to deepen the crisis of confidence. At the very least, demonstration effects given off by a rising and successful China increase the likelihood of its way of politics becoming an increasingly important international exemplar.

Conclusion

This chapter has considered some but not all possibilities for democracy's future. At the heart of this discussion is the observation that understandings of democracy have never stood still, but have evolved through space and time alongside social conditions and forms of political organization. The rise of nation-states and markets, and shifting ideas about the nature, role and worth of the individual, had profound impacts on the way we think about democracy. Most of us would no doubt consider it inevitable, as well as right and proper, that we think of and practice democracy differently from the ancient Athenians. However, if we accept that interpretations of democracy are apt to change, and that it is good that they do so, why would we assume that liberal or electoral democracy as currently practised cannot or ought not evolve further?

Anticipating this issue, many liberal democracies have begun to explore new ways of engaging citizens in the political process, including alternative methods for choosing those who serve in public office. Here, we have noted in particular experiments in sortition, as well as deliberative institutional arrangements, and the pros and cons of e-democracy. These we classified as attempts to reform liberal democracy from within, something which implies that while democracy has deep worth, it can nevertheless be improved upon. However, the latter portion of the chapter also explored the practice of 'whole-process people's democracy' in China, how its proponents regard it as superior to liberal democracy and what China's geopolitical ascendance and influence implies for liberal democracy globally. Sobering though it may seem, future textbooks on democratization and democratic theory may need to incorporate aspects of Xi Jinping's thought if they are to accurately capture the state of thinking about democracy around the globe.

Much of what we have written in this volume points to a gloomy outlook for democracy and democratization worldwide. While we cannot ignore the troubling trends we have detailed, we close here with a note of qualified optimism. In this chapter and throughout this book we have repeatedly pointed out the modularity and flexibility of democracy's character, geographically and through the centuries. However, this argument should be tempered with a mention of democracy's durability. Indeed, innovation to democratic models at many historic turning points suggests that while it remains a work in progress, core elements of democracy have been consistently recognized as worth retaining. It is notable that for all of the changes the concept of democracy has undergone, and may yet undergo, it has not been outright discarded. Even in places like China, where there is deep scepticism over the suitability of democratic models practised elsewhere, developing democracy is talked about as a worthy and desirable goal. The democratic moment is far from over.

Questions for discussion

1 How have understandings of democracy changed over time and space? What factors have influenced understandings of democracy?
2 What problems or challenges can you anticipate with the institution of e-democracy? Does the internet hold the power to exclude certain groups from political participation?
3 In your view, is random selection (sortition) a more equitable or efficient way of making public policy?
4 Is the Chinese model of democracy commensurate with liberal democracy as discussed throughout this book, or is it a fundamentally different system of government?
5 If you could innovate or change some aspect of the way democracy is practised, what would it be?

Further reading

Blühdorn, Ingolfur, and Felix Butzlaff, 'Democratization beyond the Post-Democracy Turn: Towards a Research Agenda on New Conceptions of Citizen Participation', *Democratization*, Vol. 27, No. 3 (2020): 369–88.
Bouricius, Terrill, 'Why Hybrid Bicameralism Is Not Right for Sortition', *Politics and Society*, Vol. 46, No. 3 (2018): 435–51.
Fenton, Natalie, 'Post-Democracy, Press, Politics and Power', *The Political Quarterly*, Vol. 87, No. 1 (2016): 81–5.
Fishkin, James S., Robert C. Luskin and Roger Jowell, 'Deliberative Polling and Public Consultation', *Parliamentary Affairs*, Vol. 53 (2000): 657–66.
Gamble, Andrew, and Tony Wright, eds, *Rethinking Democracy* (Chichester: Wiley, 2019).
Goodin, Robert E., *Innovating Democracy: Democratic Theory and Practice after the Deliberative Turn* (Oxford: Oxford University Press, 2012).

Karlsson, Martin, Joachim Åström and Magnus Adenskog, 'Democratic Innovation in Times of Crisis: Exploring Changes in Social and Political Trust', *Policy and Internet*, Vol. 13, No. 1 (2021): 113–33.

Nyabola, Nanjala, *Digital Democracy, Analogue Politics: How the Internet is Transforming Politics in Kenya* (New York: Bloomsbury, 2018).

Vaccari, Cristian, *Digital Politics in Western Democracies: A Comparative Study* (Baltimore, MD: Johns Hopkins University Press, 2013).

Whitehead, Laurence, 'The Alternatives to "Liberal Democracy": A Latin American Perspective', *Political Studies*, Vol. 40, No. 1 (1992): 146–59.

References

Introduction

Carothers, T. (2002), 'The End of the Transition Paradigm', *Journal of Democracy*, Vol. 13, No. 1: 5–21.

Collier, D., and S. Levitsky (1997), 'Democracy with Adjectives: Conceptual Innovation in Comparative Research', *World Politics*, Vol. 49, No. 3: 430–51.

Crozier, M., S. P. Huntington and J. Watanuki (1975), *The Crisis of Democracy* (New York: New York University Press).

Dahl, R. (1971), *Polyarchy: Participation and Opposition* (New Haven, CT: Yale University Press).

Diamond, L. (2002), 'Elections without Democracy: Thinking about Hybrid Regimes', *Journal of Democracy*, Vol. 13, No. 2: 21–35.

Durant, R. F. (1995), 'The Democratic Deficit in America', *Political Science Quarterly*, Vol. 110, No. 1: 25–47.

Fukuyama, F. (1992), *The End of History and the Last Man* (New York: Free Press).

Huntington, S. P. (1991), *The Third Wave: Democratization in the Late Twentieth Century* (Norman: University of Oklahoma Press).

Huntington, S. P. (1996), *The Clash of Civilizations and the Remaking of World Order* (New York: Simon & Schuster).

Keck, M. E., and K. Sikkink (1998), *Activists beyond Borders: Advocacy Networks in International Politics* (Ithaca, NY: Cornell University Press).

Levitsky, S., and L. A. Way (2010), *Competitive Authoritarianism: Hybrid Regimes after the Cold War* (Cambridge: Cambridge University Press).

Murtazashvili, J. B. (2022), 'The Collapse of Afghanistan', *Journal of Democracy*, Vol. 33, No. 1: 40–54.

O'Donnell, G. (1996), 'Illusions about Consolidation', *Journal of Democracy*, Vol. 7, No. 2: 34–51.

Putnam, R. D. (1993), *Making Democracy Work: Civic Traditions in Modern Italy* (Princeton, NJ: Princeton University Press).

Sartori, G. (1987), *Theory of Democracy Revisited* (Chatham, NJ: Chatham House Publishers).

Schmitter, P. C., and Terry Lyn Karl (1991), 'What Democracy Is ... and Is Not', *Journal of Democracy*, Vol. 2, No. 3: 75–88.

V-Dem Institute (2021), 'Autocracy Turns Viral, Democracy Report 2021'.

Zakaria, F. (1997), 'The Rise of Illiberal Democracy', *Foreign Affairs*, Vol. 76, No. 6: 22–43.

Chapter 1

Acemoglu, D., and J. A. Robinson (2012), *Why Nations Fail: The Origins of Power, Prosperity, and Poverty* (New York: Crown Publishing Co.).

Acemoglu, D., and J. A. Robinson (2015), 'The Rise and Decline of General Laws of Capitalism', *Journal of Economic Perspectives*, Vol. 29, No. 1: 3–28.

Almond, G. A. (1991), 'Capitalism and Democracy', *PS: Political Science and Politics*, Vol. 24, No. 3: 467–74.

Auty, R. M. (1993), *Sustaining Development in Mineral Economies: The Resource Curse Thesis* (London and New York: Routledge).

Beblawi, H. (1987), 'The Rentier State in the Arab World', *Arab Studies Quarterly*, Vol. 9, No. 4: 383–98.

Beetham, D. (1991), *The Legitimation of Power* (Basingstoke: Palgrave Macmillan).

Beetham, D. (1997), 'Market Economy and Democratic Polity', *Democratization*, Vol. 4, No. 1: 76–93.

Berman, S. (2006), *The Primacy of Politics: Social Democracy and the Making of Europe's Twentieth Century* (New York: Cambridge University Press).

Carothers, T. (2002), 'The End of the Transition Paradigm', *Journal of Democracy*, Vol. 13, No. 1: 5–21.

Clayton, R., and J. Pontusson (1998), 'Welfare-State Retrenchment Revisited: Entitlement Cuts, Public Sector Restructuring, and Inegalitarian Trends in Advanced Capitalist Societies', *World Politics*, Vol. 51, No. 1: 67–98.

Dahl, R. (1990), *After the Revolution? Authority in a Good Society* (New Haven, CT: Yale University Press).

Diamond, L. (1992), 'Economic Development and Democracy Reconsidered', *American Behavioural Scientist*, Vol. 35, Nos 4–5: 450–99.

Dunning, T. (2008), *Crude Democracy: Natural Resource Wealth and Political Regimes* (Cambridge: Cambridge University Press).

Esping-Andersen, G. (1990), *The Three Worlds of Welfare Capitalism* (Cambridge: Polity Press).

Fukuyama, F. (1992), 'Capitalism & Democracy: The Missing Link', *Journal of Democracy*, Vol. 3, No. 3: 100–10.

Giddens, A. (1998), *The Third Way: The Renewal of Social Democracy* (Cambridge: Polity Press).

Gilley, B. (2009), *The Right to Rule: How States Win and Lose Legitimacy* (New York: Columbia University Press).

Hall, P. A., and D. Soskice, eds (2001), *Varieties of Capitalism: The Institutional Foundation of Comparative Advantage* (Oxford: Oxford University Press).

Hirschman, A. (1986), *Rival Views of Market Society* (New York: Viking).

Karl, T. L. (1997), *The Paradox of Plenty: Oil Booms and Petro-States* (Berkeley: The University of California Press).

Katzenstein, P. J. (2019), *Corporatism and Change: Austria, Switzerland, and the Politics of Industry* (Ithaca, NY: Cornell University Press).

Levitsky S. R., and L. A. Way (2012), 'Beyond Patronage: Violent Struggle, Ruling Party Cohesion and Authoritarian Durability', *Perspectives on Politics*, Vol. 10, No. 4: 869–89.

Lindblom, C. E. (1982), 'The Market as Prison', *Journal of Politics*, Vol. 44, No. 2: 324–36.

Lipset, S. M. (1959), 'Some Social Requisites of Democracy: Economic Development and Political Legitimacy', *American Political Science Review*, Vol. 53, No. 1: 69–105.

Lipset, S. M. (1994), 'The Social Requisites of Democracy Reconsidered', *American Sociological Review*, Vol. 59, No. 1: 1–22.

Mahdavy, H. (1970), 'Patterns and Problems of Economic Development in Rentier States: The Case of Iran', in M. A. Cook, ed., *Studies in the Economic History of the Middle East*, 428–67 (London: Routledge).

Merkel, W. (2014), 'Is Capitalism Compatible with Democracy?' *Zeitschrift für Vergleichende Politikwissenschaft*, Vol. 8: 109–28.

Molina, O. and M. Rhodes (2002), 'Corporatism: The Past, Present, and Future of a Concept', *Annual Review of Political Science*, Vol. 5: 305–31.

Moore, B. (1966), *Social Origins of Dictatorship and Democracy: Lord and Peasant in the Making of the Modern World* (Boston, MA: Beacon Press).

Offe, C. (1984), *Contradictions of the Welfare State* (Cambridge, MA: MIT Press).

Piketty, T. (2014), *Capital in the Twenty-first Century* (Cambridge, MA: Harvard University Press).

Przeworski, A. and F. Limongi (1997), 'Modernization: Theories and Facts', *World Politics*, Vol. 49, No. 2: 155–83.

Ross, M. L. (2015), 'What Have We Learned about the Resource Curse?' *Annual Review of Political Science*, Vol. 18: 239–59.

Schmitter, P. C. (1975), 'Liberation by *Golpe*: Retrospective Thoughts on the Demise of Authoritarian Rule in Portugal', *Armed Forces & Society*, Vol. 2, No. 1: 5–33.

Starke, P. (2008), *Radical Welfare State Retrenchment: A Comparative Analysis* (Houndmills: Palgrave Macmillan).

Svolik, M. (2008), 'Authoritarian Reversal and Democratic Consolidation', *American Political Science Review*, Vol. 102, No.2: 153–68.

Swank, D. (2005), 'Globalisation, Domestic Politics, and Welfare State Retrenchment in Capitalist Democracies', *Social Policy & Society*, Vol. 4, No. 2: 183–95.

Vaswani, K. (2018), 'Why Asia Turned to China during the Global Financial Crisis', *BBC News* (13 September). https://www.bbc.com/news/business-45493147. Accessed 5 August 2020.

Ware, A. (1992), 'Liberal Democracy: One Form or Many?' *Political Studies*, Vol. 40, No. 1: 130–45.

Chapter 2

Albini, J. L., and J. Anderson (1998), 'Whatever Happened to the KGB?' *International Journal of Intelligence and Counter-intelligence*, Vol. 11, No. 1: 26–56.

Aminzade, R. (1992), 'Historical Sociology and Time', *Sociological Methods & Research*, Vol. 20, No.4: 456–80.

Bennett, A., and J. T. Checkel, eds (2014), *Process Tracing: From Metaphor to Analytic Tool* (Cambridge: Cambridge University Press).

Bratton, M., and N. Van de Walle (1994), 'Neopatrimonial Regimes and Political Transitions in Africa', *World Politics*, Vol. 46, No. 4: 453–89.

Brooker, P. (2014), *Non-Democratic Regimes: Theory, Governments and Politics*, 3rd edn (Houndmills: Palgrave Macmillan).

Bueno de Mesquita, B., and A. Smith (2012), *The Dictator's Handbook: Why Bad Behavior Is Almost Always Good Politics* (New York: PublicAffairs).

Bueno de Mesquita, B., A. Smith, R. M. Siverson and J. D. Morrow (2003), *The Logic of Political Survival* (Cambridge, MA: MIT Press).

Capoccia, G., and R. D. Kelemen (2007), 'The Study of Critical Junctures: Theory, Narrative, and Counterfactuals in Historical Institutionalism', *World Politics*, Vol. 59, No. 3: 341–69.

Capoccia, G., and D. Ziblatt (2010), 'The Historical Turn in Democratization Studies: A New Research Agenda for Europe and Beyond', *Comparative Political Studies*, Vol. 43, Nos 8–9: 931–68.

Carothers, T. (2002), 'The End of the Transition Paradigm', *Journal of Democracy*, Vol. 13, No.1: 5–21.

Collier, D. (2011), 'Understanding Process Tracing', *PS: Political Science and Politics*, Vol. 44, No. 4: 823–30.

Collins, R. (1999), *Macro History: Essays in Sociology of the Long Run* (Stanford, CA: Stanford University Press).

Evans, P. B., D. Rueschemeyer and T. Skocpol, eds (1985), *Bringing the State Back In* (Cambridge: Cambridge University Press).

Fishkin, J. S., B. He, R. C. Luskin and A. Siu (2010), 'Deliberative Democracy in an Unlikely Place: Deliberative Polling in China', *British Journal of Political Science*, Vol. 40: 435–48.

Gerring, J. (2001), *Social Science Methodology: A Criterial Framework* (New York: Cambridge University Press).

Gilley, B. (2009), *The Right to Rule: How States Win and Lose Legitimacy* (New York: Columbia University Press).

Huntington, S. P. (1990), *The Third Wave: Democratization in the Late Twentieth Century* (Norman: University of Oklahoma Press).

Karl, T. L. (1995), 'The Hybrid Regimes of Central America', *Journal of Democracy*, Vol. 6, No. 3: 72–86.

Klandermans, B., and C. Van Stralen, eds (2015), *Movements in Times of Democratic Transition* (Philadelphia, PA: Temple University Press).

Klotz, A. (2002), 'Transnational Activism and Global Transformations: The Anti-Apartheid and Abolitionist Experiences', *European Journal of International Relations*, Vol. 8, No. 1: 49–76.

Levitsky, S., and L. A. Way (2010), *Competitive Authoritarianism: Hybrid Regimes after the Cold War* (Cambridge: Cambridge University Press).

Linz, J. J. (1978), 'Crisis, Breakdown, and Reequilibration', in J. J. Linz and A. Stepan, eds, *The Breakdown of Democratic Regimes*, Vol. 1, 1–124 (Baltimore, MD: Johns Hopkins University Press).

Linz, J. J. (1990), 'The Perils of Presidentialism', *Journal of Democracy*, Vol. 1, No. 1: 51–69.

Linz, J. J., and A. Stepan (1996), *Problems of Democratic Transition and Consolidation: Southern Europe, South America, and Post-Communist Europe* (Baltimore, MD, and London: Johns Hopkins University Press).

Mahoney, J. (2000), 'Path Dependence in Historical Sociology', *Theory & Society*, Vol. 29, No. 4: 507–48.

Munck, G. L. (1994), 'Democratic Transitions in Comparative Perspective', *Comparative Politics*, Vol. 26, No. 3: 355–75.

Nordlinger, E. A. (1981), *On the Autonomy of the Democratic State* (Cambridge, MA, and London: Harvard University Press).

O'Donnell, G., and P. C. Schmitter and L. Whitehead (1986), *Transitions from Authoritarian Rule: Tentative Conclusions about Uncertain Democracies* (Baltimore, MD: Johns Hopkins University Press).

Pan, J. C. (2020), *Welfare for Autocrats: How Social Assistance in China Cares for Its Rulers* (New York: Oxford University Press).

Pierson, P. (2000), 'Increasing Returns, Path Dependence, and the Study of Politics', *American Political Science Review*, Vol. 94, No. 2: 251–67.

Rotberg, R. I., ed. (2003), *When States Fail: Causes and Consequences* (Princeton, NJ: Princeton University Press).

Rustow, D. A. (1970), 'Transitions to Democracy: Toward a Dynamic Model', *Comparative Politics*, Vol. 2, No. 3: 337–63.

Schedler, A. (2002), 'Elections without Democracy: The Menu of Manipulation', *Journal of Democracy*, Vol. 13, No. 2: 36–50.

Share, D., and S. Mainwaring (1986), 'Transitions through Transaction: Democratization in Brazil and Spain', in W. A. Selcher, ed., *Political Liberalization in Brazil: Dynamics, Dilemmas, and Future Prospects*, 175–216 (Boulder, CO: Westview Press).

Slater, D., and J. Wong (2013), 'The Strength to Concede: Ruling Parties and Democratization in Developmental Asia', *Perspectives on Politics*, Vol. 11, No. 3: 717–33.

Sly, L. (2015), 'The Hidden Hand behind the Islamic State Militants? Saddam Hussein's', *The Washington Post* (4 April). https://www.washingtonpost.com/world/middle_east/the-hidden-hand-behind-the-islamic-state-militants-saddam-husseins/2015/04/04/aa97676c-cc32-11e4-8730-4f473416e759_story.html. Accessed 22 February 2022.

Snyder, J. L. (2000), *From Voting to Violence: Democratization and Nationalist Conflict* (New York: W. W. Norton).

Tilly, C. (1975), 'Reflections on the History of European State-making', in C. Tilly, ed., *The Formation of Nation States in Western Europe*, 3–83 (Princeton, NJ: Princeton University Press, 1975).

Weber, M. (1964), 'The Fundamental Concepts of Sociology', in T. Parsons, ed., *The Theory of Social and Economic Organization*, 94–164 (New York: Free Press).

Chapter 3

Barron, P., and A. Burke (2008), *Supporting Peace in Aceh: Development Agencies and International Involvement*, Policy Studies No. 47 (Washington, DC: ISEAS Publishing).

Bartusevicius, H., and S.-E. Skaaning (2018), 'Revisiting Democratic Civil Peace: Electoral Regimes and Civil Conflict', *Journal of Peace Research*, Vol. 55, No. 5: 625–40.

Besaw, C. (2021), 'Election Violence Spiked Worldwide in 2020 – Will this Year be Better?' *The Conversation*, 19 February 2021. Available at https://theconversation.com/election-violence-spiked-worldwide-in-2020-will-this-year-be-better-153975. Accessed on 4 May 2021.

Colaresi, M., and S. C. Carey (2008), 'To Kill or Protect: Security Forces, Domestic Institutions and Genocide', *Journal of Conflict Resolution*, Vol. 52, No. 1: 39–67.

Des Forges, A. (1999), *'Leave None to Tell the Story': Genocide in Rwanda* (New York: Human Rights Watch).

Gleditsch, K. S., and A. Ruggeri (2010), 'Political Opportunity Structures, Democracy, and Civil War', *Journal of Peace Research*, Vol. 47, No. 3: 299–310.

Gleditsch, N. P., L. S. Christiansen and H. Hegre (2007), 'Democratic Jihad? Military Intervention and Democracy', World Bank Policy Research Paper, No. 4242, pp. 1–62.

Hedman, E. E., ed. (2008), *Conflict, Violence, and Displacement in Indonesia* (Ithaca, NY: Cornell University Press).

Hegre, H. (2014), 'Democracy and Armed Conflict', *Journal of Peace Research*, Vol. 51, No. 2: 159–72.

Horowitz, D. L. (1985), *Ethnic Groups in Conflict* (Berkeley and Los Angeles: The University of California Press).

Jervis, R. (2002), 'Theories of War in an Era of Leading Power Peace', *American Political Science Review*, Vol. 96, No. 1: 1–14.

Klinken, G. van (2007), *Communal Violence and Democratization in Indonesia: Small Town Wars* (London and New York: Routledge).

Lemarchand, R. (2009), *The Dynamics of Violence in Central Africa* (Philadelphia: University of Pennsylvania Press).

Levy, J. S. (1988), 'Domestic Politics and War', *The Journal of Interdisciplinary History*, Vol. 18, No. 4: 653–73.

Lijphart, A. (1977), *Democracy in Plural Societies: A Comparative Exploration* (New Haven, CT: Yale University Press).

Mansfield, E. D., and J. Snyder (2005), *Electing to Fight: Why Emerging Democracies Go to War* (Cambridge, MA: MIT Press).

McDoom, O. S. (2012), 'The Psychology of Threat in Intergroup Conflict: Emotions, Rationality, and Opportunity in the Rwandan Genocide', *International Security*, Vol. 37, No.2: 119–55.

Raknerud, A., and H. Hegre (1997), 'The Hazard of War: Reassessing the Evidence for the Democratic Peace', *Journal of Peace Research*, Vol. 34, No. 4: 385–404.

Reyntjens, F. (1996), 'Rwanda: Genocide and Beyond', *Journal of Refugee Studies*, Vol. 9, No. 3: 240–51.

Russett, B., C. Layne, D. E. Spiro and M. W. Doyle (1995), 'The Democratic Peace', *International Security*, Vol. 19, No. 4: 164–84.

Snyder, J. (2000), *From Voting to Violence: Democratization and Nationalist Conflict* (New York: W. W. Norton).

Spodek, H. (2010), 'In the Hindutva Laboratory: Pogroms and Politics in Gujarat, 2002', *Modern Asian Studies*, Vol. 44. No. 2: 349–99.

Straus, S. (2006), *The Order of Genocide: Race, Power and War in Rwanda* (Ithaca, NY: Cornell University Press).

Wilkinson, S. I. (2004), *Votes and Violence: Electoral Competition and Ethnic Riots in India* (Cambridge: Cambridge University Press).

Chapter 4

Ali, M. (2009), 'Civil Society in Afghanistan: Issues and Prospects', *Pakistan Horizon*, Vol. 62, No. 2/3: 77–94.

Almond, G. A., and S. Verba (1963), *The Civic Culture: Political Attitudes and Democracy in Five Nations* (Princeton, NJ: Princeton University Press).

Asian Development Bank (2009), 'Overview of Civil Society Organizations: Afghanistan' (June).

Bates, R. H., R. J. P. de Figueiredo Jr and B. R. Weingast (1998), 'The Politics of Interpretation: Rationality, Culture, and Transition', *Politics & Society*, Vol. 26, No. 4: 603–42.

Beissinger, M. R. (2002), *Nationalist Mobilization and the Collapse of the Soviet State* (Cambridge: Cambridge University Press).

Berman, S. (2001), 'Ideas Norms, and Culture in Political Analysis', *Comparative Politics*, Vol. 33, No. 2: 231–50.

Bob, C. (2011), 'Civil and Uncivil Society', in M. Edwards, ed., *The Oxford Handbook of Civil Society*, 209–19 (Oxford: Oxford University Press).

Brenan, M. (2020), 'Americans Remain Distrustful of Mass Media', *Gallup News* (30 September). https://news.gallup.com/poll/321116/americans-remain-distrustful-mass-media.aspx. Accessed 25 April 2021.

Buttigieg, J. A. (1995), 'Gramsci on Civil Society', *Boundary 2*, Vol. 22, No. 3: 1–32.

Carothers, T. (2007), 'How Democracies Emerge: The Sequencing Fallacy', *Journal of Democracy*, Vol. 18, No. 1: 12–27.

Chambers, S., and J. Kopstein (2011), 'Bad Civil Society', *Political Theory*, Vol. 29, No. 6: 837–65.

Cooley, A., and J. Ron (2002), 'The NGO Scramble: Organizational Insecurity and the Political Economy of Transnational Action', *International Security*, Vol. 27, No. 1: 5–39.

Dahl, R. A. (1961), 'The Behavioral Approach in Political Science: Epitaph for a Monument to a Successful Protest', *American Political Science Review*, Vol. 55, No. 4: 763–72.

Davis, J.-M. (2019), 'Real "Non-governmental" Aid and Poverty: Comparing Privately and Publicly Financed NGOs in Canada', *Canadian Journal of Development Studies*, Vol. 40, No. 3: 369–86.

Diamond, L. (1999), *Developing Democracy* (Baltimore, MD: Johns Hopkins University Press).

Dionne, E. J. (2013), *Why Americans Hate Politics* [Reissue Edition] (New York: Simon & Schuster).

Easton, D. (1953), *The Political System: An Inquiry into the State of Political Science* (New York: Alfred A. Knopf).

Filali-Ansary, A. (1999), 'Muslims and Democracy', *Journal of Democracy*, Vol. 10, No. 3: 18–32.

Fonseca, M. (2016), *Gramsci's Critique of Civil Society: Towards a New Concept of Hegemony* (London and New York: Routledge).

Fukuyama, F. (1995), 'Confucianism and Democracy', *Journal of Democracy*, Vol. 6, No. 2: 20–33.

Geertz, C. (1973), *The Interpretation of Cultures* (New York: Basic Books).

Goddard, C. (2009), 'Cultural Scripts', in G. Shenft, J. Östman and J. Verschueren, eds, *Culture and Language Use*, 68–80 (Amsterdam and Philadelphia, PA: John Benjamins Publishing Company).

Grigsby, E. (2004), *Analysing Politics: An Introduction to Political Science*, 5th edn (Boston, MA: Cengage Learning).

Harpviken, K. B., A. Strand and K. Ask (2002), 'Afghanistan and Civil Society', Norwegian Ministry of Foreign Affairs (8 December). https://www.cmi.no/publications/file/1765-afghanistan-and-civil-society.pdf. Accessed 28 April 2021.

Helmke, G., and S. Levitsky, eds (2006), *Informal Institutions and Democracy: Lessons from Latin America* (Baltimore, MD: Johns Hopkins University Press, 2006).

Hildebrandt, T. (2013), *Social Organizations and the Authoritarian State in China* (Cambridge: Cambridge University Press).

His Holiness the Dalai Lama (1999), 'Buddhism, Asian Values, and Democracy', *Journal of Democracy*, Vol. 10, No. 1: 3–7.

Hough, J. F., and M. Fainsod (1979), *How the Soviet Union Is Governed* (Cambridge, MA, and London: Harvard University Press).

Hsu, J. Y. J., C. L. Hsu and R. Hasmath (2017), 'NGO Strategies in an Authoritarian Context and their Implications for Citizenship: The Case of the People's Republic of China', *Voluntas*, Vol. 28: 1157–79.

Khatab, S., and G. D. Bouma (2007), *Democracy in Islam* (London and New York: Routledge).

Lecy, J. D., G. E. Mitchell and H. P. Schmitz (2010), 'Advocacy Organizations, Networks, and the Firm Analogy', in A. Prakash and M. K. Gugerty, eds, *Advocacy Organizations and Collective Action*, 229–51 (Cambridge: Cambridge University Press).

March, J. G., and J. P. Olsen (2009), 'Elaborating the "New Institutionalism"', in S. A. Binder, R. A. W. Rhodes and B. A. Rockman, eds, *The Oxford Handbook of Political Science*, 1–19 (Oxford: Oxford University Press).

Mlambo, V. H., S. P. Zubane and D. N. Mlambo (2020), 'Promoting Good Governance in Africa: The Role of the Civil Society as a Watchdog', *Journal of Public Affairs*, Vol. 20, No. 1: e1989.

Putnam, R. D. (1993), *Making Democracy Work: Civic Traditions in Modern Italy* (Princeton, NJ: Princeton University Press).

Putnam, R. D. (2000), *Bowling Alone: The Collapse and Revival of American Community* (New York: Simon & Schuster).

Rosenbaum, W. A. (1972), *Political Culture* (New York: Praeger, 1972).

Safi, M. (2012), 'Civil Society in Afghanistan: A Decade of Progress and Challenges', Peace Insight (20 December 2012). www.peaceinsight.org. Accessed 28 April 2021.

Swedish International Development Cooperation Agency (SIDA), (2007), 'SIDA's Support to Civil Society' (16 May). https://cdn.sida.se/publications/files/ sida37855en-sidas-support-to-civil-society.pdf. Accessed 23 August 2022.

The West Wing, Season 7, Episode 14. Originally aired 19 March 2005. National Broadcasting Corporation.

Teets, J. C. (2014), *Civil Society under Authoritarianism: The China Model* (Cambridge: Cambridge University Press).

Tocqueville, A. (1835), *Democracy in America*, Vol. 1 (n.p).

Van Rooy, A. ed. (1990), *Civil Society and the Aid Industry* (New York: Earthscan).

Chapter 5

Abdullah, W. J. (2020), '"New Normal" No More: Democratic Backsliding in Singapore after 2015', *Democratization*, Vol. 27, No. 7: 1123–41.

Curato, N. (2017), 'Flirting with Authoritarian Fantasies? Rodrigo Duterte and the New Terms of Philippine Populism', *Journal of Contemporary Asia*, Vol. 47, No. 1: 142–53.

Diamond, L. (2021), 'Democratic Regression in Comparative Perspective: Scope, Methods, and Causes', *Democratization*, Vol. 28, No. 1: 22–42.

Dressel, B., and C. R. Bonoan (2019), 'Southeast Asia's Troubling Elections: Duterte versus the Rule of Law', *Journal of Democracy*, Vol. 30, No. 4: 134–48.

Hafner-Burton, E. M., S. D. Hyde and R. S. Jablonski (2013), 'When Do Governments Resort to Election Violence?' *British Journal of Political Science*, Vol. 44, No. 1: 149–79.

Hutchcroft, P. D. (2008), 'The Arroyo Imbroglio in the Philippines', *Journal of Democracy*, Vol. 19, No. 1: 141–55.

Iyekekpolo, W. (2021), 'How Insurgent Groups Emerge: The Political Process in Democratic Nigeria', PhD Dissertation, University of Auckland.

Levitsky, S., and L. A. Way (2010), *Competitive Authoritarianism: Hybrid Regimes after the Cold War* (Cambridge: Cambridge University Press).

Linantud, J. L. (2005), 'The 2004 Philippine Elections: Political Change in an Illiberal Democracy', *Contemporary Southeast Asia*, Vol. 27, No. 1: 80–101.

Ortmann, S. (2011), 'Singapore: Authoritarian but Newly Competitive', *Journal of Democracy*, Vol. 22, No. 4: 153–64.

Smith, P. H., and M. R. Ziegler (2008), 'Liberal and Illiberal Democracy in Latin America', *Latin American Politics and Society*, Vol. 50, No. 1: 31–57.

Worthington, R. (2001), 'Between Hermes and Themis: An Empirical Study of the Contemporary Judiciary in Singapore', *Journal of Law and Society*, Vol. 28, No. 4: 490–519.

Zakaria, F. (1997), 'The Rise of Illiberal Democracy', *Foreign Affairs*, Vol. 76: 22–43.

Chapter 6

Bermeo, N. (2016), 'On Democratic Backsliding', *Journal of Democracy*, Vol. 27, No. 1: 5–19.

Curato, N. (2017), 'Flirting with Authoritarian Fantasies? Rodrigo Duterte and the New Terms of Philippine Populism', *Journal of Contemporary Asia*, Vol. 47, No. 1: 142–53.

Diamond, L. (2021), 'Democratic Regression in Comparative Perspective: Scope, Methods, and Causes', *Democratization*, Vol. 28, No. 1: 22–42.

Gerbaudo, P. (2018), 'Social Media and Populism: An Elective Affinity?' *Media, Culture & Society*, Vol. 40, No. 5: 745–53.

Guia, A. (2016), 'The Concept of Nativism and Anti-Immigrant Sentiments in Europe', European University Working Paper 20: 1–16.

Haggard, S., and R. Kaufman (2021), 'The Anatomy of Democratic Backsliding', *Journal of Democracy*, Vol. 32, No. 4: 27–41.

Higham, J. (1988), *Strangers in the Land: Patterns of American Nativism, 1860–1925* (New Brunswick, NJ: Rutgers University Press).

Huntington, S. P. (1985), *The Soldier and the State: The Theory and Politics of Civil-Military Relations* (Cambridge, MA: Harvard University Press).

Jaffrelot, C. (2021), *Modi's India: Hindu Nationalism and the Rise of Ethnic Democracy* (Princeton, NJ: Princeton University Press).

Laclau, E. (2005), *On Populist Reason* (London: Verso).

Merkel, W., and A. Lührmann (2021), 'Resilience of Democracies: Responses to Illiberal and Authoritarian Challenges', *Democratization*, Vol. 28, No. 5: 869–84.

Mudde, C. (2010), 'The Populist Radical Right: A Pathological Normalcy', *West European Politics*, Vol. 33, No. 6: 1167–86.

Mudde, C., and C. R. Kaltwasser (2017), *Populism: A Very Short Introduction* (New York: Oxford University Press).

Pildes, R. H. (2021), 'Why so Many Democracies are Floundering', *New York Times Online*, 29 December. https://www.nytimes.com/2021/12/29/opinion/democracy-fragmentation-america-europe.html. Accessed 23 August 2022.

Repucci, S., and A. Slipowitz (2021), 'Freedom in the World 2021: Democracy under Siege' (Washington, DC: Freedom House).

Weiner, M. (1978), *Sons of the Soil: Migration and Ethnic Conflict in India* (Princeton, NJ: Princeton University Press).

Chapter 7

Anheier, H., M. Glasius and M. Kaldor, eds (2001), *Global Civil Society 2001* (New York: Oxford University Press).

Barber, B. (1995), *Jihad vs. McWorld: Terrorism's Challenge to Democracy* (New York: Times Books).

Barnett, M., and R. Duvall, eds (2005), *Power in Global Governance* (Cambridge: Cambridge University Press).

Beetham, D. (2009), 'Democracy: Universality and Diversity', *Ethics & Global Politics*, Vol. 2, No. 4: 284–96.

Bolt, P. J., and S. N. Cross (2018), *China, Russia, and Twenty-first Century Global Geopolitics* (Oxford: Oxford University Press).

Bowman, J. (2006), 'The European Union Democratic Deficit: Federalists, Sceptics, and Revisionists', *European Journal of Political Theory*, Vol. 5, No. 2: 191–212.

Brancati, D., and A. Lucardi (2019), 'Why Democracy Protests do not Diffuse', *Journal of Conflict Resolution*, Vol. 63, No. 10: 2354–89.

Castells, M. (2008), 'The New Public Sphere: Global Civil Society, Communication Networks and Global Governance', *Annals of the American Academy of Political and Social Science*, Vol. 616, No. 11§§§1: 78–93.

Clark, J. D. (2014), *Worlds Apart: Civil Society and the Battle for Ethical Globalization* (Abingdon, UK: Earthscan Publications).

Collier, G. A., and J. F. Collier (2005), 'The Zapatista Rebellion in the Context of Globalization', *The Journal of Peasant Studies*, Vol. 32, Nos. 3–4: 450–60.

Cordesman, A., (2014), 'Russia and the Colour Revolution: A Russian Military View of a World Destabilized by the US and the West', Center for Strategic and International Studies, 28 May 2014. https://www.csis.org/analysis/russia-and-%E2%80%9Ccolor-revolution%E2%80%9D. Accessed 14 April 2021.

Deibert, R. J. (2020), *Reset: Reclaiming the Internet for Civil Society* (Toronto: House of Anansi Press).

Diamond, L. (2021), 'Rebooting Democracy', *Journal of Democracy*, Vol. 32, No. 2: 179–83.

Edwards, M., and J. Gaventa, eds (2001), *Global Citizen Action* (Abingdon, UK: Earthscan Publications).

Evans, P. (1997), 'The Eclipse of the State? Reflections on Stateness in an Era of Globalization', *World Politics*, Vol. 50, No. 1: 62–87.

Featherstone, K. (1994), 'Jean Monnet and the "Democratic Deficit" in the European Union', *Journal of Common Market Studies*, Vol. 32, No. 2: 149–70.

Finkelstein, L. S. (1995), 'What is Global Governance?' *Global Governance: A Review of Multilateralism and International Organizations*, Vol. 1, No. 3: 367–72.

Friedman, T. L. (2000), *The Lexus and the Olive Tree: Understanding Globalization* (London: HarperCollins).

Guidry, J. A., M. D. Kennedy and M. N. Zald (2000), 'Globalizations and Social Movements', in J. A. Guidry, M. D. Kennedy and M. N. Zald, eds, *Globalizations and Social Movements: Culture, Power, and the Transnational Public Sphere*, 1–32 (Ann Arbor, MI: University of Michigan Press).

Haas, P. M. (1992), 'Epistemic Communities and International Policy Coordination', *International Organization*, Vol. 46, No. 1: 1–35.

Haynes, J. (2005), *Comparative Politics in a Globalizing World* (Cambridge: Polity Press).

Hopgood, S. (2006), *Keepers of the Flame: Understanding Amnesty International* (Ithaca, NY: Cornell University Press).

Huntington, S. P. (1991), *The Third Wave: Democratization in the Late Twentieth-Century* (Norman: University of Oklahoma Press).

Huntington, S. P. (1993), 'The Clash of Civilisations?' *Foreign Affairs*, Vol. 72, No. 3: 22–49.

Inglehart, R., and C. Welzel (2005), *Modernization, Cultural Change, and Democracy: The Human Development Sequence* (Cambridge: Cambridge University Press).

Kaldor, M. (2003), 'The Idea of Global Civil Society', *International Affairs*, Vol. 79, No. 3: 583–93.

Keohane, R. O. (2002), 'The Globalization of Informal Violence, Theories of World Politics, and the "Liberalism of Fear"', *Dialog-IO*, Vol. 1, No. 1: 29–43.

Kumar, K. (2007), 'Global Civil Society', *European Journal of Sociology*, Vol. 48, No. 3: 413–34.

Landers, C. S., ed. (2017), *The Digital Divide: Issues, Recommendations, and Research* (Hauppauge, NY: Nova Science Publisher).

Levitsky, S., and L. A. Way (2002), 'Linkage versus Leverage: Rethinking the International Dimension of Regime Change', *Comparative Politics*, Vol. 38, No. 4: 379–400.

Levitsky, S., and L. A. Way (2005), 'International Linkage and Democratization', *Journal of Democracy*, Vol. 16, No. 3: 20–34.

Martinez-Torres, M. E. M. M. (2001), 'Civil Society, the Internet, and the Zapatistas', *Peace Review*, Vol. 13, No. 3: 347–55.

Mearsheimer, J. (2001), *The Tragedy of Great Power Politics* (New York, NY: W. W. Norton).

Norris, P. (2001), *Digital Divide: Civic Engagement, Information Poverty and the Internet Worldwide* (Cambridge: Cambridge University Press).

Parekh, B. (1992), 'The Cultural Particularity of Liberal Democracy', *Political Studies*, Vol. 40, No. 1: 160–75.

People's Republic of China (2015), Information Office of the State Council, '中国的军事战' [China's Military Strategy], May. http://www.china.org.cn/china/2015-05/26/content_35661433.htm. Accessed 14 April 2021.

Ragnetta, M., and G. W. Muschert, eds (2013), *The Digital Divide: The Internet and Social Inequality in International Perspective* (New York and London: Routledge).

Ronfeldt, D. F. (1998), *The Zapatista 'Social Netwar' in Mexico* (Santa Monica, CA: Rand).

Sen, A. (1999), 'Democracy as a Universal Value', *Journal of Democracy*, Vol. 10, No. 3: 3–17.

Strange, S. (1996), *The Retreat of the State: The Diffusion of Power in the World Economy* (Cambridge: Cambridge University Press).

Chapter 8

Albright, M. (1999), 'American Political and Economic Leadership: The Challenges of the Global Economy', Remarks to the U.S. Chamber of Commerce, Washington, DC, 14 April. https://1997-2001.state.gov/statements/1999/990414.html. Accessed 3 June 2020.

Borzyskowski, I. von (2016), 'Resisting Democracy Assistance: Who Seeks and Who Receives Technical Election Assistance', *Review of International Organizations*, Vol. 11: 247–82.

Burnell, P. (2000), 'Democracy Assistance: The State of the Art', in P. Burnell, ed., *Democracy Assistance: International Co-operation for Democratization*, 3–33 (London: Frank Cass).

Bush, S. S. (2015), *The Taming of Democracy Assistance: Why Democracy Promotion Does not Confront Dictators* (Cambridge: Cambridge University Press).

Carothers, T. (1999), *Aiding Democracy Abroad: The Learning Curve* (Washington, DC: Carnegie Endowment).

Carothers, T. (2006), *Confronting the Weakest Link: Aiding Political Parties in New Democracies* (Washington, DC: Carnegie Endowment).

Carothers, T. (2015), 'Democracy Aid at 25: Time to Choose', *Journal of Democracy*, Vol. 26, No. 1: 59–73.

Carothers, T. (2017), 'Democracy Promotion under Trump: What has Been Lost? What Remains?' Carnegie Endowment for International Peace, 6 September. https://carnegieendowment.org/2017/09/06/democracy-promotion-under-trump-what-has-been-lost-what-remains-pub-73021. Accessed 29 March 2021.

Catón, M. (2007), 'Effective Party Assistance: Stronger Parties for Better Democracy', International Institute for Democracy and Electoral Assistance (IDEA), 27 November. https://www.idea.int/publications/catalogue/effective-party-assistance-stronger-parties-better-democracy. Accessed 16 June 2020.

Council of Europe (2018), 'State of Democracy, Human Rights, and the Rule of Law: Role of Institutions, Threats to Institutions', Report by the Secretary-General, 18 May.

Dahinden, M. (2013), 'Democracy Promotion at a Local Level: Experiences, Perspectives and Policy of Swiss International Cooperation', *International Policy Development*, Vol. 4.3. https://journals.openedition.org/poldev/1517. Accessed 29 March 2021.

Elections Canada (2020) 'International Affairs'. https://www.elections.ca/content.aspx?section=abo&dir=int&document=index&lang=e. Accessed 17 June 2020.

European Union (2019), 'Promoting Democracy and Observing Elections', November. https://www.europarl.europa.eu/factsheets/en/sheet/166/promoting-democracy-and-observing-elections. Accessed 17 June 2020.

Finkel, S. E., A. Pérez-Liñán, M. A. Seligson, and C. N. Tate (2008), 'Deepening Our Understanding of the Effects of US Foreign Assistance on Democracy Building Final Report', USAID, 28 January.

Finnemore, M., and K. Sikkink (2001), 'Taking Stock: The Constructivist Research Program in International Relations and Comparative Politics', *Annual Review of Political Science*, Vol. 4: 391–416.

Gilley, B. (2010), 'Democratic Enclaves in Authoritarian Regimes', *Democratization*, Vol. 17, No. 3: 389–415.

International IDEA (2018), 'Political Party Strengthening Toolkit'. https://www. idea.int/sites/default/files/news/news-pdfs/2018-10-18-PPR-Tools_for_ Political_party_strengthening.pdf. Accessed 17 June 2020.

Lawson, M. L., and S. B. Epstein (2019), 'Democracy Promotion: An Objective of US Foreign Assistance', Congressional Research Service, 4 January.

Layne, C. (1994), 'Kant or Can't: The Myth of the Democratic Peace', *International Security*, Vol. 19, No. 2: 5–49.

Layne, C. (2001), 'Shell Games, Shallow Gain and the Democratic Peace', *International History Review*, Vol. 23, No. 4: 799–813.

McIntosh-Sundstrom, L. (2006), *Funding Civil Society: Foreign Assistance and NGO Development in Russia* (Stanford, CA: Stanford University Press).

Mendelson, S. E., and J. K. Glenn, eds (2002), *The Power and Limits of NGOs: A Critical Look at Building Democracy in Eastern Europe and Eurasia* (New York: Columbia University Press).

O'Donnell, G. (1996), 'Illusions about Consolidation', *Journal of Democracy*, Vol. 7, No. 2: 34–51.

Ottaway, M. and T. Carothers, eds (2000), *Funding Virtue: Civil Society Aid and Democracy Promotion* (Washington, DC: Carnegie Endowment).

Paris, R. (2010), 'Saving Liberal Peacebuilding', *Review of International Studies*, Vol. 36, No. 2: 337–65.

Perlin, G., D. Sully, V. Ashford, N. O'Connor and S. Noakes (2008), 'Literature Review of Applied Research on Democratic Development', International Development Research Centre, 15 October.

Reynolds, M. (2003), 'Bush Says U.S. Must Spread Democracy', *Baltimore Sun*, 7 November.

Russett, B., (2005), 'Bushwacking the Democratic Peace', *International Studies Perspectives*, Vol. 6, No. 4: 395–408.

Schattschneider, E. E. (1942), *Party Government* (New York: Holt, Rinehart and Winston).

Schedler, A., L. Diamond, and M. F. Plattner (1999), *The Self-Restraining State: Power and Accountability in New Democracies* (Boulder, CO: Lynne Rienner Publishers).

Shapiro, I., and C. Hacker-Cordón (1999), 'Promises and Disappointments: Reconsidering Democracy's Value', in I. Shapiro and C. Hacker-Cordón, eds, *Democracy's Value*, 1–20 (Cambridge: Cambridge University Press).

Søndergaard, R. S. (2015), 'Bill Clinton's "Democratic Enlargement" and the Securitisation of Democracy Promotion', *Diplomacy & Statecraft*, Vol. 26: 534–51.

Talbott, S. (1996), 'Democracy and the National Interest', *Foreign Affairs* (November/December). https://www.foreignaffairs.com/articles/1996-11-01/ democracy-and-national-interest. Accessed 3 June 2020.

Travis, R. (1998), 'The Promotion of Democracy at the End of the Twentieth Century: A New Polestar for American Foreign Policy?' in J. M. Scott, ed., *After the End: Making U.S. Foreign Policy in the Post-Cold War World*, 251–76 (Durham, NC: Duke University Press).

Uberti, L. J., and D. Jackson (2018), 'Promoting Electoral Integrity through Aid: Analysis and Advice for Donors', U4 Anti-Corruption Resource Centre, May. https://www.u4.no/publications/promoting-electoral-integrity-through-aid-analysis-and-advice-for-donors. Accessed 17 June 2020.

United Nations, Department of Political and Peacebuilding Affairs (2017), 'Electoral Assistance Factsheet'. https://dppa.un.org/en/elections#Types%20of%20Assistance. Accessed 15 June 2020.

Van Rooy, A. ed. (1998), *Civil Society and the Aid Industry* (London and Sterling, VA: North-South Institute/ Earthscan).

Wersch, J. van, and J. de Zeeuw (2005), 'Mapping European Democracy Assistance: Tracing the Activities and Financial Flows of Political Foundations', Working Paper 36, Netherlands Institute of International Relations Conflict Research Unit.

White House (2009), 'Remarks by the President to the Ghanaian Parliament', Accra, Ghana, 11 July 2009. https://obamawhitehouse.archives.gov/the-press-office/remarks-president-ghanaian-parliament. Accessed 3 June 2020.

Chapter 9

Abizadeh, A. (2021), 'Representation, Bicameralism, Political Equality, and Sortition: Reconstituting the Second Chamber as a Randomly Selected Assembly', *Perspectives on Politics*, Vol. 19, No. 3: 791–806.

Aristotle, *Politics*, 4.

Abramowitz, A., and J. McCoy (2018), 'United States: Racial Resentment, Negative Partisanship, and Polarisation in Trump's America', *The Annals of the American Academy of Political and Social Science*, Vol. 681, No. 1: 137–56.

Bell, D. A. (2015), *Political Meritocracy and the Limits of Democracy* (Princeton, NJ: Princeton University Press).

Boehlen, M., J. Gamper, W. Polasek and M. A. Wimmer, eds (2005), *E-Government: Towards Electronic Democracy*, International Conference Proceedings, TCGOV 2005, Bolzano, Italy, 2–4 March.

Burnheim, J. (2006), *Is Democracy Possible?* (Sydney: Sydney University Press).

Chwalisz, C. (2019), 'A New Wave of Deliberative Democracy', Carnegie Europe, November.

Chwalisz, C. (2020), 'Innovative Citizen Participation and New Democratic Institutions: Catching the Deliberative Wave', OECD, 10 June.

Coppedge, M., A. Alvarez and C. Maldonado (2008), 'Two Persistent Dimensions of Democracy: Contestation and Inclusiveness', *Journal of Politics*, Vol. 70, No. 3: 632–47.

Crombez, C. (2003), 'The Democratic Deficit in the European Union: Much Ado about Nothing?' *European Union Politics*, Vol. 4, No. 1: 101–20.

Crouch, C. (2004), *Post-Democracy* (Cambridge: Polity Press).

Crouch, C. (2013), '5 Minutes with Colin Crouch'. https://blogs.lse.ac.uk/politicsandpolicy/five-minutes-with-colin-crouch. Accessed 6 January 2022.

Dahlberg, L. (2011), 'Reconstructing Digital Democracy: An Outline of the Four "Positions"', *New Media and Society*, Vol. 13, No. 6: 855–72.

Dickson, B. J. M. Shen and J. Chan (2016), 'Generating Regime Support in Contemporary China: Legitimation and Local Legitimacy Deficit', *Modern China*, Vol. 43, No. 2: 123–55.

Dijk, J. van (2012), 'Digital Democracy: Vision and Reality', in I. Snellen, M. Thaens and W. van de Donk, eds, *Public Administration in the Information Age: Revisited*, 49–62 (Amsterdam: IOS Press).

Ebert, H. (2020), 'Hacked IT Superpower: How India Secures its Cyberspace as a Rising Digital Democracy', *India Review*, Vol. 19, No. 4: 376–413.

Fishkin, J. S. (2003), 'Consulting the Public through Deliberative Polling', *Journal of Policy Analysis and Management*, Vol. 22, No. 1: 128–33.

Fishkin, J. S. (2009), *When the People Speak: Deliberative Democracy and Public Consultation* (Oxford: Oxford University Press).

Fishkin, J. S. and R. C. Luskin (2005), 'Experimenting with a Democratic Ideal: Deliberative Polling and Public Opinion', *Acta Politica*, Vol. 40: 284–98.

Follesdal, A., and S. Hix (2006), 'Why there is a Democratic Deficit in the EU: A Response to Majone and Moravcsik', *Journal of Common Market Studies*, Vol. 44, No. 3: 533–62.

Gagnon, A., and M. Keating, eds (2012), *Political Autonomy and Divided Societies: Imagining Democratic Alternatives in Complex Settings* (Houndmills: Palgrave Macmillan).

Gastil, J., and E. O. Wright (2019), *Legislature by Lot: Transformative Designs for Deliberative Government* (London and New York: Verso).

Graham, M. H., and M. W. Svolik (2020), 'Democracy in America? Partisanship, Polarisation, and the Robustness of Support for Democracy in the United States', *American Political Science Review*, Vol. 114, No. 2: 392–409.

Greco, B. (2021), 'Paris: This is How the New Citizens' Assembly, Made up of 100 Inhabitants Drawn by Lot, Will Work', *Le Journal du Dimanche*, 28 November. https://www.lejdd.fr/JDD-Paris/paris-voici-comment-fonctionnera-la-nouvelle-assemblee-citoyenne-composee-de-100-habitants-tires-au-sort-4079459. Accessed 19 January 2022.

Hacker, K. L. and J. van Dijk, eds (2000), *Digital Democracy: Issues of Theory and Practice* (London: SAGE Publications).

Hanson, F., S. O'Connor, M. Walker and L. Courtois (2019), 'Hacking Democracies: Cataloguing Cyber-enabled Attacks on Elections', Analysis and Policy Observatory, 15 May. https://apo.org.au/node/236546. Accessed 25 January 2022.

Hindman, M. (2009), *The Myth of Digital Democracy* (Princeton, NJ: Princeton University Press).

Information Office of the State Council of the People's Republic of China (2019), 'Full Text: China: Democracy that Works'. http://english.scio.gov.cn/whitepapers/2021-12/04/content_77908921.ht. Accessed 25 August 2022.

Keane, J. (2011), 'Monitory Democracy?' in J. Kean and W. Merkel, eds, *The Future of Representative Democracy*, 212–35 (Cambridge: Cambridge University Press).

Landemore, H. (2013), 'Deliberation, Cognitive Diversity, and Democratic Inclusiveness: An Epistemic Argument for the Random Selection of Representatives', *Synthese*, Vol. 190: 1209–31.

Lape, S. (2009), *Reproducing Athens: Meander's Comedy, Democratic Culture, and the Hellenistic City* (Princeton, NJ: Princeton University Press).

Library of Congress (n.d.), 'Voting Rights'. https://www.loc.gov/collections/civil-rights-history-project/articles-and-essays/voting-rights. Accessed 14 January 2022.

Mill, J. S. (1861), *Considerations on Representative Government* (London: Parker, Son, and Bourn).

Moravcsik, A. (2004), 'Is there a Democratic Deficit in World Politics? A Framework for Analysis', *Government and Opposition*, Vol. 39, No. 2: 336–63.

Nabatchi, T., and M. Leighninger, eds (2015), *Public Participation in Twenty-first Century Democracy* (Hoboken, NJ: John Wiley and Sons).

National Low Income Housing Coalition (2020), 'A History of Voter Suppression', 23 September. https://nlihc.org/resource/history-voter-suppression. Accessed 14 January 2022.

Perry, E. J. (2019), 'Is the Chinese Communist Regime Legitimate?' in J. Rudolph and M. Szonyi, eds, *The China Questions: Critical Insights into a Rising Power*, 11–17 (Cambridge, MA: Harvard University Press).

Rhodes, P. J., ed. (2017), *The Athenian Constitution: Written in the School of Aristotle* (Oxford: Oxford University Press).

Schapals, A. K., A. Bruns and B. McNair, eds (2018), *Digitising Democracy* (London and New York: Routledge).

Schill, D., and J. A. Hendricks, eds (2017), *The Presidency and Social Media: Discourse, Disruption, and Digital Democracy in the 2016 Presidential Election* (London and New York: Routledge).

Sortition Foundation (2021), 'Deliberative Democracy in Australia: An Update from Down Under', 25 August. https://www.sortitionfoundation.org/australia_update. Accessed 19 January 2022.

UK National Archives (n.d.), 'The Struggle for Democracy: Getting the Vote', https://www.nationalarchives.gov.uk/pathways/citizenship/struggle_democracy/getting_vote.htm. Accessed 11 January 2022.

UK Parliament (n.d.), '19th Century Elections', https://www.parliament.uk/about/living-heritage/transformingsociety/electionsvoting/elections-and-voting-in-the-19th-century/reforming-election-methods/controverted-elections/. Accessed 11 January 2022.

Yew Lun Tian (2021), 'As US Promotes Democracy, China Touts its Own Version', *Reuters*, 4 December. https://www.reuters.com/world/china/us-promotes-democracy-china-touts-its-own-version-2021-12-03/. Accessed 27 January 2022.

Yu Keping (2009), *Democracy is a Good Thing: Essays on Politics, Society and Culture in Contemporary China* (Washington, DC: Brookings Institution).

Zeng, J. (2014), 'The Debate on Regime Legitimacy in China: Bridging the Wide Gulf between Western and Chinese Scholarship', *Journal of Contemporary China*, Vol. 23, No. 89: 612–35.

Zhang, W. (2021), 'How People's Democracy Works in China', *Beijing Review*, Vol. 19, No. 6, May.

Index

www.ingramcontent.com/pod-product-compliance
Lightning Source LLC
Chambersburg PA
CBHW050417280326
41932CB00013BA/1895